CONFLICT & CONNECTION

THE JEWISH-CHRISTIAN-ISRAEL TRIANGLE

MOSHE AUMANN

gefen
publishing house
JERUSALEM ◆ NEW YORK

Typesetting: Raphaël Freeman, Jerusalem Typesetting
Cover Design: Studio Paz, Jerusalem

1 3 5 7 9 8 6 4 2

Gefen Publishing House
POB 36004, Jerusalem 91360, Israel
972-2-538-0247 • orders@gefenpublishing.com

Gefen Books
12 New Street Hewlett, NY 11557, USA
516-295-2805 • gefenny@gefenpublishing.com

www.israelbooks.com

Printed in Israel   *Send for our free catalogue*

ISBN 965-229-299-0

Library of Congress Cataloging-in-Publication Data:
Aumann, Moshe
Conflict and Connection: The Jewish-Christian-Israel Triangle / Moshe Aumann.
p. cm.

1. Judaism – Relations – Christianity – History. 2. Christianity and other religions –
Judaism – History. 3. Judaism – Relations – Christianity – 1945 – Sources.
4. Christianity and other religions – Judaism – 1945 – Sources.
I. Title: Conflict and Connection. II. Title

BM535.A8265 2003 • 261.2′6 – DC21 • CIP NO: 2002192856

This book is dedicated
to the blessed memory of my parents
Siegmund and Miriam Aumann ז״ל
whose open hand
genuine piety
and unfettered spirit
provided preparation and inspiration
not to be acquired
in any other way

"Can two walk together without having met?"

Amos 3:3

Contents

Contents

Acknowledgments

First and foremost, I give thanks to Him who has granted us the power of speech, and who gives strength to the weary, for allowing me to see this work through to its culmination.

A special note of thanks goes to my beloved wife, Shirah Miriam / Mimi. Her assistance, support and wise counsel, throughout the years in which this book was in preparation, were a wellspring of inspiration and encouragement. I also wish to express my appreciation to my sons and daughter, the children of my first wife, Miriam / Mady ז"ל: Benny, Uri and Giti – may they be granted long and fruitful lives – who have stood by me and with me, each in his or her own way, as I faced the challenges and pitfalls an author will encounter in a venture of this kind.

My employer, the Israel Ministry of Foreign Affairs, opened for me a wondrous window to the Christian world when, in 1987, it appointed me Minister-Counselor for Relations with the Christian Churches at the Embassy of Israel in Washington. This appointment introduced me to a story that, with the passage of time, began to "grow on me" and ultimately created the irresistible urge to write this book. Upon my return to Jerusalem in 1990, it was Ambassador Moshe Gilboa, at the time the Foreign Minister's Adviser on Inter-religious Affairs, who encouraged me to continue my involvement in Israel-Christian relations; and, much later, one of his successors, Ambassador Gadi Golan, read the manuscript of this book and offered some timely comments.

I feel privileged to have had the critical input of Rabbi Aharon Lichtenstein, head of the Har Etzyon Yeshiva, whose insightful comments I have endeavored to reflect in the final text of this book.

Special thanks are due to several good friends in the scholastic and ecclesiastic domains, who willingly gave of their time to read the manuscript and to make valuable and often quite detailed observations, comments and suggestions. In this category I wish, in particular, to note here the contributions of Moshe Kohn of Jerusalem and Charles Siegman of Silver Spring, both of them true gentlemen and scholars; Rabbi Aaron Borow of Jerusalem, formerly the spiritual leader of the Nusach H'ari B'nai Zion Congregation in St. Louis; Dr. Eugene J. Fisher, Associate Director of the Secretariat for Ecumenical and Interreligious Affairs, US Conference of Catholic Bishops in Washington; Rabbi Joshua O. Haberman, Senior Rabbi Emeritus, Washington Hebrew Congregation; Rev. Petra Heldt, Executive Secretary of the Ecumenical Theological Research Fraternity in Israel; Malcolm Lowe, New Testament scholar, writer and lecturer; Rabbi A. James Rudin, Senior Interreligious Adviser at the American Jewish Committee; Dr. Franklin Sherman, Associate for Interfaith Relations, Evangelical Lutheran Church in America, and a former Dean at the Lutheran School of Theology in Chicago; and my brother, Prof. Robert J. Aumann, who would probably skin me alive if I were to mention more about him here than the bare fact that he is a retired professor of mathematics at the Hebrew University of Jerusalem, specializing in game theory and economics, and today a member of the university's Rationality Center.

My friend Ruth S. Frank, a public relations consultant, was most helpful in steering me to the right publisher and letting me have the benefit of her experience and expertise in the field.

A final word: The readiness of these good people to read my manuscript and to offer comments and suggestions in no way constitutes an endorsement, by any of them, of its contents, the responsibility for which is mine alone.

Foreword

THE WORLD is in the throes of convulsive change.

The cataclysmic events that rocked our globe in the middle of the twentieth century – the Shoah, World War II, the Atomic Bomb and, in counterpoise, the rebirth of Israel and, in decades to follow, the emergence of over a hundred new nation-states the world over – have set in motion a series of developments so vast in their magnitude and in the speed of their unfolding, that they seriously challenge our capacity to comprehend their full meaning and their potential impact on the future of the human race.

Within the short span of just a few years in the late 1980s, the vaunted Soviet Union collapsed and, with it, virtually the entire Communist empire. That collapse generated a worldwide movement towards more freedom, more democracy and the resolution of international conflicts by peaceful means. An anachronistic, ill-conceived act of naked aggression by Iraq's Saddam Hussein against neighboring Kuwait encountered the determined opposition of a broad coalition of nations. In the 1991 Gulf War, that coalition, led by the United States of America, drove Saddam's troops out of Kuwait and placed the Iraqi dictator's regime under the ongoing scrutiny of the United Nations. The United States emerged from this test as the world's sole remaining superpower.

Of course there have also been other developments, not all of them potential blessings to mankind like those enumerated above. Pockets of armed strife continue to exist and to erupt from time to time in various corners of the world, some of them spawned by the very phenomena we have just described. Terrorism is spreading across the globe; and the development and control of nuclear weaponry are no longer exclusively in the hands of the so-called great powers. Indeed, nuclear proliferation threatens the continued "balance of terror" that has played such an important role in preventing the outbreak of major conflicts involving the dreaded possibility of the actual use of nuclear weapons. Not least of the dangers threatening the future peace of the human race is the woeful and, in some cases, worsening economic condition of many peoples the world over – and particularly the growing imbalance of wealth between the industrialized nations of the North and the far less developed societies of the South.

Subtly interwoven in this large-as-life fabric of worldwide political and social transformation, one may discern two far more delicate strands. Forming an integral part of the overall pattern, they may, in the long term, prove of much greater impact on future developments than now seems likely. One of these was the courageous positive response of Egypt's President Anwar Sadat, in 1977, to a peace overture by Israeli Prime Minister Menachem Begin. In March 1979, a peace treaty was concluded between Egypt and Israel, designed to terminate Egypt's long and bitter conflict with Israel, based on the full recognition of Israel's right of national existence in the region. This act on the part of the leading country among Israel's Arab neighbors set in motion a process that may one day put an end to one of the most enduring and seemingly intractable conflicts of the twentieth century: that between the Arab states of the Middle East and the nation of Israel.

The "peace process" spawned by the Middle East Peace Conference at Madrid in 1991, and supposedly buttressed by the Oslo Accords signed by Israel and the Palestine Liberation Organization in 1993 and in subsequent years, came crashing to the ground with the Palestinian Arab assault on Israel in September 2000 – a deadly combination of warlike acts and terrorist outrages that at the time of writing, in mid-2002, had not yet been brought to a complete halt. Nevertheless, this rather stormy period in the quest for peace in the region did witness the ceding by Israel of significant areas to the Palestinian Authority (PA), as well as the signing, in October 1994, of the Israel-Jordan Peace Treaty – the second peace treaty between Israel and an Arab country.

The other strand of the fabric is still more delicate, and less apparent to the eye of the casual observer. Yet, in its potential for profound political and social change on the world scene in the twenty-first century, it probably is of greater importance than the political developments in the Middle East. This is so because it is a basically religious phenomenon and involves not only international relationships but also the pattern of relations between two of the world's major faiths: Judaism and Christianity.

There has been a dramatic positive change in the attitude of some of the major Christian Churches – Protestant, Catholic and, to a lesser extent, Orthodox – towards the Jewish religion. Many among the general public, Jews and Christians, are unaware – or only dimly aware – of this change. But it is a matter of record, and it is pregnant with meaning and with the possibility of a thoroughgoing transformation, in the long term, of the entire Church-Synagogue relationship, with all that this would imply with regard to (a) relations between the Christian and Jewish communities and (b) the attitude of the Churches towards the modern rebirth and regeneration of Israel and towards the State of Israel as such.

In my capacity as an Israeli diplomat, I have spent several years familiarizing myself with "the Christian scene" and becoming acquainted, in the process, with Christian leaders and functionaries, mainly in the United States. Much of this took place in the three years (1987–1990) that I served as Consul General and Minister-Counselor for Church Relations at the Embassy of Israel in Washington. What most impressed me, during my tenure as Israel's envoy to the Churches, was the great complexity of the three-way relationship involving the State of Israel, the Jewish community and religion, and the Christian Churches. The longer I was on the job, the more firmly I became convinced that it was impossible to give a simple, unencumbered answer to the oft-asked question, "What is the Church's attitude toward Israel?" One cannot, in honesty, give a simple answer to this question – because one cannot speak of a single, uniform attitude, on the part of the Christian Churches, toward Israel, any more than one can speak of a single, uniform attitude, on the part of these Churches, toward Jews and Judaism. Nor will one find a necessary correlation between the attitude toward the Jewish religion and that toward the State of Israel. Similar variances, naturally enough, may be perceived among Jews and Israelis with respect to their attitudes toward Christians and Christianity.

As the subtitle of this book indicates, we will be dealing here with the three sides of the Jewish-Christian-Israel triangle – and how they relate to each other. However, while the Jewish religion is an element in this presentation, Christianity *per se* is not – and for good reason. For one thing, as a religiously observant Jew, I feel confident and competent in offering the reader an exposition of the Jewish faith (as I have done in Chapter 1) – but do not feel the same confidence or competence with regard to the Christian faith, my knowledge of which, in the nature of things, is second- or third-hand.

More to the point in this context, however, is the fact – noted by many participants in the Christian-Jewish dialogue – that this dialogue is asymmetrical in the sense that, while the Jewish partner's self-definition does not necessarily require a familiarity with Christianity, the Christian partner's self-definition does require a familiarity with Judaism. (At the same time, it goes without saying that both partners need to show more than a cursory interest in each other's teachings and traditions in order for the dialogue to bear fruit.) In the words of a World Council of Churches document to which we shall refer in a later chapter:

> While an understanding of Judaism in New Testament times becomes an integral and indispensable part of any Christian theology, for Jews, a 'theological' understanding of Christianity is of a less than essential or integral significance.

One may go further and say – again, with the support of our Christian partners-in-dialogue – that "an understanding of Judaism" must include also the history of a dynamic development of Jewish religious thought and literature throughout the nearly two thousand years that have elapsed since New Testament times. Thus, the National Commission for Catholic-Jewish Religious Dialogue, affiliated with the National Conference of Brazilian Bishops, in 1984 found that –

> Judaism cannot be considered a purely social and historical entity, or a leftover from a past that no longer exists. We must take into account the vitality of the Jewish people, which has continued throughout the centuries to the present.

This recognition of the historical continuity and ongoing vitality of Judaism and the Jewish people is reflected in numerous Church documents published since the 1960s. Some of these declarations are quoted in Chapter 6 – the structural backbone of this book since it documents the systematic, steadily persevering change of course in Church doctrine that constitutes the central theme of this work.

The documents cited in this book provide convincing proof that much of the Christian world is today moving firmly, and with growing confidence, in a new direction: the direction of ecumenism, reconciliation and a spirit of inquiry aimed at a better mutual understanding among various and differing faith communities – but particularly between the Christian and Jewish communities. What we are witnessing here is an ongoing series of constructive changes in Christian theology and practice relating to the Jewish people and the Jewish religion. At the same time, many millions of Christians recognize the reborn nation of Israel as the realization of biblical prophecy and thus as a palpable part of God's plan.

Essentially, this book poses the question: Do these developments bear the seeds of a fundamental and historic resolution of the centuries-old conflict between Christianity and Judaism?

After nearly two thousand years of hatred, inquisition and persecution, suspicion and rancor, separation and isolation, an encounter has taken place – or, rather, a series of encounters. A connection has been made; a dialogue has been launched. The first faltering steps have been taken in what appears to be an honest and earnest effort, on the part of some major Churches, as well as many Christian communities and individuals, to atone for the sins of an inglorious past and to pave the way for a more salutary future in the relationship between the two closely related faith systems and communities that, together, make up what is known as the Judeo-Christian civilization.

The purpose of this book is, first of all, to bring the very fact of this extraordinary transformation to the attention of a Christian *and* Jewish public that, for the most part, is barely conscious of it today. Moreover, this process represents an opportunity not to be missed for a historic reconciliation between the Christian and Jewish communities, on the basis of the new thinking in the Churches, coupled with the need for a loud-and-clear positive Jewish response and for effective Jewish-Christian cooperation, particularly in the social and humanitarian domains. The first two chapters of the book are designed to demonstrate how Jewish religion and history have prepared the Jewish people to meet this modern social challenge in a positive spirit.

The last three chapters deal with problem areas that obviously exist in this kind of situation and relationship – highlighting such issues as anti-Judaism, proselytism and hostility towards the State of Israel. Contradictions and dilemmas will, of course, crop up when such issues are examined. Yet the very fact that, on the whole, the Churches have not flinched from facing these problems and challenges, and making an apparently honest effort to overcome them, opens up the hope that, after two millennia of conflict, the connection that has finally been made between these two faith communities will, in time, develop into a genuine and lasting reconciliation.

Part One
Background

Chapter 1

The Jewish Ethos

THE DAILY MORNING PRAYER in the Jewish liturgy begins with a paean of praise for the Jewish people uttered by the gentile prophet Balaam (*"How goodly are thy tents, o Jacob, thy dwelling places, o Israel!"* – Num. 24:5) – and ends with a ringing statement on the universal dominion of God by the Hebrew prophet Zechariah (*"And the Lord shall be king over all the earth: On that day shall the Lord be One and His Name – One."* – Zech. 14:9).

The choice of precisely these two scriptural verses as "book-ends" for the Jewish daily prayer service represents a near-perfect encapsulation of the two-fold essence of the Jewish faith: (1) recognition of the all-embracing, universal oneness of God; and (2) awareness of the particular mission of the Jewish people within the human family.

We shall have more to say, later in this book, about the very complex and controversial figure of this gentile prophet named Balaam, when we discuss the attitude of the Hebrew Bible – and of later Jewish exegetes – to non-Jewish biblical figures in general. For the moment, let it be noted that the authors of the Jewish liturgy chose a direct quotation from a non-Jewish source as the opening verse of the daily prayer service. Let it be noted further that the focus of the message contained in this verse is Jacob/Israel, Jacob traditionally representing the Jewish people, and Israel – the nation or body politic.

"You Are One"

"You are One, and Your Name is One," begins the central portion of the Sabbath afternoon prayer service, and it goes on: *"...and who is like unto Your people Israel – one nation in the world."* Actually, the wording in the original Hebrew is – *"...oomee ke'amcha Israel goy ehad ba-aretz."* The word *aretz* may mean "world" or "earth"; at other times it denotes "land" or "country." Either interpretation would give us an eminent fit in the context of this verse. What we have here, then, is a most succinct expression of the dual approach of Jewish religious philosophy: juxtaposing and, simultaneously, intertwining the cognizance of the universal – the all-embracing Oneness of the Divine Presence – with the realization that the Jewish people has a particular, well-defined role to play in the general order. A rudimentary understanding of this philosophy is essential to any consideration of Jewish attitudes towards "the other," in general – and towards Christians and Christianity in particular.

Let us, therefore, take a closer look at this philosophy, beginning with its universal aspect.

THE WHOLE (Thesis)

"...the Lord is One." (Deuteronomy 6:4)
"...His Presence fills all the earth." (Isaiah 6:3)
"...on that day shall the Lord be One and His Name – One." (Zechariah 14:9)

What message does the Bible wish to convey when it avers that "the Lord is One"?

On the face of it, the statement seems almost meaningless. Every first-grader knows that one plus one equals two. The existence, then, of X as "one" should not preclude the coexistence of Y as another "one" – and, for that matter, of Z and Q and R. Clearly, the oneness referred to in the Bible as the essential divine attribute is a different concept altogether.

The 16th century Italian Bible exegete Ovadiah Seforno suggests that the word "one" in this context should be understood as meaning "unique":

> Having granted existence to all that exists, He is also separate from all that exists in the universe... in a manner that leaves Him alone [i.e., unique]...

Other Bible commentators, as we shall see, take a quite different approach to this question. Instead of *exclusiveness*, they speak of *inclusiveness*. Here we are introduced to the concept of the one-ness of all existence, the "macro-oneness" made up of a myriad "micro-onenesses" – from the tiniest atomic particle to all the elements comprising the mineral, vegetable and animal kingdoms, to the component parts of the human body, the human being as such, the family, the social community, the political community, the faith community, the nation, the region, the world, merging ultimately with the macrocosm that may be defined as all the worlds ever created – the universe itself.

In a very real sense, God is this all-embracing Oneness, a concept that finds graphic expression in the following *Midrash* (hermeneutical exegesis of the Jewish Bible) relating to the biblical command, in Deuteronomy 6:5, to "love the Lord your God with all your heart *and with all your soul...*":

> Note that God fills His world, as the human soul fills the body; God suffers the world, as the soul suffers the body; God is unique in His world, as the human soul is unique; God does not slumber, as the soul does not slumber; God is unsullied in His world, as the soul is unsullied in the body; God sees but is not seen: Let, then, the human soul that sees but is not seen extol the Holy One Who sees but is not seen. (*Devarim Rabba* 2)

We may be doing an eminently irrational thing when we express and act upon our belief in a God we cannot perceive with the aid of our physical senses. Yet this act of faith is a very natural aspect of the human condition, which of course includes vital non-rational components. One could even say that faith in God has in it a quasi-rational element: After all, we are ready to accept the notion of infinity without really being capable of fathoming this concept intellectually. Why, then, should we feel that we are precluded from accepting the existence of a Supreme Being that we cannot see or hear or touch and that, therefore, we cannot fully comprehend?

King Solomon, reputedly the wisest of all men, wrote in the Book of Ecclesiastes (3:11), "He brings everything to pass precisely in its time; He also puts eternity in their [i.e., the human] mind – [but] without man ever finding [i.e., being able to understand fully] what God has wrought, from first to last."

That says it all.

The Tabernacle

The Oneness-theme recurs in the biblical story of the Holy Tabernacle that the Children of Israel were commanded to erect in the desert. Chapters 25, 26 and 27 of the Book of Exodus deal exclusively with the divine instructions to Moses, in the minutest detail, concerning the construction of the Tabernacle; Chapters 35 (from Verse 4), 36 (in its entirety) and 37 (to Verse 20) describe, with the same devotion to detail, how those instructions were carried out.

The centerpiece of both of these biblical passages is the rather enigmatic statement, in the first passage, that "*the Tabernacle shall be one*" (Exodus 26:6) and, in the second, that "*the Tabernacle was one*" (Ex. 36:13). There is something awesomely stark yet profoundly meaningful in the seemingly paradoxical appearance of this laconic statement of unity in the midst of that ocean of minutiae dealing with the erection of God's Dwelling Place among the Israelites. Two classic Jewish Bible commentators turn their attention to this paradox – and come up with much the same remarkable explanation.

Abraham Ibn Ezra, the 12th century Spanish poet, philosopher and exegete, wrote this succinct yet penetrating commentary on Exodus 26, Verse 6:

> ...and the Tabernacle was called one – inclusive of everything. For every object is not one thing; rather, it is composed of parts

[lit., "ones"]. And thus it is with the Revered Name [i.e., God], who is One, inclusive of everything, and is called The One. Thus, too, the micro-world and the macro-world.

The same idea is set forth in somewhat greater detail by Rabbi Meir Leibush, better known as Malbim, a practicing rabbi and Bible commentator in 19th century Poland and Romania:

> It is well known that all the worlds unite as one man, and all that exists [i.e., the universe] is called the Great Man. This means that just as all the organs that make up a human being, though each has its own particular nature and characteristics, combine to form one person, and all of them are linked together and complement one another – so that if one should be deficient, that would constitute a defect in the body as a whole – thus, too, all of existence and the infinite number of worlds that God has created have been placed and arranged as a comprehensive organism, all of whose component parts are interrelated and, in their interaction, enable the organism as a whole to function as an organism. (*Remazei Hamishkan*, Exodus, Ch. 25)

There are very few texts in the entire Bible that come as close as these passages in the Book of Exodus, as illuminated and elucidated by Ibn Ezra and Malbim, to stating the essence of the Jewish philosophy.

Children of One Man

"We are all the children of one man!" (Gen. 42:11) plead Joseph's brothers when, standing before him in Egypt, they find themselves inexplicably accused of espionage. Aside from its plain connotation in the immediate context of the Joseph story, this plea becomes one of the most powerful – and fundamental – messages in the Bible, a message later to be echoed by the Prophet Malachi (2:10): *"Have we not all one father? Did not God create us?"*

The "first man" (*adam harishon*) – a phrase taken not from the Bible but from later rabbinic literature – was neither Jew nor Christian, neither Buddhist nor Muslim. He was the progenitor of humankind, no more and no less, with all that this proposition implies, from that day to this, concerning human relationships and interaction. It is the original, as well as the ultimate, message of the universality of humankind.

We are all "children of one man."

The Talmud – that titanic compendium of Jewish law and lore, completed in the fifth century CE – is probably not the place where one would look for expression of the universal idea. And yet it is there. In a discussion of the meaning of the biblical verse, *"You shall keep My statutes and My ordinances, by the pursuit of which man shall live..."* (Levit. 18:5), one of the Talmudic sages, Rabbi Meir, comments: "It does not say Priests, Levites and Israelites; it says 'man.' This means that even a gentile, if he busies himself with Torah, is like a high priest..." (*Avodah Zarah* 3a).

"Let Every Creature Understand..."

Yet another major manifestation of the centrality of the universal idea in Jewish thought is the prayer service for the High Holy Days, and particularly *Rosh Hashanah*, the Jewish New Year. There is no better way to illustrate this point than simply to quote from the opening passage of the Rosh Hashanah section of the *Amidah* – the central prayer of the daily service:

> And so, O Lord our God, instill Your awe upon all Your works, and Your dread upon all that You have created. Let all works revere You and all creatures prostrate themselves before You. Let them all become one society, to do Your will wholeheartedly. For...the dominion is Yours...and Your Name inspires awe over all that you have created....

> Our God and God of our forefathers, reign over the entire universe in Your glory, be exalted over all the world in Your splendor, reveal Yourself in the majestic grandeur of Your strength over all the dwellers of Your inhabited world. Let everything that has been made know that You are its Maker, let every creature understand that You are its Creator, and let every being with life's breath in

its nostrils proclaim: The Lord, God of Israel, is King, and His kingship rules over everything!

The prayer, to be sure, is not exclusively universalist in its character and outlook. It contains particularist elements as well, which are likewise an integral part of the Jewish tradition and religious philosophy. The same is true of the *Aleinu Leshabe'ah* prayer, also featured prominently in the Amidah of Rosh Hashanah. It is replete with affirmations of God's universal sovereignty:

> It is our duty to praise the Maker of all, to ascribe greatness to the Molder of primeval creation... We express our hope... for the perfection of the universe through the Almighty's sovereignty.... All the world's inhabitants will recognize and know that to You every knee should bend, every tongue should swear, and they will accept the yoke of Your kingship, that You may reign over them, soon and forevermore....

There can be no doubt – as a thorough perusal of the High Holy Days prayer book will bear out – that the keynote of the divine service for these special days on the Jewish Calendar is Almighty God's reign over the entire human family and, indeed, over all that lives and breathes in our universe.

THE PART (Antithesis)

"You shall be My treasured possession among all the peoples."

(Exodus 19:5)

What does it mean to be God's "treasured possession" (*segulah*) – or, in terms of the more commonly used phrase, a "chosen people"? It may be well to clarify, first of all, what it does *not* mean. Dr. J.H. Hertz, former Chief Rabbi of the British Empire (1913–1946), in his commentary on Deuteronomy 7:6, quotes the German-Jewish historian Moritz Güdemann on this score:

> The character of Israel as the Chosen People does not involve

the inferiority of other nations. The universality of Israel's idea of God is sufficient proof against such an assumption.

He then goes on to suggest what chosenness does imply:

> Every nation requires a certain self-consciousness for the carrying out of its mission. Israel's self-consciousness was tempered by the memory of its slavery in Egypt and the recognition of its being the servant of the Lord. It was the *noblesse oblige* of the God-appointed worker for the entire human race.

Much in line with this proposition, some Jewish thinkers have postulated that Jewish peoplehood is predicated on the notion that, in a manner of speaking, God needed someone to deliver His message at the human level, and so He "chose" Abraham (after Abraham "discovered" Him) and his descendants to perform this task for Him.

Even the most cursory examination of the biblical sources themselves will reveal that the proclamation of Israel's being a "chosen people" (or, as many translate, a "treasured people"), far from being merely an announcement of privileged status, is actually very closely linked to the observance of God's commandments; in fact, it may be said to be *conditioned upon* such observance. In the Torah's first mention of the chosenness concept (Exodus 19:5), the condition is stated explicitly:

> Now then, if you will obey Me faithfully and keep My covenant, you shall be My treasured possession among all the peoples.

Deuteronomy 7:6 – "...*of all the peoples on earth the Lord your God chose you to be His treasured people*" – is followed, in Verse 11, by this "rider:" "*Therefore observe faithfully the instruction, the statutes and the ordinances with which I charge you today.*"

The last occasion on which the Torah cites Israel's elevation (Deuteronomy 26:16–19) again makes it clear that it is a two-way street:

> The Lord your God commands you this day to observe these laws...
> You have affirmed this day that the Lord is your God, that you will walk in His ways ... and that you will obey Him. And the Lord

has affirmed this day that you are, as He has promised you, His
treasured people who shall observe all His commandments...

The 19th century German-Jewish spiritual leader Rabbi Samson
Raphael Hirsch, a noted Bible commentator, went so far as to aver
that "if Israel should ever become unfaithful to its sacred calling,
even the youngest lad from any of the other nations of mankind
could remind it of its mission and of its commitment." (*The Pentateuch – With Excerpts from the Hirsch Commentary*, Judaica Press
1986, p. 772)

What, then, is this calling, this mission, this commitment?

THE COMMITMENT (Synthesis)

> "*Hear O Israel, the Lord is our God, the Lord is One.*"
>
>   (Deuteronomy 6:4)

Rabbi Hirsch, in his commentary on the passage in Deuteronomy
26 cited at the end of the previous section, defines the commitment
thus:

> ...Israel's appearance on the scene of world history should serve
> to proclaim the acts of God and redound to His Name and to
> His glory ... a revelation of God's sovereignty among men;
> indeed, an emanation reflecting the Divine origin of all natural
> and historical phenomena, and confirming God's existence and
> supreme sovereignty. More than that,... Israel is to bring to the
> world a specific, clearly defined conception of the existence and
> the will of this One God ... so that 'nations shall walk by your
> light'... (Isaiah 60:3)

We have come full circle.

The seeming inward thrust of the Jewish people's particularism
turns out, in essence, to be something quite different. Fundamen-
tally, and taking the historical "long view," the Jewish commitment
is oriented outward, rather than inward. Its ultimate aim is, precisely, to achieve worldwide recognition of its own universalist

understanding of God. But the stress here is on the words "ultimate" and "long view." Until the time is ripe for this worldwide recognition to blossom in full, the Jewish people is duty-bound to preserve and nurture its own identity, cultivate its sense of mission and never cease aspiring to become "a crown of glory in the hand of the Lord, a royal diadem in the palm of God" (Isaiah 62:3). For how can Israel hope to be "a light unto the nations" (Isaiah 49:6) if it does not take care to keep its own flame burning?

Nowhere does this twin calling of Judaism find more succinct expression than in a central dictum of the Judeo-Christian ethos, recorded in the Book of Deuteronomy (6:4) and re-stated in Mark 12:28–29:

> *Shema Israel Adonai Eloheinu Adonai Ehad*
> ("Hear O Israel! The Lord is our God, the Lord is One").

No single verse in the Hebrew Scriptures has exercised so profound an impact on the Jewish psyche as has this verse. The Jewish individual is enjoined to recite it, together with the verses that follow (*"And you shall love the Lord your God with all your heart, etc."*), twice each day, morning and evening – in the language that he or she understands, if Hebrew is not that language. This ringing statement of the Oneness of God is solemnly proclaimed by the synagogue cantor as he removes the Torah scroll from its Ark, at the height of the Sabbath morning service, and is sung out in unison by the entire congregation. It forms the dramatic climax of the annual *Yom Kippur* (Day of Atonement) liturgy. And it is the last utterance to cross the lips of the believing Jew when his soul is about to depart his body. Indeed, many – alas, too many! – have been the Jewish men and women who spoke these words with their dying breath in countless massacres down the ages.

The verse has been variously translated (a) as above – i.e., two separate statements, a particularist one and a universalist one, and (b) as a single statement, "...the Lord our God [the Lord] is One." (The Hebrew language, in this instance, allows the translator this latitude.)

For the purpose of our analysis, however, it makes no difference which way we translate it; the message remains the same, and it is this:

The self-same deity that we know as the God of Israel – the God of Abraham, Isaac and Jacob Who redeemed the Children of Israel from Egypt's bondage, revealed Himself to His people at Mount Sinai, brought a new generation of Israelites into the Promised Land and guides this people's destiny – is the timeless, omnipotent Creator of the universe, the Father of humankind, the first and last manifestation of the all-embracing oneness of all that exists, has ever existed and will ever exist.

Creation and Exodus

The Sabbath Eve meal is introduced by a prayer, recited over a cup of wine and two loaves of bread, sanctifying the Sabbath Day; this prayer is known as the *kiddush* (sanctification). It is addressed to "our God, King of the Universe," and it recalls the Sabbath Day as being "a remembrance of Creation" and "of the Exodus from Egypt." Both of these juxtapositions – *our God* vis-à-vis *King of the Universe*, and *Exodus* vis-à-vis *Creation* – underscore the synthesis, in Jewish thought, between the universal and the particularist views.

Even in the Exodus itself – which, incidentally, features very prominently in Jewish liturgy, as it does of course in the Bible itself, and which must be understood, first of all, as the prime manifestation of Jewish nationhood and Jewish particularism – the synthesis is also present. In fact, the further the account of the Israelites' departure from the Egyptian "house of bondage" is developed, in the biblical story, the more powerfully emerges the portrayal of the omnipotent nature of God and of His all-embracing control of the universe.

The 13th century Spanish-Jewish Bible commentator Nahmanides (Ramban) refers to the Exodus as God's demonstration to humanity that He controls nature and manipulates it at will. Moreover, Nahmanides continues, the events of the Exodus bear witness to God's creation – and mastery – of the universe. (See his commentaries on Exodus 13:16 and Deuteronomy 5:15.)

No single fact, probably, illustrates this universalist aspect of the Exodus more tellingly than the Giving of the Torah on Mount Sinai in the midst of the wide-open wilderness, rather than in the Land of Israel. The Midrash (*Shmot Rabba* 28) expands on the verse, "*And all the people witnessed the voices and the lightnings…*" (Exodus 20:15) as follows:

> Why "voices"? Because The Voice was converted into seven voices, and from seven into seventy tongues. And why seventy tongues? So that all the nations might hear.

"Why," says another Midrash (*Bemidbar Rabba* 1) "was not the Torah given in the Land of Israel? So as not to give the nations of the world the pretext to say, since the Torah was given [to Israel] in its land, we did not take it to be ours." And it concludes this passage with the following statement:

> The Torah was given with three elements: Wilderness – as it is written (Num. 1:1), "…the Lord spoke to Moses in the Wilderness of Sinai…"; Fire – as it is written (Ex. 19:18), "Now Mount Sinai was all in smoke, for the Lord had come down upon it in fire…"; and Water – as it is written (Jud. 5:4), "…the heavens dripped, yea, the clouds dripped water…before the Lord, Him of Sinai…" – to make the point: Just as these elements are freely available to all the creatures of the world, so too the words of the Torah are freely available to all, as it is written (Isa. 55:1), "Ho, all who are thirsty, come for water…"

The Talmud (*Zevahim* 116a) relates that –

> When the Holy One gave the Torah to Israel, His voice reverberated from one end of the world to the other, and the kings of all the nations, seized with trembling, burst into song. And they went to the Prophet Balaam and asked him, What is this great outcry that we have heard? Is it a flood? Or a conflagration? And Balaam answered them, The Holy One has sworn that He would neither inundate the world again, nor destroy all living flesh. The Holy One has bestowed the Torah upon His people and its friends, as it is written: "The Lord shall grant His people strength…" (Psalms

29:11) – to which they all responded, "…The Lord shall grant His people peace!"

Again, the synthesis: The Torah was given to Israel – and its friends; its eternal message was broadcast throughout the world – and (at least according to this particular Midrash) accepted.

Mission Accomplished?

Looking back, now, across the millennia, to that moment in antiquity when the people of Israel was charged with its momentous task – to serve as the vehicle for the transmission of the Divine message to the world – we may properly ask the question: In what measure has Israel realized this mission?

One could say, of course, that the mission has been accomplished. Ancient Judaism proclaimed to the world the concept of monotheism and produced a nation that, for over a thousand years, strove to live and act out that concept in its faith, its religious practices and the recorded utterances of its leaders and prophets. Later, it gave birth to another monotheistic faith – Christianity – which was, in the course of the centuries, to spread to every corner of the globe. One could add that the subsequent emergence, from this budding Judeo-Christian civilization, of what many regard as a third monotheistic religion, Islam, constitutes a forceful affirmative response to the question posed above.

In fact, no less a figure than the renowned Jewish medieval scholar and commentator Maimonides (Rambam) acknowledged the possibility that, in the larger scheme of things, Christianity played an important role in spreading the Word of God to the human race worldwide. Maimonides, of course, did not accept Jesus's messiahship, as he made clear in writing on this subject. (For this reason, the Christian authorities of his time censored those portions of Maimonides's text in which he negated that messiahship, and so in many editions of that text the reader will not find these passages.)

The text that will be quoted here – from Maimonides's *Laws of Kings,* Chapter 11 – was taken from an uncensored version of the book. It is presented here not in order to expose the author's critical attitude towards Jesus, but to underscore his remarkable recognition, notwithstanding that attitude, of Christianity's positive role in disseminating the truth of the Biblical Word throughout the world:

> Jesus of Nazareth, who imagined that he would be the Messiah and was put to death, was prophesied over by Daniel, as it is written (11:14), "...and the lawless sons of your people will assert themselves to confirm the vision, but they will fail." And could there be a greater failure than this?...And yet man has not the capacity to fathom the thoughts of the Creator – for our ways are not His, and our thoughts are not His (Isaiah 55:8), and all of these words of Jesus of Nazareth, and of the Ishmaelite who rose after him, have only as their purpose to pave the way for the Messiah-King, and to ready the whole world to serve the Lord together, as it is written, "For then I will make the peoples pure of speech, so that they all invoke the Lord by name and serve Him with one accord" (Zephaniah 3:9). How? Already all the world is filled with the words of that Messiah and with the words of the Torah and its precepts, and these things have spread to the farthest regions and among numerous peoples of uncircumcised hearts...

Still, when all is said and done, the fulfillment of Israel's mission is far from complete. After all, there still are billions of people, the world over, who do not acknowledge the Almighty, let alone serve Him. And even among the vast number who do, there are many, too many, who fail to live up to their faith, and that is true of nations as it is of tribes, clans, families and individuals. The conclusion is inescapable: Israel's biblical call – to ptroclaim the existence and sovereignty of the One God and, in the rather picturesque wording of Lloyd George, to bear God's "choicest wines to the lives of humanity, and to stimulate and strengthen their faith" – continues unabated and, indeed, will not cease until the day dawns on which every creature on earth will acknowledge that "the Lord is One and His Name – One."

Chapter 2

Historic Encounters

The deeds of the Fathers are signposts for the Children.
(Talmud, Sota 34a)

THIS COMMON JEWISH ADAGE is another way of expressing the thought that many of the events taking place today, many of the problems and challenges we face, were foretold thousands of years ago, in the form of similar situations described in the Bible.

The theme of this book – Conflict and Connection – is a case in point. Indeed it is astounding, upon reflection, to what extent the process of reconciliation between Church and Synagogue that we have been witnessing in recent decades was foreshadowed in a whole series of narratives and incidents related in the Bible. There is hardly a major dispute or conflict in the Bible that does not, at one point, reach an amicable solution. The reconciliation factor does not always come quickly, nor is it always prominent in the narrative – but, to the discerning eye, it is there. Surely it holds a message for humankind!

Let us, then, take a closer look at some well-known biblical episodes and try to learn something from them concerning the attitude of the Jew – then and now – to "the other," the "stranger in our midst."

Abraham and the Nations

The first Jew, of course, was Abraham. He was also the forefather of the first Christian – and, through his son Ishmael, of the first Muslim: "the father of a multitude of nations" (Genesis 17:4).

For the purpose of this discussion, however, we shall consider him in his capacity as the Father of the Jewish People. Abraham's encounter with his heathen environment was at times negative, even explosive, and at other times positive. His bold action in destroying his father's idols (and then blaming the "head idol" for the deed) is related in the Midrash (*Bereshit Rabba* 38), as is his and his wife Sarah's "missionary" activity (*ibid.* 39) – based on the cryptical biblical phrase, "and the souls they made in Haran" (Gen. 12:5). Other episodes are detailed in the Bible, such as his encounters with the kings of Egypt (Gen. 12:10–20), of Sodom (Gen. 14:17, 21–24), of Salem (Gen. 14:18–20) and of the Philistines (Gen. 20:1–18).

For sheer poignancy, it would be difficult to rival the account (Gen. 18:22–33) of Abraham's spirited plea to the Almighty on behalf of the inhabitants of the wicked city of Sodom: to spare them the Divine retribution that was about to be meted out to them. "Will you sweep away the righteous along with the wicked?" Abraham remonstrates with the Lord. "Shall the Judge of all the earth not do justice?!" (Gen. 18:25)

Upon Sarah's death, Abraham, describing himself as "a stranger and a resident" (Gen. 23:4), approaches the local community in Hebron and its leader, Ephron the Hittite, with the request to sell him a burial estate where he might inter his departed spouse, and which would subsequently serve as the family burial plot. The Hittites' response is both unhesitating and forthcoming: "...*you are a mighty prince among us! In the choicest of our sepulchers shall you bury your dead: None of us will withhold his burial-place from you...*" (Gen. 23:6) Ephron exacted from Abraham a not insubstantial price for the transaction; the point is, however, that the Hittites' attitude towards this "stranger in their midst" was one of full acceptance and cooperation.

The late Jewish scholar and teacher, Rabbi Joseph B. Soloveitchick, for many decades the Nestor of American Orthodox rabbis, utilized this self-stylization of Father Abraham's as an illustration of the essential ambivalence that, to this day, characterizes the Jewish people's relationship with the outside world. In an essay entitled "Confrontation" (*Studies in Judaica*, edited by Leon D. Stitskin, Ktav Publishing House, Yeshiva University Press 1964, pp. 65–66), Rabbi Soloveitchick writes:

> We cooperate with the members of other faith communities in all fields of constructive human endeavor; but, simultaneously with our integration into the general social framework, we engage in a movement of recoil and retrace our steps. In a word, we belong to the human society and, at the same time, we feel as strangers and outsiders.... Our first patriarch, Abraham, already introduced himself in the following words: "I am a stranger and a sojourner with you." Is it possible to be both – stranger and sojourner – at the same time?...the Jew of old did think of himself in contradictory terms. He knew well in what areas he could extend his full cooperation to his neighbors and act as a *toshav*, a resident, a sojourner, and at what point this gesture of cooperation and goodwill should terminate and he must disengage as if he were a *ger*, a stranger.

Sibling Rivalry – and Reconciliation

Isaac and Ishmael, Jacob and Esau, Joseph and his brethren provide prototypal examples of sibling rivalries that invariably culminated in reconciliation. In the latter two cases, the "happy endings" receive considerable emphasis in the biblical account and are therefore well known.

One of the most dramatic – and poignant – moments in the biblical story of the Hebrew Patriarchs is described in Chapter 33 of the Book of Genesis. Following the episode in which Jacob uses a subterfuge to deprive his brother Esau of the paternal blessing he had expected, a deeply wounded and disappointed Esau threatens to kill his brother, and Jacob is compelled to flee his home. Some twenty years later, the two brothers are reunited when Jacob returns to his homeland. Jacob is highly apprehensive as the moment of the meeting approaches, but his fears prove unfounded. *"And Esau ran to meet him,"* the Bible tells us (Gen. 33:4), *"and he embraced him and fell on his neck, and he kissed him, and they wept."*

The noted 19th century Bible commentator, Rabbi Naftali Zvi Yehuda Berlin (the "Netziv") of Volozhin, relating to this dramatic moment in his commentary, *Ha'mek Davar*, wrote:

> **"...and they wept"** – Both of them wept. Thus we learn that Jacob, too, at this moment in time finds it in his heart to love his brother Esau. And thus it has been down the generations: When the descendants of Esau are inspired to acknowledge the descendants of Israel and their intrinsic worth, then we for our part feel inspired to acknowledge Esau, for he is our brother – viz., Rabbi Yehudah Hanassi's genuine appreciation for Antoninus, and many similar cases.

By way of a footnote to this commentary, it should be pointed out to the reader that, in Jewish tradition, Christendom has at times been associated with the descendants of Esau. Considering, then, that these words were written in the latter half of the 19th century, they may indeed be described not only as insightful – but as prophetic, as well.

Less famous is the reconciliation between Isaac and Ishmael – only hinted at in Genesis Chapter 25, Verse 9, which tells us that, when Abraham passed away, he was laid to rest by his sons Isaac and Ishmael – to which the Midrash (*Bereshit Rabba* 62) adds: "Here the son of the maidservant [Hagar] honored the son of the lady [Sarah]." In other words, at the graveside of their father, the half-brothers were reconciled. Are today's descendants of Isaac and Ishmael ready for a similar reconciliation?

Other forms of rivalry – and peacemaking – also make their frequent appearance in the Bible:

Abraham-Isaac / Philistines

Abraham had to battle the Philistines over a water-well he had dug and that had been sabotaged by the Philistines. King Abimelech later apologized for the incident, and the two made a peace pact, based on Abimelech's recognition, expressed to Abraham (Gen. 21:22), that *"God is with you in everything that you do."* The idyll, alas, was shattered when, in Isaac's day, fighting broke out once more over a number of wells in the region – and, again, Abimelech (the same as above, or his son) sues for peace. This time an interesting dialogue ensues (Gen. 26:26–31):

> And Isaac said to them, Why have you come to me, seeing that you hated me and sent me away from you? And they replied, We have seen repeatedly that the Lord is with you, and so we said, Let there now be an oath between us, and let us make a covenant with you.... After all, you are blessed of the Lord!

Nearly 4,000 years later – in 1977–79 – an Egyptian President, Anwar Sadat, after three decades of deep Arab hatred of Israel, and hostilities with it, finally made his peace with the Jewish state, motivated in no small measure by the conviction that Israel "is here to stay" and cannot be defeated militarily.

Jacob / Laban

Jacob, repeatedly deceived, degraded and exploited by his uncle Laban, finally flees his uncle's estate, taking his family and his livestock with him, and heads for home. Laban pursues him, and words are exchanged when he catches up with him. But in the end the two "make up" and erect a "mound of witness," or watchpost, on the spot (Gen. 31:44–54) – with this prayer: *"May the Lord watch between you and me when we can no longer see each other..."*

Joseph / Pharaoh

Thanks to his God-given talent for dream interpretation, Joseph rises to phenomenal heights in Egypt's political hierarchy. Indeed, so great is his influence over the Pharaoh of that day, that some history scholars have speculated that this Egyptian monarch may well have been Akhnaton, or Amenhotep IV (1378–1361 BCE) of Egypt's 18th dynasty, the first (indeed the only) Pharaoh to depart from the prevailing multi-deity religious concept of ancient Egypt to promulgate the faith in a supreme deity – the sun-god – as the principal source of nourishment, the shaper of natural forces, the supreme ruler over all the other deities: a concept he may well have developed under the influence of Joseph.

Moses / Jethro

The monumental figure of Moses, moving from his early existence as an "Egyptian" prince to the status of heroic redeemer of his own downtrodden Hebrew kinfolk and, ultimately, that of national leader and lawgiver, is constantly and repeatedly exposed to gentile encounters.

After being rescued from the waters of the Nile by Pharaoh's daughter, he not only grows up at the royal court but actually lives most of his life there. Aware, however, of his Hebrew origins, thanks to ongoing contacts with his sister Miriam, Moses begins at last to take an active interest in the fate of his oppressed brethren. Encountering an Egyptian taskmaster belaboring a Hebrew slave, he slays the Egyptian – and, threatened with exposure, is forced to flee to Midian. There he is again cast in the role of hero, rescuing a group of "damsels in distress," among them Tsipporah, daughter of the Midianite priest Jethro and later to become Moses's wife.

As it turns out, Jethro is to play a key role in subsequent events connected with the Israelites' wanderings in the desert. He joins Moses at Mount Sinai and offers him some invaluable counsel concerning the dispensation of justice among his people (Chapter 18 in the Book of Exodus). *"And Moses,"* the Bible tells us towards the end of that chapter, *"hearkened to the voice of his father-in-law and did all that he had said."*

Jethro distinguished himself in yet another way: This Midianite priest, of whom it was said (*Rashi/Siftei Hachamim* on Exodus 2:16) that no form of idol worship existed in his day in which he did not indulge, now fully and openly acknowledged the supremacy and omnipotence of Israel's God – and proclaimed his acknowledgment for all to hear: *"Blessed be the Lord,"* Jethro said, *"who delivered you from the Egyptians and from Pharaoh, and who delivered the people from under the hand of the Egyptians. Now I know that the Lord is greater than all the gods..."* (Exodus 18:10–11). The Midrash (*Mechilta* 2) salutes Jethro for this public acknowledgment in these words: "Scripture here reprimands Israel. For here were 600,000 people, and not one of them stood up to bless the Almighty, until Jethro came along and blessed the Almighty."

Had he lived today, Jethro would surely have been awarded the title of "Righteous Gentile." As it is, he is remembered and honored in another way: An entire Weekly Portion of the Torah (read in the synagogue during the Jewish Sabbath service) is named after him.

While on the subject of Moses, we might add a word about the intriguing episode, referred to in Numbers 12:1, concerning his Cushite (Ethiopian?) wife. Miriam and Aaron spoke out against Moses "regarding the dark-skinned ('Cushite') woman he had married – for he had indeed married a dark-skinned woman." The commentators differ as to whether this woman was an Ethiopian (as the name Cushite seems to indicate) or whether the reference is to the Midianite Tsipporah, daughter of Jethro. In any event, the Lord's ire is aroused by this casting of aspersions on His trusted servant Moses, and Aaron and Miriam are severely reprimanded (Num. 12:5–9).

Joshua / Rahab

Rahab was the harlot in whose house, built into the walls of Jericho, two Israelites, sent by Joshua to spy out the land, found refuge (Joshua 2). In return for her protection, the two pledged that Rahab and her family would be spared when Joshua and his army captured the town; and this pledge was honored. Moreover, according to Jewish tradition, Rahab not only adopted the Jewish faith but is said to have been surpassed only by Moses himself in the vigor and depth of her commitment to God's kingship. She married Joshua, and their descendants included eleven prophets, among them Jeremiah, Ezekiel and Hulda, as well as the kings of the Hasmonean dynasty. When the Jews do right, the Jerusalem Talmud relates, "God finds righteous gentiles like Jethro and Rahab to join the Jewish people; when they incur His wrath, He removes the righteous from their midst."

Balaam: Blessing – and Curse

An exceedingly strange encounter was that between the schizophrenic Aramean prophet Balaam and the Children of Israel. Summoned by the King of Moab, Balak, to curse the Israelites as they prepared to pass through his land (Numbers, Chapters 22–24), Balaam, after first hesitating to respond to this call, finally consented; but, instead of uttering the requested curses, he was led by God to recite a paean of praise and blessing for Israel. Jewish scholars down the centuries have rendered differing assessments of this gentile seer – some regarding him as an unregenerate mischief-maker, the very epitome of evil, whose blessings had to be forced from his lips; while others perceived him as a prophet of great stature, on a par with the greatest of the Jewish prophets, Moses. Here is how the Midrash (*Bemidbar Rabba* 20) puts it:

> Just as God provided kings, wise men and prophets for the Children of Israel, so did He provide these for the nations of the world.... If greatness was granted to Israel – so it was with the nations. Thus was Moses given to Israel – and Balaam to the nations of the world.

All agree, however, that Balaam's character was flawed, and that it was he who counseled Balak, after the "blessing fiasco" (from Balak's point of view), to corrupt the Israelite community by having "the daughters of Moab" entice them into acts of immorality culminating in the brazen worship of the Moabite deity Baal Peor, also known as "the god of shamelessness." In the ensuing plague that broke out among the Israelites, 24,000 died. Ultimately, Balaam was made to pay with his own life for his evil counsel. And yet – as we have already mentioned – it is one of Balaam's inspired utterances that holds pride of place in the Jewish liturgy: The first six words of the morning prayer are words that were spoken by this gentile prophet.

Good Neighbors and Bad

How should Israel relate to the nations of the world? The Torah carefully and deliberately discriminates, in this respect, among various groups of nations. One illuminating example of this, from the ethical point of view, is the set of instructions issued the Israelites, in Deuteronomy 23:4–9, as to how they are to relate to the Ammonites, the Moabites, the Edomites and the Egyptians. On Ammon and Moab, we read the following:

> An Ammonite or a Moabite shall not enter into the assembly of the Lord; even their tenth generation shall not enter into the assembly of the Lord, forever; because they did not meet you with bread and water on your journey after you left Egypt, and because they hired Balaam… to curse you. … You shall never concern yourself with their welfare or their benefit as long as you live.

Note, however, a different approach to Edom and Egypt – and the reasons given:

> You shall not abhor an Edomite, for he is your kinsman. You shall not abhor an Egyptian, for you were a stranger in his land. Children born to them may enter into the assembly of the Lord in the third generation.

The precise reasons – for the rejection in one instance, and for a conditioned acceptance in the other – are not so important here as the implied proposition that there are nations, or societies, that are unredeemable and with whom, therefore, one should have no dealings of any kind. And there are nations or societies which, though they may have a history of conflict with you and wrongdoing against you, are nevertheless potentially worthy of communion and friendship, in spite of their faults and blemishes.

Wise – and blessed – is the nation that knows how to make the distinction.

The Case of Amalek

We must, in this context, mention an encounter of a very different kind between Jew and gentile. This encounter, which took place very early in the history of the Jewish people, sparked a conflict that not only left an indelible scar on the Jewish psyche but that, contrary to most of the other conflicts mentioned in this chapter, has no redeeming feature and is not destined to culminate in reconciliation. The treacherous assault upon the Israelites in the desert by the tribe of Amalek became an event to be remembered by the Jewish people for all eternity. Indeed, the Torah (Deuteronomy 25:17–19) impresses upon Israel the crucial importance of this act of remembrance:

> Remember what Amalek did to you on your journey, when you went out of Egypt: how, undeterred by fear of God, he fell upon you on the way, when you were famished and weary, and massacred your stragglers. Therefore, when the Lord your God will have given you respite from all your enemies round about, in the land that the Lord your God is giving you as an inheritance to take possession of it, you shall blot out the memory of Amalek from under the heaven: Do not forget this!

Through the ages, the injunction to "remember Amalek" has been etched in the consciousness of the Jewish people. But the tribe and its offspring have not been blotted out. And whenever a particularly vile and brutal foe of the Jewish people has acted to decimate that people – whether it was Persia's Haman in biblical times, Torquemada of the Spanish Inquisition in the Middle Ages or Adolf Hitler in the 20th century – Jews would say: Amalek lives on.

This, too, is part of the history of the relations between the Jew and "the other."

Chapter 3

Parting of the Ways

With the emergence of Christianity in the first two centuries of the Common Era, the Jewish-gentile encounter took on a new character. What began as a falling-out between rabbinic Jewry and other Jews of the time who felt inclined to follow the Apostles and to accept Jesus as Messiah later became a far wider-ranging conflict. With the passage of time, the Christian faith was accepted by more and more people outside the Jewish community; by the mid-fourth century, under the Emperor Constantine, it had become the official religion of the Roman Empire.

It is not within the scope or purpose of this book to delve into the details, circumstances and motivating factors that make up the history of the 2,000-year-old conflict between Christianity and its mother-religion, Judaism. Countless books and articles have been written on this subject, and on the long record of anti-Jewish dogmas and teachings, policies and practices of the Christian Church, and the deep wounds these policies and practices have inflicted on the Jewish people over the centuries. These things are too well known to bear repetition. For the purposes of our discussion, let us accept this history as a given – and cull from it only some less-familiar episodes having a direct bearing on the subject of this book.

Conversion
Two millennia have elapsed since the end of the biblical era. Needless to say, dialogue (often on the personal level) and debate (generally

before large audiences) between Jew and gentile have continued, in various forms and with varying results, throughout this time. Such contacts, when conducted between individuals, have at times culminated in the conversion of the Christian partner to Judaism or in the conversion of the Jewish partner to Christianity. Most of the time, however, these encounters did not produce a meeting of the minds, and the existing animosities remained in place.

The Jewish attitude towards the phenomenon of gentile conversions to Judaism has varied over the centuries. When things went well for the Jews, there was a tendency to welcome converts; when things went badly, they tended to discourage conversions. Since the latter was the more commonly prevailing condition, it may be said that, generally speaking, potential converts to Judaism have been discouraged from taking the step. Indeed, over time, a procedure was established, in Jewish law (*halachah*) and practice, whereby the candidate for conversion is rebuffed again and again, and only if he demonstrates his strong will and determination by coming back after each of these rejections, is he permitted to enter the next phase: a thoroughgoing course of instruction in the rudiments of the Jewish faith, preparatory to becoming a member of that faith community. But once he is accepted, the convert (*ger*) becomes a full-fledged Jew, with all the rights, privileges and obligations of one who is born into the faith. (For a discussion of the Jewish view concerning the conversion of Jews to Christianity, see Chapter 8, pp. 129–130.)

The Hebrew word for convert is *ger*. Derived from the root *goor*, meaning "to dwell," the term is used in two different combinations having, actually, three different meanings: A *ger-toshav* (dweller-resident), in the social sense, is one who has come from another land to settle (see *Abraham*, on p. 24); in the religious sense, the term denotes a gentile who has accepted the seven Noahide commandments (to establish courts of law and to refrain from murder, from stealing, from incest, from cruelty to animals, from idolatry and from blasphemy) but not the remaining portions of the Torah; a *ger-tse-dek* (authentic convert) is one who, having held another faith, has converted fully to Judaism, not for material or other personal gain, but out of conviction.

The classic case of conversion to Judaism is that of Ruth the Moabite. It is also an apt illustration – indeed the source and origin, one might say – of the rule, mentioned earlier, that in bad times (as were those described in the Book of Ruth) conversions to Judaism should be discouraged. Ruth, however, the Bible tells us, would not take no for an answer, and went on to distinguish herself as the progenitor of King David – and thus of the Messiah.

Onkelos: The Ideal Convert

A later example of the full integration and acceptance of a former gentile, through conversion, into Jewish peoplehood is the case of the second-century scholar Onkelos, best known perhaps for his translation of the Torah (Pentateuch) into Aramaic. This translation has been universally accepted and respected, in the world of Jewish learning, as a highly authoritative, even inspired, rendition of the biblical text, whose profound and incisive insights have, on innumerable occasions to this very day, served Bible commentators and exegetes in their own commentaries and interpretations of the sacred text.

The Talmud, in the tractate of *Gitin* (56b–57a), relates that Onkelos was a nephew of the Roman emperor Titus and that, when he began to think about becoming a Jew, he invoked the spirits of Titus, Balaam and Jesus and sought their counsel: All of them testified that in the world to come it would be the Children of Israel who would be held in the highest regard. According to another Talmudic account (*Avodah Zarah* 11a), after Onkelos's conversion, the Roman emperor summoned him to the royal palace, but each time the emperor's guards, sent to bring the convert to Rome, were themselves converted by Onkelos to Judaism!

As we have indicated, Onkelos in his translation of the Hebrew Bible exhibits a profound understanding not only of the biblical text but also of root concepts that underlie that text and make it more meaningful to the reader and to the student of the Bible. One example of this insight will have to suffice for our purposes:

Former MIT physics professor Dr. Gerald Schroeder is one of several scientist-authors who have advanced the thesis that the biblical account of the creation of the universe, when correctly understood, corresponds very closely to the most widely held current cosmological perceptions. One of these is what Schroeder – in his book, *Genesis and the Big Bang* (Bantam Books) – calls "a flow from chaos to cosmos." In this connection, Schroeder makes a remarkable linguistic discovery, worth sharing here with our readers in the author's own words (and please note his observation, in the second paragraph, concerning Onkelos's Aramaic translation):

> Our study of the evening and morning sequences in the first chapter of Genesis has taught us that days and nights are not the main topic of conversation here. Each "day" marked an epoch, a flow from disorder toward increasing order in the material of the universe. This transition from disorder toward order is hinted at in the evening to morning phrasing of the biblical text. The root meaning of the Hebrew word for evening (*erev*) is "disorder" (*eruv, irbuv*) and for morning (*boker*) is "order" (*bakarah, bikoret*). "And there was evening and there was morning" is telling us that in each "daily" episode, at a specific location within the universe, order was imposed by God on the disorder that had existed.
>
> In a brilliant insight into the quality of the world present at the close of the six days of Genesis, Onkelos translates the "and it was very good" of Genesis 1:31 as "and it was a unified order." The physical universe was prepared, and mankind was in place. The social evolution that was to follow was no longer dominated by the inherent forces of matter that until now had played a major role in the world's development. From this time forward, there would be an interplay between man's free will and his knowledge of the will of the Creator. This interplay would be imprinted on future events. (Parenthetical glosses added.)

The fact of Onkelos having been a convert to Judaism never for a moment stood in the way of his literary offerings being accepted and recognized by Jewish scholars down the centuries as the monumental contributions that indeed they are to a fuller and better understanding of God's Word.

Dialogue and Debate

The Talmud in several places alludes to a series of theological discussions held by the editor of Israel's Oral Torah, the Mishnah, Rabbi Yehudah Hanassi, with a second-century Roman statesman identified only as "Antoninus." It was, you might say, the first interfaith dialogue, conducted – to judge from the Talmudic account – in a spirit of candor, mutual respect and genuine intellectual curiosity.

This, however, is hardly the way one would describe the debates or religious disputations that were to characterize the Christian-Jewish encounter in later centuries. More in the nature of "command performances," these asymmetrical disputations invariably placed the minority Jewish partner at an impossible disadvantage vis-à-vis the Christian representative.

With the passage of time, Judaism and Christianity – and the two faith communities as such – grew farther and farther apart. It is hardly surprising, therefore, that the fourth-century public theological debate, in Caesarea, between the Jewish sage Rabbi Abahu and the Christian ecclesiastic Bishop Eusebius, at the invitation of the Roman governor and in his presence, was held in a more tolerant atmosphere than two similar disputations, nearly a thousand years later, in Paris and Barcelona.

In the year 1240, a religious debate between Nicolaus Donin, an ex-Jewish apostate, and the head of the Paris Talmudic Academy, Rabbi Yehiel, ended in the public burning of 24 wagonloads of Talmudic volumes, rendering continued Jewish religious study in France all but impossible.

Twenty-three years later, Nahmanides, Chief Rabbi of Catalonia, Spain, and one of the great Jewish biblical and Talmudic scholars and commentators, responded to a challenge from another apostate, the Dominican priest Pablo Christiani. With the bitter memory of the ill-fated Paris debate still vivid in the Jewish community's memory, the rabbis in Spain were strongly opposed to any kind of Jewish participation in such a debate. The King of Spain, however, exploiting his personal friendship with Nahmanides, was able to persuade him to act as the advocate of Judaism at the public spectacle in Barcelona upon which he had set his heart. However, Nahmanides was not given the opportunity to present the Jewish case in the manner in which he had planned to do, the proceedings being rudely cut short by the riotous intervention of the spectators, from which the learned rabbi barely escaped with his life.

Persecution / Protection

The Middle Ages are notorious in Jewish history for the manner in which Christian Europe dealt with its Jewish communities. The record is there for all to note: blood libels, massacres, socio-economic discrimination, incarceration of spiritual leaders, forced conversions, mass expulsions. We mention this briefly "for the record," though – once again – it must be emphasized that this aspect of the Jewish-Christian encounter down the centuries, while extremely significant in its own right, and highly germane to the subject of this book, will not be discussed or documented here in detail. Our purpose is not to dwell on these well-known facts of history, but to direct the reader's attention to what appears to be developing – right now, in our own generation – into an epoch-making change in the very nature of the encounter.

It is a change that has the potential for reversing the negative relationship that has characterized this encounter ever since the inception of Christianity two thousand years ago. And yet, so few are aware of it, in both the Christian and the Jewish communities, that its continuation and full fruition in the years and decades to come is truly in jeopardy. For, clearly, such a process can feed only on widespread active participation by the members of both communities; and how can we have such participation in a process of which most people are still unaware? The central purpose of this book, therefore, is to help more people, Christians and Jews, to learn of what has been happening – and, as a natural consequence, to become actively involved.

Before moving into the realm of 20th-century developments, however, we must point to yet another little-known aspect of that earlier history.

Bleak and terrible as they were, the events of Middle Age Europe did not present a tapestry of unrelieved hatred and woe. At various times, and in various parts of the continent, there were episodes in which the Christian ruler of a country would take his Jewish subjects under his wing, legislate for their protection and in this way actually improve their lot.

One such episode took place in Poland, where King Boleslav IV ("The Pious") in 1264 granted the Jews of Poland a Charter of Protection – a kind of "bill of rights" specifying a whole series of measures that would protect them from the arbitrary acts of vengeance and rank discrimination by the government that were so much the order of the day in that age and in most countries. The Jews of Bohemia and those living under the reign of the German emperor, Frederick II, were granted similar charters, but Boleslav's document – issued in the face of stiff papal opposition – went beyond those.

A common feature of these charters were specific clauses calling for strict penalties against Christians violating the rights of Jews, committing acts of vandalism against them or inflicting personal injury. Some even provided legal safeguards against the notorious blood libel so common in those days. Thus, the Boleslav charter contains the following provision:

> We emphatically forbid that any Jews in our state be in future accused of using human blood, since all Jews, by the tenets of their religion, abstain from blood altogether. Should a given Jew be accused of murdering a Christian child, the charge shall be proved by the testimony of three Christians and three Jews, whereupon the usual punishment shall be meted out. Should he, however, be exonerated by such witnesses as being innocent of the alleged crime, the Christian shall, for his false accusation, be

accorded the punishment that the Jew would have borne, had he been found guilty.

The last two clauses of the Polish charter, quoted below, contain a new set of privileges, not granted in any other country of the time:

- If any Jew raises an alarm at night and his Christian neighbors fail to come to his aid, they shall each be liable to a fine of 30 solids.

- Jews shall be free to buy or sell any item whatsoever and touch bread in the same way as Christians, and whosoever interferes with them shall be liable to a fine.

To be sure, the motivation for these protective measures may have had more to do with political and economic considerations than with the genuine soul-searching that appears to be in progress in the Christian world today. Nonetheless, the very fact of their existence in those truly "Dark Ages" is worthy of note.

The "Black Death"

The year 1348 was a black year for Europe: It marked the outbreak of the pestilence that, by the time it had run its course, was – according to some accounts – to take the lives of more than 20 million people, or more than one-third of the continent's population! It was a black year, in particular, for the Jews of Europe, who – not for the first time in a situation of this kind – were falsely accused by their Christian neighbors of being the cause of the "Black Death" by "poisoning the wells and the rivers." And, not for the first time, mobs incited by their leaders all over Europe rampaged through the Jewish quarters of their cities, massacring tens of thousands of innocent men, women and children in the process.

Yet, once again, we must record several redeeming incidents in what must otherwise be regarded as one of the darkest chapters in the annals of Christian-Jewish relations.

- One is the publication, in Avignon, of a papal bull signed by Pope Clement vi, which states, in part:

Recently we heard the rumor, or rather the ignominy, that certain Christians were incited by the devil to look for the causes of the Plague, which the Lord inflicted on the Christian peoples for their sins, in alleged acts of poisoning committed by the Jews. By their covetousness and their greed, Christians have been induced to seek their own profit at the expense of Jews, to whom they were owing major sums of money, by killing them off, regardless of age or sex. Although the Jews were prepared to stand trial for this libellous charge, these Christians did not desist from their accusations and, in their madness, took the law into their own hands...

Had these Jews been guilty of this heinous crime, this certainly could on no account be condoned. However, since the epidemic has affected different parts of the world, including those where there are no Jews at all, and is raging at the Lord's secret counsel, so that it is inconceivable for the Jews to have had a hand in it, I order your entire flock, by this Apostolic epistle,...to reprove your citizens, your nobles, your priests and your commons...and explicitly, on the threat of excommunication, to order them not to seize, beat, wound or kill Jews on this pretext...

• Another noteworthy incident, in this context, grew out of a Muslim initiative – but also involved Christians and Jews. In Damascus, the Muslim governor, Seif ad-Din Argun Sha'ah, proclaimed a three-day fast, at the conclusion of which the Emirs, bearing copies of Islam's holy book, the Koran, led a procession of the Muslim faithful from the Great Mosque in Damascus to the Mosque of Al-Akdam, on the Jerusalem road, south of Damascus. With them, at the invitation of the Muslim authorities, marched the Jews, carrying Scrolls of the Law, and the Christians, bearing the Gospel.

Was this the first public interfaith event in the annals of human-kind? Whether it was or not, it certainly brought together the leaders of these three faith communities that were facing the same common threat to their very existence – and were driven to the realization that their only recourse, at that point, was to Him who had created them all, and in whose hands rested their collective fate.

- In a message of welcome, in 1348, to the Jews of Greater and Smaller Poland (the union of which had taken place a year earlier), King Casimir III declared that all the privileges granted to them in the past would remain in force, and that anyone who dared spread the well-poisoning libel in his country would be severely punished. Casimir was not fazed by the mocking references to him as "the king of the peasants and the Jews." His customary retort to this "charge" was that he had nothing to be ashamed of, since Jesus himself was called *rex judeorum* – King of the Jews.

- Meanwhile, in Spain, King Peter IV of Aragon issued the following notice to the Jews of Saragossa:

    > The Jewish community of Saragossa having been stricken so severely by the present epidemic that barely one-fifth of it remains alive, reduced to a state of dire poverty, I do hereby provide that no claims for taxes or other payments due may be pressed against it or against any of its members until God in His great mercy will put an end to the Plague, at which time demand notices may be issed to the survivors.

- While we are distributing "Honorable Mentions," we might mention some other 14th and 15th century personalities (and political entities) who, in one way or another, moved against the anti-Jewish tide of that day:

    Kings Henry II and Henry III of Seville – for acting vigorously (if not always successfully) to curb the anti-Jewish excesses of the Archdeacon of Castille, Fernando Martinez;

    Pope Benedict XIII (Pedro de Luna) – for opening the gates of Avignon, the seat of his papacy, to French Jews seeking refuge following the expulsion order against the Jews of France issued by King Charles VI in 1394; and for having earlier (as Cardinal of Pamplona) refused permission to the antisemitic Paulus de Santa Maria to conduct a conversion campaign among the local Jews;

    The French provinces of Dauphine, Provence, Arles and Marseilles – for refusing to honor King Charles's expulsion order;

    Pope Sixtus IV – for his strong principled stand against the Span-

ish Inquisition, and particularly for his April 1482 letter to Queen
Isabella, in which he condemned the judicial methods adopted by
the Inquisition in the Seville trial where 300 Marranos (undercover
Jews) were burned to death: These trials, the Pope averred, were being
conducted "not for love of our faith or to mend souls, but from sheer
greed" (*non zelo fidei et salutis animarum, set lucri cupiditas*).

The Righteous Gentile

The *Haggadah shel Pesach* (Passover Narrative) – the traditional text
that forms the backbone of the Passover Seder Night ritual in Jewish
homes – contains this passage:

> And it is this that has stood by our fathers and us: For not only
> one has risen up against us to destroy us, but in all ages they
> have risen up to destroy us – and the Holy One Blessed Be He
> has delivered us from their hands.

The passage cites two themes: the ever-present threat of destruction…and the promise – and fulfillment – of Divine deliverance. The
Jewish people, scattered across the world among often hostile societies, has been buffeted by many a human tempest, sometimes at a
frightful cost in lives, but it was guaranteed survival as a people, so
long as it kept the faith – and survive it did. *"But while a tenth part
yet remains, it shall repent,"* says the Prophet. *"It shall be ravaged like
the terebinth and the oak, of which stumps are left even when they are
felled: Its stump shall be a holy seed"* (Isaiah 6:13).

On more than one occasion, the Lord has chosen a gentile as
the human instrument by means of which to effect the deliverance
of His people.

Moses, who led the Israelites out of the Egyptian "house of bondage," was a Hebrew. But he spent his youth in Egypt's royal palace,
the daughter of the Egyptian Pharaoh having saved him from certain death when he was yet a tiny babe, in defiance of her father's
genocidal order to cast every Israelite baby boy into the waters of
the river. The "Bitya, daughter of Pharaoh" mentioned in 1 Chronicles

4:18, was, according to the Talmud, the woman who rescued Moses from the waters of the Nile. (The role of Jethro, Moses's father-in-law, as a Righteous Gentile is discussed in Chapter 2 – see p. 28.)

Bitya (Hebrew for "Daughter of God") was the illustrious forerunner of those courageous Christians in mid-20th century Europe who risked their lives by sheltering Jewish neighbors from the Nazis' murderous clutches. Asked later how they had mustered the courage to do this noble deed at such terrible risk to their own and their families' safety and very lives, the response offered, often as not, was: "It was the Christian thing to do."

Those deeds – shining through all the more because of their relative rareness in the Nazi inferno – bespoke Christian witness in its most exalted sense. It was a "voice in the wilderness" – part of that wilderness being the silence of the established Christian Churches in the face of what was happening. But it was a voice the Jewish people, and the State of Israel that today speaks for the Jewish people, will never forget.

On October 10, 1996, a French pastor's wife named Magda Trocmé died, aged 94, in a Paris hospital. It was Mme. Trocmé and her husband André who had inspired the successful wartime effort of Le Chambon-sur-Lignon, a small mountain community in central France, to rescue thousands of local (and other) Jews from the Nazis. Through word of mouth, the village, together with other villages in the area, became a haven for some 5,000 refugees, most of them Jews, during World War II. Le Chambon has been honored by Yad Vashem, the Holocaust memorial institution in Jerusalem, for its collective rescue effort, and its exploits have been immortalized in a feature film – in French and English versions – entitled *Les armes de l'esprit* ("Weapons of the Spirit"). In July 1986, Magda Trocmé received the Righteous Gentile award in a ceremony at the Embassy of Israel in Paris. Mme. Trocmé never quite understood all the attention she received for doing something she considered her natural duty. "She just always thought that there should be more justice and more love in the world for people of all classes," her son

Jacques said after her death. "She believed that what she was doing was perfectly normal."

That, indeed, was the attitude displayed by many of these Christians – alas, there were too few of them! – Germans, Poles, Dutch, Danes, French, Lithuanians, Ukrainians, Italians and others who, in Europe's darkest hour, responded in selfless bravery to the divine command to "Love thy neighbor as thyself."

Another of those courageous Christian voices that could not be silenced was that of Dr. Klara Schlink (later to become known as Mother Basilea) of Darmstadt, Germany, who dared in those dark years to speak out on Israel's "great future" as "the foundation for humankind's redemption." Twice, Dr. Schlink was interrogated by the Nazi Secret Police, the Gestapo, but, by the grace of the Lord, she was spared. In 1947, only two years after the war, Dr. Schlink, together with her co-worker Erika Madauss (later Mother Martyria), founded the Evangelical Sisterhood of Mary, as part of the German Protestant Church. In the Foreword to Mother Basilea's book, "Israel, My Chosen People," the Sisters of Mary describe the birth of the Sisterhood in these words:

> At the end of the war, clearly perceiving God's hand of judgment in the destruction of many German towns, including her hometown Darmstadt, she [Mother Basilea] was used by the Lord to start a movement of repentance, which was to have nationwide repercussions. Repentance was the keynote of the revival among the Girls' Bible Study Groups, which gave rise to our Evangelical Sisterhood of Mary, and it was repentance that gave birth to a deep love for Israel in our fellowship.

The Sisterhood has since grown into an international, interdenominational organization with branches in ten countries – including Israel (Beth Abraham, in Jerusalem) and the United States (Canaan in the Desert, in Phoenix, Arizona). Its members have devoted their lives to the service of God, and, through prayer, fasting and good deeds, they are helping to heal the deep wounds inflicted on Israel and the

Jewish people. Interestingly, those first post-war signs of repentance and change in the Christian Church that, much later, were to blossom into a wide-ranging pattern of theological re-thinking and revision took place in Germany itself – the country where Church-inspired antisemitism had sprouted in its most horrific form.

In that same year of 1947, another significant milestone was implanted on the new road of Christian repentance: the Ten Points published by the International Council of Christians and Jews in the Swiss town of Seelisberg. But more on that in a later chapter (see p. 72), where we shall see how these bridging events in the early years following the Shoah / Holocaust culminated in the series of revisionary moves, by major Catholic and Protestant Churches and institutions, to which we have alluded.

One particular voice – that of The Assemblies of God in the United States – deserves separate and special mention in this context. As early as 1927 – 21 years before the advent of the State of Israel in its modern reincarnation – the Assemblies' General Council, in Article 14 of its Statement of Fundamental Truths, referred explicitly to "the salvation of national Israel." And, in 1945, in the wake of World War II and the Shoah, it took a firm principled stand on antisemitism, going on to define in some detail its position concerning the restoration of Israel and the ingathering of its exiled sons and daughters: an event that was to come to full fruition only years later! More on this, too, in a later chapter (see pp. 70–71).

Part Two
Sea-Change

Chapter 4

The Christian Churches Today

THE FIRST AND MOST important thing to be noted, as we move to the Christian side of the Jewish-Christian encounter, and to contemporary developments in this encounter, is that we are not dealing here with a monolith. The use of the plural form – "Churches" – in this context is deliberate. It is designed to eliminate, from the outset, the kind of question that I was so frequently asked (though rarely by a Christian!) when I served as Israel's envoy to the Christian Churches in the United States: "What is the Christian (or the Christian Church's) attitude towards Israel (or towards Jews)?" This kind of question presupposes a Christian community that is uniform in the way its members think, believe and act. In point of fact, doctrinal and attitudinal differences among the various Churches and denominations are at least as numerous, in the Christian community, as they are in the Jewish. We have not, in the previous chapters, discussed the latter, because the intracommunal variances in Jewry are essentially irrelevant to the theme of this book, the main thrust of which is the sea-change that has substantially altered the face of Chrisendom in its attitude towards the Jewish people, the Jewish religion and the reborn Jewish nation-state.

Jewish internal differences will be brought into play when we deal, later, with the Jewish response to this change. Up to this point, however, these differences have not been relevant to our presentation. The purpose thus far has been to paint a background picture of the Jewish-Christian encounter in history, to set the stage for the veritable revolution in the nature of that encounter that has taken place in the second half of the 20th century and into the 21st.

From Supersessionism to Contempt

Historically, Christian attitudes towards Jews and Judaism have been shaped, in large measure, by such interrelated doctrinal and attitudinal concepts as supersessionism, triumphalism and the teaching of contempt.

Supersessionism maintains that, following the Jews' rejection of the messiahship of Jesus of Nazareth, the divine election of the Jews was replaced by that granted to the Christian Church – "the new (or true) Israel" or "the new Chosen People," replacing the old. By extension, this doctrine was also applied to the New Testament – or, better stated perhaps, the New Covenant – as essentially replacing the Old as the valid Word of God. From doctrines such as this it was but a short step to concepts like triumphalism – celebrating "the victory of the Church over the vanquished Jewish people, condemned to wander endlessly over the face of the earth," and the teaching of contempt – which, in effect, gave license, to Christians disposed to do so, to demean, persecute, despoil and massacre Jews at will. Under the circumstances, and with this theological background, it was not difficult for those who engaged in these practices to do these things in the sincere belief and conviction that they were merely "doing the will of the Lord" in thus punishing these "infidels."

Adolf Hitler and his Nazi cohorts were not Christians; in fact, they were avowed and unabashed opponents of Christianity. However, in conceiving, planning, directing and executing their satanic and unprecedented campaign of genocide against the Jewish people, they were able to exploit to the fullest the anti-Jewish doctrines of the Christian Church that, for centuries, had rendered the members of this people so vulnerable to unbridled abuse and persecution.

The Situation in America

Even in countries and societies – such as the United States of America – where the dominant Christian population followed an entirely different path in its relationship with the Jewish community, and where news of the Nazi Holocaust in Europe belatedly aroused horror and revulsion, the traditional antisemitic doctrines of the Church could not but leave their imprint on the minds and souls of the faithful. Supersessionism and its various doctrinal by-products were preached regularly from the pulpit, and the relegation of the Old Testament to the sidelines, in favor of the New, was common-place. This is true particularly of the so-called "mainline" Protestant Churches, notably the United Church of Christ and the Presbyterian, Methodist, Lutheran, Episcopalian and Baptist Churches.

(The continuing decline in membership, in recent decades, among many of these denominations has given birth – in some Christian think-tanks – to the alternate term "sideline Churches" to denote this branch of Protestantism. I preferred to stay with the more widely used "mainline" – and to place it within quotation marks.)

Among these denominations, it was not uncommon to reduce the Old Testament, though considered part of Holy Scripture, to a somewhat lesser status, some of it being assigned allegorical mean-ing rather than being understood literally.

There is, on the other hand, a growing body in Christendom that relates quite differently to the Old Testament – the *Tanach*. These are the Evangelical Christians: Pentecostals, Charismatics, Southern Baptists and others, many of them belonging to churches that do not identify with any particular denomination. They are Christians who believe in making a conscious personal commitment to Jesus, a spiritual encounter often referred to as the born-again experience. To them, the Jewish Bible, or Old Testament, is revered on the same level as is the New. Indeed, many Evangelicals regard themselves as fundamentalist Christians, in relating to both parts of their Bible as the literal and living Word of God; in other words, as history – or "history with a message for humankind."

The way in which the various Protestant denominations and groupings relate to the Jewish Bible was bound to impact the way these denominations viewed the national resurgence of the Jew-ish people in the 20th century. For "mainline" Protestants, at that time still imbued with the anti-Jewish doctrines and teachings that shaped so much of Christianity's behavior down the centuries, the establishment of the State of Israel in 1948 and the concomitant, and subsequent, large-scale "ingathering of the exiles" from the four corners of the earth was very difficult to understand and assimilate: Here was a people that, according to what they had been taught, God had rejected and relegated to a status of homelessness and suffering; how could this people now suddenly be the beneficiary of the blessings of reunification, nationhood and prosperity?! The resultant confusion in the minds of many Christians evoked two kinds of reaction: one was aggravated hostility towards the Jews and their state; the other – a profound re-thinking of traditional beliefs and doctrines, leading eventually to acceptance of a new and different kind of truth from the one that had informed the Christian ethos up to that point.

Initially, in the nature of things, the first of these reactions proved to be the prevailing one in these circles, and, for a number of years following the attainment of Israel's independence, much of "mainline" Protestantism translated its doctrinal consternation into an attitude ranging from reserve to outright hostility vis-à-vis Jews and the Jewish state. Then, gradually, under the growing impact of developments in the Church that began, in a serious way, in the 1960s, there came a perceptible if gradual shift to the second option – as will be discussed further (and documented) in Chapter 6. Still, traces of the initial theological difficulty that plagued this segment of the Protestant world appear to have remained, and they find repeated expression in the pointedly anti-Israel statements issued, from time to time, by these Churches and their umbrella organization, the World Council of Churches. (This subject is treated, and documented, at greater length in Chapter 9.)

Evangelicals and the State of Israel

Not so, however, in the Evangelical community. Evangelicals, by and large, did not view the national resurgence of Israel, the ingathering of the exiles and the social and economic revival of the Holy Land as in any way contradicting Christian theology and tradition. Quite the contrary. They understood all of these developments as nothing less than the wondrous fulfillment of biblical prophecy – the realization, "in spades," of the prophecies of Isaiah, Jeremiah, Ezekiel, Amos, Zechariah and others concerning the return of the people of Israel to their land; the confluence, in the land, of its dispersed sons and daughters from every corner of the globe; the rejuvenation and fructification of the long-neglected soil and the rebuilding of "the waste cities." God (so it was felt in these circles) was bringing His people home, as He had promised He would, and those of the human race living in this generation have truly been privileged to witness this glorious event in their own lifetime and – if they so choose – actually to be a part of it. Could there be a greater blessing? Could there be a more exhilarating climax to the biblical story and its ultimate promise? Well, perhaps not the *ultimate* promise: That, in Christian eyes, would be the Second Coming of Christ; but the anticipation of that event, too, is part of the great turn-of-the-millennium drama unfolding before our very eyes. Believing Christians do not know when that eagerly awaited happening will take place. What they do know, however, is that the return of the Jewish people to its ancestral homeland is the necessary forerunner of the return of Jesus – and is to be celebrated for that if for no other reason.

Episcopalians, Evangelicals… Presbyterians, Pentecostals: Christians all, yet what a difference in outlook on one of the central events of the 20th century!

Hidden Agenda?
Coming back, though, for a moment, to the above-mentioned Evangelical "celebration" of Israel Reborn as the necessary forerunner of the return of Jesus: The truth is that many in the Jewish community have a problem with this "hidden agenda." How – they maintain – can we trust these Evangelicals and their friendship and support, when their agenda includes the Second Coming, at which time they will seek to convert all of us to their faith? The authentic Jewish response to these reservations would appear to be a simple one: That dreaded "agenda" is, after all, a Christian agenda, not a Jewish one. And Jews should feel firm enough and strong enough in their ancestral faith

to withstand attempts to convert them – in the future as in the present and the past.

Besides, Jews too await the advent of Messiah, do they not? – though clearly in a different way from the way Christians do. The difference, to be sure, is an important, indeed a vital, one – and one to be kept in mind at all times in relating to the Jewish-Christian encounter. This, however, need not and should not prevent our two communities from pursuing a wholesome relationship, and "walking together" when that portion of our spiritual heritage that we do hold in common enables us – no, commands us – to walk together. Chapter 8 of this book (dealing with Mission, Witness and Dialogue) develops this theme further: thus, for example, Prophet Micah's (4:5) wise counsel (p. 146); the fascinating "Converging Verticality" theory of Father Marcel Dubois (p. 130); and the musings on the Messiah in a new and little-noticed Vatican study (p. 153).

A quite remarkable footnote to this recital of the Evangelical view of The Return is a parallel belief in the Jewish community – based on the writings of Maimonides and other Jewish commentators and philosophers – that the attainment of Jewish national independence and sovereignty in the Land of Israel is a prior condition for the advent of the Messiah. And, while we are on the subject of parallels between the Jewish ethos and that of Evangelical Christianity, here is another: The reader may recall our definition of the Jewish commitment (see p. 17). Oriented outward rather than inward, we said, its ultimate aim is "to achieve worldwide recognition of its own universalist understanding of God." However, "Until the time is ripe for this worldwide recognition to blossom in full, the Jewish people is duty-bound to preserve and nurture its own identity, cultivate its sense of mission and never cease aspiring to become 'a crown of glory in the hand of the Lord...' For how can Israel hope to be 'a light unto the nations'...if it does not take care to keep its own flame burning?" Now compare this, if you will, to the words of Manhattan Evangelist Bill Bray: "We want to change the world – but we want to change ourselves first" (TIME, Dec. 26, 1977). A leaf from the same book?

President Ezer Weizman receives first Papal Nuncio in Israel, Msgr. Andrea di Montezemolo

Prime Minister Shimon Peres greets Vatican Secretary of State Msgr. Jean-Louis Tauran (1996)

Israel's Chief Rabbi Israel Meir Lau and Pope John Paul II meet at the Vatican (1993)

Rome, July 1992: Vatican-Israel Commission that paved the way for diplomatic relations - headed by Msgr. Claudio M. Celli (fifth from right) and Ambassador Yossi Hadas (sixth from left)

Pope John Paul II receives Israel's first Ambassador to the Vatican, Shmuel Hadass (left), as Israel Ambassador to Rome, Avi Pazner, looks on

*Msgr. Claudio M. Celli (Vatican) and Deputy Foreign Minister
Dr. Yossi Beilin (Israel) sign 1993 Fundamental Agreement*

*Cardinal Carlo Maria Martini and
Chief Rabbi Israel Meir Lau meet in Jerusalem in 1999*

Pope John Paul II at Western Wall of Temple Mount
(March 2000)

Jewish worshiper at Western Wall pays his respects to the pope,
as Minister for Diaspora Affairs Rabbi Michael Melchior looks on

President Ezer
Weizman receives Latin
Patriarch H.B. Michel
Sabbah, as Armenian
Patriarch H.B. Torkom
Manoogian looks on

Author meets Cardinal
John O'Connor and
Mayor of Jerusalem,
Teddy Kollek (1992)

Father-Son Reunion in
Jerusalem: Fr. George
Edelstein, of Russian
Orthodox Church, with
son Yuli, then Israel's
Absorption Minister
(and an Orthodox Jew)

Catholic-Anglican-Lutheran triad in Jerusalem: Fr. Marcel Dubois (r.) receiving Cross of Nails from Rev. Canon Andrew White at Ratisbonne Institute, as Rev. Petra Heldt looks on

Rabbi Michael Melchior meets (from left) Bishop Zakarias Johannes of Eritrea, Archbishop Ndingi Mwana'a Nzeki of Kenya and Archbishop John Onaiyeken of Nigeria - in Jerusalem (2000)

Philippine pilgrims at Christian Embassy's Tabernacles Feast march through downtown Jerusalem (Oct. 2000)

Christmas Caroling in Jerusalem's Safra Square, with Mayor Ehud Olmert

*In 1995, the Pentecostal World Conference came to
Jerusalem for its 17th annual meeting*

© Yoav Loeff

*Pentecostal Minister
and NCLCI Chairman
Dr. David Lewis*

*(l. to r.) Sisters Gratia and
Irene (Jerusalem) and Sister
Pista (Darmstadt) of the
Sisterhood of Mary, with
the Author at "Beth
Abraham" in Jerusalem*

Chapter 5

The Catholic Church: A Special Case

*The characteristic note of the Roman Curia is its intense
conservatism and its slowness to move, whether in approv-
ing or condemning new developments of opinion or action.*
(Encyclopedia Britannica, 11th Edition, 1910–1911)

OUR OMISSION of the Roman Catholic Church from the previous chapter is not accidental or haphazard. The discussion of that Church and its relationship to Jews and to the State of Israel merits a separate chapter – and this for three reasons:

1. The Roman Catholic Church is unique in that it is the only Church that, side by side with its spiritual "personality," has a temporal-political one as well.

2. The Roman Catholic Church bears the brunt of the historic responsibility for the promulgation of the anti-Jewish doctrines that have been the cause of so much suffering and anguish among the Jewish people over the centuries.

3. The Roman Catholic Church, ever since the 1960s, has played a pioneering role in instituting the theologically wrenching revisions in those doctrines that have moved other major Christian Churches to follow in its footsteps, and that have paved the way for recognition of the Jewish State of Israel by the Holy See and the establishment of full diplomatic relations with it.

The first point cited above, while important in its own right for our understanding of the distinction that must be drawn between this Church and all the others, is in this context merely a necessary introduction to the third point. The second point concerns a subject that has already been elucidated in earlier chapters. It remains for us, therefore, only to discuss the third point – by way of a preface leading directly to the documentation presented in Chapter 6.

As was pointed out in the previous chapter, the twin upheavals that impacted the Jewish people in the middle of the 20th century – the Shoah and the national renascence of this people – sent theological shock waves through the Christian world. The largest single organized component of this world, with close to a billion members worldwide, is the Roman Catholic Church, headed by the Bishop of Rome, the Pope, residing in the sovereign state known as Vatican City. For this reason alone, it would not be unreasonable to expect the primary and most authoritative reaction to the events mentioned to emanate from that Church. And, to all intents and purposes, that was indeed the case.

True, as will be shown in Chapter 6, other Christian voices were heard, here and there, before that of the Catholic Church. But neither by the content of their messages nor by the impact they had in Christendom could any of them compare to the content and impact of the 1965 *Nostra Aetate* declaration of the Second Vatican Council (see p. 73). Nostra Aetate was important, first of all, in its own right: as a landmark theological document. Its greater importance, however, lies in the process it set in motion throughout the Christian world, generating further doctrinal and attitudinal changes, in increasing detail, and of growing significance to the whole pattern of Christian-Jewish relations. In a manner of speaking, Nostra Aetate created a shock wave of its own – a shock wave still reverberating through the Christian world as well as the world of Christian-Jewish relations, probably the most fitting possible response to the twin shock waves, mentioned earlier, that preceded it.

The publication of Nostra Aetate – the ground-breaking declaration, by the highest collective authority in the Catholic Church, that Jews were not to be held collectively and eternally responsible for the death of Jesus – served as a signal for the launching of yet another ground-breaking development: an ongoing dialogue between the Catholic Church and the Jewish people, a dialogue that, over the years, has generated a continuing series of statements, notes and guidelines designed to elaborate on the Nostra Aetate statement – and carry it further.

Before long, the Catholic-Jewish dialogue was carried over into the world of Protestantism, whose Churches (Presbyterian, Lutheran, Methodist and others) soon began to produce documents of their own, involving theological revisions and rectifications that, in several instances, went beyond the Catholic ones in extent, detail and quality. All in all, it was a wholesome, healing process that eventually was to embrace, in addition to the Catholic and Protestant Churches, some of the Orthodox denominations and such umbrella organizations as the World Council of Churches.

The Vatican and Israel

As this process unfolded, in the years between 1965 and 1985, it became clear that if the Church appeared ready to mend its theological fences with Judaism and the Jewish people, it was not yet ready to face up to the new political reality that had emerged on the scene: the national embodiment of the Jewish people – the State of Israel. Neither Nostra Aetate nor the "Guidelines" published by the Vatican in 1974 (see p. 74) made any mention of the State of Israel; nor did most of the Protestant documents that were published during this period. Even as late as 1987, in the American Presbyterian Church's study entitled "A Theological Understanding of the Relationship Between Christians and Jews" (see pp. 87–89), the most the authors of that study were ready to say about Israel was to pledge "a willingness to investigate the continuing significance of the promise of 'land' and its associated obligations, and to explore the implications for Christian theology." Taken as a whole, however, that Presbyterian study represents one of the most candid, searching and self-critical of all the Christian documents issued during this entire period; for this reason, we have decided to present it to the reader in its original, unabridged version (see Appendix L). Yet, as we have pointed out, on the question of Israel it is strangely reticent.

Could this reticence, one has to wonder, be a reflection of a similar reticence on this subject, at that point in time, in the Catholic documents? After all, the Protestant Churches appear to have followed the Vatican's lead on this entire subject of Christian-Jewish reconciliation. They may well have done the same on the question of how to relate to Israel.

Nevertheless, the fact is that the Vatican, in the 1970s and 1980s, was undergoing a very slow, subtle, incremental change in its position vis-à-vis the Jewish State. This found expression in several ways. For one thing, somewhere along the line, the Holy See quietly and unobtrusively abandoned the stance it had taken initially with regard to the UN General Assembly's 1947 call for the internationalization of Jerusalem – a stance that had been totally supportive of that call. Responding, apparently, some years later, to the total rejection of that proposal – not only by Israel but by Jordan as well, which from 1948 to 1967 held the eastern portion of the city – and also perhaps to widespread objections being voiced to internationalization as an impractical as well as essentially unworkable solution to the issue, the Vatican eventually stopped calling for that solution and, instead, began urging the adoption of an international statute that would guarantee the inviolability and accessibility of the holy places in Jerusalem.

Dr. Shlomo Slonim, Professor Emeritus of American History at the Hebrew University in Jerusalem, calls this "the pragmatic phase" in Vatican policy on Jerusalem – following the earlier theological and ideological phases. In an article appearing in a 1998 book edited by Nahum Rakover, *Jerusalem, City of Law and Justice* (Library of Jewish Law, Jerusalem), Professor Slonim writes:

> The Vatican continued to deal with Israel as the administering state, *de facto*, as it had in the past, regardless of the absence

of any formal diplomatic relations. This phase can properly be called the pragmatic stage, when the Vatican limited its sights to ensuring freedom of access to the Holy Places, freedom of worship and education, etc., without seeking to impart thereto a territorial dimension.

Two developments, shortly after the 1967 Six-Day War, helped contribute to this result. On June 30, 1967, a draft resolution submitted by a group of Latin American countries at the UN General Assembly in support of the internationalization of Jerusalem was defeated. This confirmed the fact that even the UN itself no longer considered this solution viable. The second development was an Israeli diplomatic initiative suggesting a legal formula designed to give the Holy Places a status comparable, in rights and immunity, to that of diplomatic missions.

Beginning in August 1967, the Vatican, in its pronouncements on Jerusalem, dropped its earlier references to the territorial internationalization of the city, adopting instead a formulation that stressed a demand for "a special internationally guaranteed statute for Jerusalem and the Holy Places." As the Associate Director of the Secretariat for Ecumenical and Interreligious Affairs of the US Conference of Catholic Bishops, Dr. Eugene J. Fisher, told me during my tour of duty at the Israel Embassy in Washington, DC, in the late 1980s, "We are satisfied with the way the Government of Israel is safeguarding Christian interests in the city; but we wish to guard against the possibility of some future government altering this benevolent policy." (Dr. Fisher is also a Consultor to the Holy See's Commission on Religious Relations with the Jews.)

The Vatican's policy on Jerusalem has since remained basically the same, on the principle, as formulated in the Fundamental Agreement Between the Holy See and Israel (see p. 89), signed in Jerusalem in December 1993, that "The Holy See, while maintaining in every case the right to exercise its moral and spiritual teaching-office, deems it opportune to recall that, owing to its own character, it is solemnly committed to remaining a stranger to all merely temporal conflicts, which principle applies specifically to disputed territories and unsettled borders." (Article 11)

What this means in the context of Jerusalem is that the Vatican will not intervene in the political dispute between Israelis and Palestinian Arabs over control and sovereignty in this city; it will, however, take an active interest in the status of its holy places.

Acts of Recognition

Further evidence of a perceptible if slow-moving softening of the Holy See's once-antagonistic attitude towards the Jewish State (and, prior to independence, to the very idea of a Jewish national renascence) may be noted in the Vatican's "creeping recognition" of Israel. A decades-long process, it began long before the diplomatic breakthrough of the 1990s, and yet remained largely unnoticed by a Jewish public that, in the post-Shoah era, was waiting with growing impatience for political overtures to Israel on the Vatican's part. One of the most frequently heard questions from Jewish audiences, during my 1987–1990 tour of duty in Washington, was: "Why hasn't the Vatican recognized Israel?" The truth is, as stated, that Vatican recognition of Israel – certainly *de facto*, though some claim even *de jure* – was developing gradually over the years. Consider the following facts:

- The Apostolic Delegate in the region was accredited to "Jerusalem, Palestine, Jordan *and Israel*" (emphasis added). Even before the establishment of diplomatic relations and the appointment by the Pope of a Nuncio accredited to Israel, the Apostolic Delegate maintained regular contacts with Israel's Foreign Ministry.

- At the same time, the Vatican maintained similar contacts with the Embassy of Israel in Rome.

- Pope John Paul II and earlier popes on several occasions received Israeli leaders in audience at the Vatican. In speeches and statements, the Pope has made explicit references to Israel.

- Beginning with the inauguration of Pope John XXIII in 1958, an official Israeli delegation has been invited to all of the papal inaugurations.

• Israel's Ambassador in Washington and the Minister for Relations with the Churches frequently were officially invited guests at diplomatic receptions at the Vatican's Embassy.

In June 1985, the Vatican issued a set of "Notes on the Correct Way to Present Jews and Judaism in Preaching and Catechesis in the Roman Catholic Church" (see p. 84), another in the series of documents published from time to time by the Vatican as an interpretative follow-up to Nostra Aetate. In the Notes, there is, for the first time, a reference to the establishment of the State of Israel according to international law; to the permanence of Israel as an historical fact; and to the attachment of Jews to the land of their ancestors.

Diplomatic Relations: Pro and Con

Various reasons have been adduced for the Holy See's reluctance, in the early decades following Israel's independence in 1948, to establish diplomatic relations with the old-new state. Some said that the motive was theological – a theory that increasingly lost validity in light of the theological revisions the Church itself was introducing on the subject of Judaism and Israel. Others insisted that the reason had more to do with the Church's fear for the safety and welfare of its institutions in the Arab states if it warmed up to Israel. That could have been a motive, albeit not one based on a very shrewd analysis of the situation: The record will show that, more often than not, when push came to shove, countries that ignored the Arab states' attempts to ostracize and boycott Israel were not penalized. Finally, we have the Vatican's own explanation: that any decision to establish formal ties – not just with Israel, but with neighboring Jordan as well – would have to await the resolution of the Arab-Israeli conflict and, specifically, the delineation of agreed borders in the area. Observers who at the time took this explanation with a grain of salt were, of course, right: As matters turned out, the Vatican did not wait, but made its

diplomatic move long before the Middle East peace process had run
its course, long before "the delineation of agreed borders."

In point of fact, as has been shown, there were numerous signs
and indications, in the 1960s, '70s and '80s, that the Holy See was
moving slowly but inexorably towards the ultimate step in international relations. Indeed, it is not unlikely that a policy decision to this
effect was taken by the Roman Curia many years before the process
was consummated, and the reason is not difficult to fathom: All of
the above-cited factors militating *against* the establishment of relations paled in comparison with the one factor that fairly shouted for
such relations to be put in place – namely, the realization that, in the
absence of diplomatic relations with one of the major players in the
Middle East game, the Holy See could not play any kind of effective
role in the region. In particular, it would find itself at a serious disadvantage if and when it wished to influence the fate of Jerusalem
and the holy places. And so, in June 1992, it agreed to the establishment of a Vatican-Israel Bilateral Commission that would prepare
for the establishment of diplomatic relations. In December 1993, a
Fundamental Agreement (see Appendix M for full text) was signed
in Jerusalem between the Holy See and Israel, defining the relationship between the two states and determining the procedures for the
establishment of diplomatic relations and the exchange of ambassa-
dors between them in the course of the following year. Upon signing
the Agreement on behalf of the Holy See, Msgr. Claudio Maria Celli,
the Vatican's Under-Secretary for Relations With the States, spoke of
the Agreement's political and religious elements:

"While clearly distinguishing," he said, "between the political
and the religious aspects of this event, the Holy See is convinced
that the dialogue and respectful cooperation between Catholics and
Jews will now be given new impetus and energy, both in Israel and
throughout the world." He went on to underscore the Agreement's
"condemnation of hatred, persecution and all other manifestations of
antisemitism directed against Jews anywhere, at any time, by anyone."
But he also stressed the Church's own special interest: "I am likewise
certain that this new situation will provide greater confidence and

security to the Catholic Church in Israel and to her leaders. This is a matter of great importance to the Holy See, which considers the establishment of official relations with states not as an end in itself, but as a means..."

Problem Areas

The establishment of full diplomatic relations between the Holy See and Israel marked, without doubt, a decisive step – a "crossing of the Rubicon" – in the developing relationship between Jews and Catholics, as between Israel and the Vatican. That is not to say, of course, that problems do not remain in the furtherance of this relationship. Points of friction and disagreement do exist; only there is another channel, the diplomatic one, in addition to the ongoing Catholic-Jewish dialogue, in which these differences can now be aired.

Since the prime purpose of this book is to set forth and document the historic theological changes that have been taking place in the Christian Churches, there would be little point (as we shall have occasion to point out again, when we present and discuss some of the documents) in dwelling unduly on the problem areas that obviously do exist; in fact, that would be counter-productive. It would serve merely to distract the reader from the book's central thesis – a thesis that is as little known among the general public as it is historically significant. For the sake, however, of maintaining our credibility, we do make mention of these differences and problem areas and may, here and there, provide examples of such differences – especially such as have been more in the public eye than others.

A rather high-profile dispute between the Jewish side and the Catholic side has been generated by the Vatican's declared intention to elevate the late Pope Pius XII (Eugenio Pacelli), the pope of the World War II era, to the status of sainthood. It is recognized, of course, on the Jewish side that this decision and the steps that it entails are matters to be dealt with by the Church alone, and normally the Jewish side would not even contemplate interposing its own views on the subject. However, the case in point is considered to be a very special case because of the questions that have been raised, over the years, concerning this pope's role during the Shoah. That he did not publicly protest the ongoing Nazi campaign of genocide against the Jews of Europe is a matter of record. The question is: What was the reason for this? And there are other questions; for example: To what extent was the Vatican aware, in those days, of what was going on? To what extent did Pope Pius XII act, behind the scenes, to try to rescue as many of the Nazis' intended victims as possible?

For years, the International Jewish Committee for Interreligious Consultations (IJCIC) appealed to the Vatican to allow Jewish scholars access to the Vatican's wartime files, so as to clear the air and, once and for all, either confirm these doubts and suspicions or lay them to rest. Again and again, these appeals were turned down.

Finally, in March 1998, the Vatican did agree to the establishment, under the joint auspices of the Vatican and IJCIC, of a team of three Catholic and three Jewish historians, that would be given the task of reviewing eleven volumes of published Vatican records from the period in question. (These had been released for publication by a special decree issued in 1964 by Pope Paul VI.) In the ensuing year, the joint team was put together, and in December 1999 it began its work. After months of study, the team in October 2000 issued a preliminary report that included a set of 47 questions that remain unanswered, coupled with a request for access to hitherto unpublished material in the Vatican archives that had the potential for casting further light on the subject.

In a letter to the members of the joint team dated June 21, 2001, Walter Cardinal Kasper, who had in March of that year succeeded Edward Idris Cardinal Cassidy as President of the Vatican's Commission for Religious Relations with the Jews, expressed his "profound sense of gratitude" for the work the team had accomplished to date and "for the enormous help you have already given us out of your own free time and desire for accurate historical research." Cardinal Kasper asked the team to reconvene and issue its final report, after receiving answers, from Father Peter Gumpel, to their 47 questions. However, the request for access to unpublished portions of the Vatican archives dating to the war years was turned down, on the grounds that "The Vatican archives are accessible only until 1923," and that "access to the Vatican archives after that date is not possible at present for technical reasons."

The team's response to this notification, dated July 20, 2001, was couched in respectful, even cordial, terms, but ended with the announcement that, under the circumstances, the team felt it had to suspend its work. The historians, Jewish and Catholic, expressed the belief that "without access, in some reasonable manner, to additional archival material, we cannot make substantial progress toward the larger goals set for us beyond what we stated in our Preliminary Report." Such access, the letter continues, "would help to promote openness and greater understanding between our communities in the mutual search for truth."

Since, presumably, the latter aspiration continues to characterize both sides of the Catholic-Jewish dialogue, one can but hope and trust that, eventually, a way will be found to resolve this impasse and bring the project to a satisfactory and generally acceptable conclusion. Cardinal Kasper himself has since then given expression to this hope and trust. During a visit to Israel in November 2001, he said:

> The Catholic Church does not fear the historical truth.... Historical research must and will go on, and the lack of success of one group of historians...cannot and will not be the end of serious historical research on this issue.

On February 15, 2002, in what may be seen as a gesture of good will and a step in the right direction, the Vatican announced that, beginning in 2003, it would open portions of its archive relating to Germany from 1922 to the outbreak of World War II in 1939. Documents dating from this period may shed some light on Eugenio Pacelli's relations with Germany when he served as the Papal Nuncio to that country (1917–1929) and, from 1930, when, after being elevated to Cardinal, he became the Papal Secretary of State. It was in this capacity that Cardinal Pacelli in 1933 negotiated a concordat with Adolf Hitler's Nazi government.

Two Papal Visits

The distance traversed, in Catholic-Jewish / Vatican-Israel relations, in the past few decades may be gauged by the profound differences between the first papal visit to Israel, by Pope Paul VI in 1964, and the second – that of Pope John Paul II in March 2000, at the turn of the millennium.

The second visit was, one could say, everything the first one was not: open and aboveboard, warm, outgoing, wide-ranging – both in geographic scope and in its reconciliatory message. In the words of Rabbi David Hartman, of Jerusalem's Shalom Hartman Institute, the Pope came to Jerusalem "not just to visit holy sites but to acknowledge the Jewish people in its homeland. We are no longer a cursed people. We are no more a wandering people. This is a major revolution in Christian thought."

The visit was a real eye-opener for Israeli Jews too. As one *Jerusalem Post* journalist put it, "Thanks to TV coverage of the papal visit [in 1964 Israel had no TV], most Israelis got to witness the celebration of a mass for the first time. They had, in fact, the opportunity to witness several. They found them …to be joyful, aesthetic events with elements echoing Jewish practices." What "won the day" for John Paul, the same reporter concluded, was "the evident piety of a 79-year-old believer resolutely soldiering on through a grueling schedule in his march towards heaven's gates…"

In Jerusalem, the Pope was welcomed by the nation's spiritual leaders, Chief Rabbis Eliyahu Bakshi-Doron and Israel Meir Lau. Responding to their welcoming remarks, the Pope said he had "always wanted to be counted among those who work, on both sides, to overcome old prejudices and to secure ever wider and fuller recognition of the spiritual patrimony shared by Jews and Christians."

During a deeply moving visit to the Yad Vashem Holocaust Remembrance Museum, where John Paul was met by then-Prime Minister Ehud Barak, the Pope spoke of the "need for silence…

because there are no words strong enough to deplore the terrible tragedy of the Shoah." He had come, he said, "to pay homage to millions of Jewish people who, stripped of everything, especially of their human dignity, were murdered in the Holocaust." There is a need, the Pope said, to remember – but "to remember for a purpose, namely, to ensure that never again will evil prevail, as it did for the millions of innocent victims of Nazism."

In his response, Prime Minister Barak extolled the Righteous Gentiles, "mostly members of your faith," who risked their lives to save the lives of others. "You have done more than anyone else," Barak continued, "to bring about the historic change in the attitude of the Church towards the Jewish people initiated by the good Pope John XXIII, and to dress the gaping wounds that festered over many centuries. And I think I can say, Your Holiness, that your coming here today, to the Tent of Remembrance at Yad Vashem, is the climax of your historic journey of healing."

The Pope also met with the President of Israel, Ezer Weizman, at the Presidential Residence in Jerusalem – another prominent difference between the two papal visits: In 1964, Pope Paul VI declined to meet President Shazar in Israel's capital, and the meeting took place, instead, near the kibbutz of Megiddo (Armageddon).

Undoubtedly one of the high points of Pope John Paul's stay in Israel was his visit to Jewry's most revered site, the Western Wall of the Temple Mount – the last remnant of the Holy Temple. There the Pope joined the countless others who had preceded him in placing their prayers and supplications, written out on pieces of paper, in the crevices of the Wall. Here is the text of the Pope's prayer:

> God of our fathers, you chose Abraham and his descendants to bring your name to the nations. We are deeply saddened by the behavior of those who in the course of history have caused these children of yours to suffer, and, asking your forgiveness, we wish to commit ourselves to genuine brotherhood with the people of the Covenant. We ask this through Christ our Lord. Amen.
>
> Jerusalem, 26 March 2000
> Johannes Paulus II

A few days later, upon his return to Rome, Pope John Paul made a public appearance at St. Peter's Square on March 29 and, in summing up the historic visit to the Holy Land, once again confessed to a loss of words:

> I am unable to express the joy and gratitude I feel in my heart for this gift from God for which I had hoped for so long!...I thank God for this unforgettable experience.

This, then, is the story of the Catholic Church and its special role in the dramatic development, over the past half-century, of the Jewish-Christian as well as the Israel-Vatican relationship. By this time, the reader will have fully understood why I felt that this particular story warranted a chapter of its own.

Chapter 6

The Documents

Having painted in the historical background of what not very long ago could rightly be called "the great divide" between the Church and the Jewish people, we can now "get down to brass tacks": the documents in the case. For it is these documents, reflecting an earnest and persevering effort by the Church to bridge that divide, that form the backbone of our thesis.

Thoughts, observations and comments, interviews and sermons, lectures and speeches, articles and books: all these have their place, to be sure, in a nation's social, educational and political discourse. And, indeed, the profound change in the way the Christian Churches have been relating to Judaism, the Jewish people and the Jewish state has found expression, over the years, in speeches, sermons and books. Yet, in a faith community, none of these forms of communication can muster the impact of a statement of theological principle or doctrine adopted at the highest levels of the Church hierarchy. Such statements, as a rule, must move through many preliminary stages of draft formulations, examination, study and discussion, amendment and revision, often lasting years, before they are approved in their final form and made known to the faithful and the general public. It is our purpose, in this chapter, to present a representative selection of Church statements relating to this subject, more or less in chronological order, so that the reader may "get a feel" for the way this process has been playing out in various parts of Christendom as time goes by.

Obviously, we are not going to publish the documents in full, except in a few cases where the document's central importance or historic value warrants it. In all other cases, we shall quote passages that are of particular interest or importance and, where appropriate, point out the relationship between a given document and its predecessors, or followers, within the same Church or in other Churches. We shall endeavor to avoid repetition and, as far as possible, indicate in each case what the particular document cited has contributed to the process as a whole.

As in the matter of full or partial citation, mentioned above, so too in the enumeration of these documents, we have been selective: Our objective is to convey a message, not to publish an encyclopedia. Clearly, any attempt to present the reader with hundreds of documents – whether by reproduction, quotation or merely by brief descriptions or even mere listings – would make this work unwieldy and, ultimately, would defeat its purpose. (The bibliography on page 275 will direct the interested reader to a number of authoritative reference books on the subject.)

And now – for the promised "brass tacks."

Reference has been made to the historic pioneering role of the Nostra Aetate declaration adopted by the Second Vatican Council in 1965. Nostra Aetate was indeed one of the first major Church statements in the realm of Christian-Jewish relations to be promulgated after World War II. Yet it was not the very first document on the subject to make its appearance on the Christian scene; there were several earlier, if less known, pronouncements, at least some of them preceding World War II. We shall here mention four such statements.

1927 / 1945: The Assemblies of God – An Early Voice

(1) As early as 1927 – six years before the Nazis' accession to power in Germany, *and more than 20 years before the advent of the State of Israel* – the General Council of one of America's largest Churches, The Assemblies of God, adopted a series of Fundamental Truths, one of which (No. 14) states: "The revelation of the Lord Jesus Christ from

heaven, *the salvation of national Israel,* and the millennial reign of Christ on the earth is the scriptural promise and the world's hope (2 Thess. 1:7; Rev. 19:11–14; Rom. 11:26, 27; Rev. 20:1–7)." (Emphasis added.)

(2) In 1945, immediately following the end of World War II, the same Assemblies General Council adopted a detailed resolution in condemnation of antisemitism, stating in part:

> WHEREAS, We have witnessed in this generation an almost universal increase in antisemitism, and this has resulted in the greatest series of persecutions perpetrated in modern times, and

> WHEREAS, Even in the United States of America there has been an alarming increase in antisemitism;

> THEREFORE BE IT RESOLVED, That the General Council hereby declare its opposition to antisemitism, and that it disapprove of the ministers of the Assemblies of God identifying themselves with those who are engaged in this propaganda. ...

> We do not fail to recognize that God has redeemed the children of Israel unto Himself to be His people *for ever.* (Emphasis in original document.) ... Should we as children of God hate those whom God our Father loves? ...

> Every child of God who finds joy in the revealed will of our Father delights in the glorious promises of Israel's restoration. Read carefully the promises in Ezekiel 37:24–28, 39:25–29; Jeremiah 32:37–41, 33:7–9, ... 30:10, 11. ...

> God gives solemn warning to those who hate and persecute Israel. He says in Jeremiah 2:3, "All that devour him shall offend; evil shall come upon them." ...

> The greatest reason why no Christian should be antisemitic is that our Savior was a Jew. ... Let us remember the word, "Pray for the peace of Jerusalem," and the promise attached: "They shall prosper that love thee." (Psalm 122:6) If you pray for the people represented by Jerusalem, you will never be guilty of being antisemitic.

1947: The Ten Points of Seelisberg – A Joint Effort

(3) Yet another document that preceded the publication of Nostra Aetate was one published in 1947 by the International Council of Christians and Jews at Seelisberg, Switzerland, and known as The Ten Points of Seelisberg.

A relatively brief and concisely worded document (from Point No. 1: "Remember that One God speaks to us all through the Old and the New Testaments" to Point No. 10: "Avoid speaking of the Jews as if the first members of the Church had not been Jews"), it deserves to be cited in full. The unabridged text of the Ten Points may be found in Appendix A.

1964: The Episcopal Church – On the Deicide Charge

(4) Just one year before the publication of the Catholic Church's Nostra Aetate, the House of Bishops of the Episcopal Church, meeting in St. Louis, Missouri, in 1964, issued a statement on "Deicide and the Jews," the conclusion of which is presented here verbatim:

> The charge of deicide against the Jews is a tragic misunderstanding of the inner significance of the crucifixion. To be sure, Jesus was crucified by *some* soldiers at the instigation of *some* Jews. But, this cannot be construed as imputing corporate guilt to every Jew in Jesus' day, much less the Jewish people in subsequent generations. Simple justice alone proclaims the charge of a corporate or inherited curse on the Jewish people to be false.

In essence, this is the same message that was to be conveyed, a year later, by the Catholic Church's Nostra Aetate (see Appendix B) – if anything, in even more explicit terms. However, it was Nostra Aetate, emerging from the deliberations of the Second Vatican Council that had been convened by Pope John XXIII, that, in the nature of things, has drawn the larger measure of attention. In retrospect, it may be said that another reason for the Catholic document's greater impact on Christian-Jewish relations is the fact that, in contrast to the Episcopalian document quoted here, Nostra Aetate subsequently had the benefit of a long and ongoing series of further studies and statements, initiated by the Vatican, along the lines set forth in Nostra Aetate, designed to deepen and expand the concepts of Christian-Jewish understanding and reconciliation.

1965: Nostra Aetate – Breaking New Ground

At the conclusion of the Second Vatican Council, in October 1965, the Roman Catholic Church, acting on the initiative of Pope John XXIII, produced the ground-breaking document known as Nostra Aetate, which seeks to put an end to the long-standing Church doctrine that the Jewish people down the ages was guilty, collectively, for the death of Jesus – a charge that, for many Christian believers in many countries, amounted to a license to kill. For the first time ever, a Catholic Church document now declared, with reference to Jesus's death, that *"what happened in His passion cannot be blamed upon all the Jews then living, without distinction, nor upon the Jews of today."*

Nostra Aetate acknowledges – indeed, emphasizes – that Christianity's roots are to be found in Judaism; that the Church "received the revelation of the Old Testament through the people with whom God in His inexpressible mercy made the ancient covenant"; and that "God holds the Jews most dear for the sake of their fathers – He does not repent of the gifts He makes or of the calls He issues..."

The finding that the Divine Covenant with the Jewish people is still valid and indeed is irrevocable – a finding stated and reiterated, as we shall see, in numerous later Catholic and Protestant declarations – is not enunciated explicitly in Nostra Aetate; but it is clearly implied, as the passages cited above demonstrate. Treading, as it were, with great caution on totally virgin theological ground, Nostra Aetate laid the effective groundwork for the more outspoken and sharply defined statements that were to follow in subsequent years and decades.

In the same manner, this pioneering document set the foundation for numerous later pronouncements on the subject of antisemitism. It "decries hatreds, persecutions and manifestations of antisemitism directed against Jews at any time and by anyone." Here, too, the dotting of the i's and the crossing of the t's were to come later.

One of the leading figures, on the Jewish side, in the ongoing Catholic-Jewish dialogue, the late Dr. Geoffrey Wigoder, referred to Nostra Aetate as "a historic turning-point, ushering in a new era" – and indeed it was. It marks the first major step by a major Church in the effort that has developed since then to make amends for the historic sins of the Church against Judaism and the Jewish people. As such, it has served as a model, or a kind of "jumping-off" place, for subsequent statements and declarations of the Catholic Church – and, indirectly, as will be shown, for those of other Churches as well.

(Point 4 of Nostra Aetate – the portion of this document relating to the Jewish religion – is reproduced in full in Appendix B.)

1974: Guidelines – From Theory to Practice

Nine years were to pass, following publication of Nostra Aetate, before the Vatican produced its next major document on the subject – the 1974 "Guidelines and Suggestions for Implementing the Conciliar Declaration 'Nostra Aetate' No. 4" – and eleven more years, after that, until the publication of the 1985 "Notes on the Correct Way to Present the Jews and Judaism in Preaching and Catechesis in the Roman Catholic Church."

One is tempted to observe, in commenting on such time-spans, that things certainly move slowly in matters pertaining to religion, particularly where the Vatican is concerned. On the other hand, when one considers that it took the Church nearly two thousand years to begin to rectify its anti-Jewish teachings, a decade more or less is not very much, in comparison!

In the Guidelines' Preamble, antisemitism is "condemned" (where Nostra Aetate had merely "decried" it):

> The spiritual bonds and historical links binding the Church to Judaism condemn – as opposed to the very spirit of Christianity – all forms of antisemitism, which in any case the dignity of the human person alone would suffice to condemn.

On the positive side, the 1974 document defines the fundamental conditions for dialogue: "respect for the other as he is," knowledge of the "basic components of the religious tradition of Judaism" and learning "by what essential traits the Jews define themselves in the light of their own religious experience."

What may well be the Guidelines' most important contribution to the promotion of Christian-Jewish understanding and harmony is Chapter 3, "Teaching and Education," which lists a number of practical things to be done, concluding with this recommendation:

> Information concerning these questions is important at all levels of Christian instruction and education. Among sources of information, special attention should be paid to the following:
>
> • catechisms and religious textbooks
> • history books
> • the mass media (press, radio, cinema, television)
>
> The effective use of these means presupposes the thorough formation of instructors and educators in training schools, seminaries and universities.

It goes without saying that the loftiest and best-intentioned declarations and statements issued by the governing bodies of major Churches will remain little more than dead letters if the message they contain does not filter down through the ranks. That is why the Guidelines perform so critical a function when they translate the ground-breaking theological findings of Nostra Aetate into the language of pedagogics – which is precisely what happens, as we have shown, in the Guidelines' chapter on "Teaching and Education."

The Notes (mentioned briefly above) took this "translation" into practical terms a step further, as will emerge when we discuss that document (see p. 84).

1974/1994: US Lutheran Church – A Courageous Confession

The same year that saw the publication of the Catholic Church's Guidelines also witnessed the birth of another pivotal Church document dealing with Christian-Jewish relations: this one on the Protestant side.

On several occasions, the American Lutheran Church explicitly linked the antisemitic writings of its own founder, Martin Luther (excerpts in Appendix C), to "the climate of hatred" that Hitler's Nazi movement found "already in existence" when it came to power in Germany in the 1930s. "That the Nazi period fostered a revival of Luther's own medieval hostility toward the Jews, as expressed in pugnacious writings, is a special cause of regret. Those who study and admire Luther should acknowledge unequivocally that his anti-Jewish writings are beyond any defense."

These words are quoted from the statement entitled "The American Lutheran Church and the Jewish Community," adopted by the Seventh General Convention of that Church in October 1974 (excerpts in Appendix D). It surely is nothing short of remarkable that the 400-year-old Lutheran Church should have displayed the courage, as it did in this and later documents, to repudiate pronouncements of its own founder!

A 1990 statement passed at the annual meeting of the Lutheran European Commission on the Church and the Jewish People (Appendix F), while containing several eminently quotable elements on this subject, does not refer at all to Martin Luther. However, the Declaration of the Evangelical Lutheran Church in America (ELCA), adopted by that denomination's Church Council on April 18, 1994 (Appendix G), did make that reference in very explicit terms.

Following on the earlier (1974) statement of a predecessor Church body, the American Lutheran Church, mentioned above, and citing, in addition, the Lutheran World Federation (see p. 82 and Appendix E), the ELCA acknowledges "Luther's anti-Judaic diatribes and the violent recommendations of his later writings against the Jews." The authors of the Declaration "reject this violent invective, and yet more do we express our deep and abiding sorrow over its tragic effects on subsequent generations." Again taking their cue from the Lutheran World Federation, they "particularly deplore the appropriation of Luther's words by modern antisemites for the preaching of hatred toward Judaism or toward the Jewish people in our day."

The conclusion is inescapable: Martin Luther's antisemitic writings helped pave the way for the Nazis' genocidal campaign of the

1940s. Who would ever have thought that the world would get to learn of this horrendous truth from the Lutheran Church itself?

1977/1988: World Council of Churches – Proselytism Rejected

At the Jerusalem Conference of the World Council of Churches (wcc) Consultation on the Church and the Jewish People, meeting June 20–23, 1977, an important statement was issued on what was termed "Authentic Christian Witness." (The wcc is the umbrella organization of Protestant Churches worldwide.)

After drawing a distinction between the concept of proselytism, on the one hand, and the concepts of mission or witness, on the other (more on this in Chapter 8), the statement goes on to reject the former "in the strongest terms...both in its gross and in its more refined forms" – a rejection termed "the more urgent where Jews are concerned," the relationship to whom is said to be "of a unique and very close character." (Full text of statement in Appendix I.)

This rejection of proselytism was reaffirmed by the same body of the wcc eleven years later, as part of a statement entitled "The Churches and the Jewish People," adopted in Sigtuna, Sweden, in 1988. Like its Presbyterian predecessor of 1987 (see p. 87), this statement consists basically of a series of affirmations, five in number. In a paper circulated at the time by the wcc's Executive Committee, these affirmations are summarized as follows:

(a) That the covenant of God with the Jewish people continues, and that Christians are to thank God for the spiritual treasures which we share with the Jewish people.

(b) That antisemitism and all forms of the teaching of contempt are to be repudiated.

(c) That the living tradition of Judaism is a gift of God, and that we, with St. Paul in his Letter to the Romans, recognize the continuing vocation of the Jewish people and the promises given to them as a sign of God's faithfulness.

(d) That Proselytism is incompatible with Christian faith, and that claims of faith when used as a weapon against anyone are against the spirit of Christ.

(e) That Jews and Christians, each from their unique perspective, have a common responsibility as witnesses in the world to God's righteousness and peace, and that they, as God's partners, have to work in mutual respect and cooperation for justice, reconciliation and the integrity of creation.

It is in the context of these affirmations that the World Council of Churches understands its calling to engage in Christian-Jewish relations.

1980: Evangelical Church in the Rhineland – Jewish Continuity

A statement adopted in 1980 by the Synod of the Protestant Church of the Rhineland explicitly assumes "the Christian share of the responsibility and guilt for the Holocaust – the defamation, persecution and murder of Jews in the Third Reich." The statement, however, lists three additional factors in moving the Rhenish Church, or Church of the Rhineland, to accept "the historical necessity of attaining a new relationship of the Church to the Jewish people:"

- The new biblical insights concerning the continuing significance of the Jewish people for salvation history (e.g., Romans 9–11), which have been attained in connection with the Church struggle.

- The insight that the continuing existence of the Jewish people, its return to the Land of Promise, and also the establishment of the State of Israel, are signs of the faithfulness of God toward His people.

- The readiness of Jews, in spite of the Holocaust, to engage in encounter, common study and cooperation.

Acknowledgment of co-responsibility for the Holocaust is spelled out further in the Preamble to a 1996 paper of the Rhenish Church called "Israel and Christian Mission," written by Dr. Jurgen Regul of the Protestant Church of the Rhineland in September 1997. Among other things, Dr. Regul wrote:

After Christianity had come to power within the Roman Empire and the subsequently emerging states, the Jews were also politically oppressed, often persecuted and killed. At the end of this disastrous development in Europe, the National Socialist terror regime in Germany (1933–1945) attempted to eliminate the Jewish people as a whole. In addition to other injustices, more than six million Jewish people were murdered through this criminal madness.

Individual Christians and the churches as a whole never realized that the beginning of this horrific end was based on the theological hostility against Jews within Christian preaching and teaching. Even if nothing is said against Jews or the Jewish faith explicitly, this hostility-in-principle against Jews exists within Christian doctrine. As a result of this fact, the Christians and the Christian Churches, with few exceptions, kept silent when the Nazis started to terrorize and to kill the Jewish population....

Why did we keep silent? Why were we blind? We were blind because we did not see the hostility against Jews and Judaism that was fused with Christian theology. We kept silent because we had marked Judaism as hostile – at least as strange and as being opposed to the Christian faith....

The reader's attention is drawn, in particular, to the point made, in the 1980 Rhenish Church document cited above, concerning "the continuing existence of the Jewish people" and "the continuing significance of the Jewish people." This point is also underscored in the 1988 World Council of Churches Sigtuna statement in terms of "the living tradition of Judaism" and "the continuing vocation of the Jewish people." We point out this recognition, in major Christian documents, of the continuing vibrancy and ongoing development of Jewish tradition and practice, because it reflects the realization, in the Christian world, that the notion that Jewish life and cultural development effectively "froze" 2,000 years ago – a notion that lies at the root of so much anti-Jewish Church doctrine – needs to be totally reassessed and, in effect, discarded. That an important beginning has been made in this direction is evident from the words of Pope John Paul II when, on December 6, 1990, addressing a Jewish audience, he said:

When we consider Jewish tradition, we see how profoundly you venerate Sacred Scripture, the *Mikra*, and in particular the *Torah*. You live in a special relationship with the Torah – the living teaching of the living God. You study it with love in the Talmud Torah, so as to put it into practice with joy. Its teaching on love, on justice and on the law is reiterated in the Prophets – *Nevi'im* – and in the *Ketuvim*. God, His holy Torah, the synagogual liturgy and family traditions, the Land of holiness, are surely what characterize your people from the religious point of view. And these are things that constitute the foundation of our dialogue and of our cooperation.

This kind of reassessment has found powerful expression in the Protestant camp as well – as, for example, in the Third Revised Text of the Guidelines on Jewish-Christian Relations, adopted in 1977 by the British Working Group for the World Council of Churches Consultation on the Church and the Jewish People. Here is the relevant passage from that text:

Christians should be aware of the vibrant and continuing development of Judaism in post-Biblical times. Between the first century and the present day there has been an enormous output of Jewish religious and philosophical literature and commentary. In modern times Jewish religious movements have made major contributions to European religious thought. European Jewry was virtually destroyed by the Nazis – and it is nothing short of a miracle that the destruction of six million Jews should have been followed by the reconstruction of Jewish life, with its special centres in Israel, America and, to a certain extent, Britain....The most remarkable of all such resurgence is the emergence of the State of Israel, which, by restoring the *Land* to its relationship with *People* and *Religion*, has made it possible for Judaism to regain its wholeness.

The acknowledgment, on the Christian side, of Jewish cultural vitality and continuity has been manifested also in a new appreciation of the Jewish Bible as a value in its own right. A particularly strong statement on the global meaning of the Jewish Bible – and not merely as the forerunner of the Christian Bible, or New Testament – is to be found in the Pastoral Recommendations for Relations Between Jews and Christians, adopted in 1970 by the Pastoral Council of the Catholic Church of The Netherlands:

> The Jewish people must be seen as the people with whom God concluded His covenant for all time. The Old Testament does not exist only as a prefiguration of the New, but has a significance of its own, in Jewish as in world history.

No less prominent an ecclesiastical personality than the Archbishop of Canterbury, Msgr. George Carey, addressed himself to this subject when, writing in the *Journal of the Council of Christians and Jews* (London, 1993), he made this observation:

> Christianity is inexplicable without Judaism. It simply is not possible to understand the world of the New Testament in isolation from its roots in the Near East and particularly against the background of Jewish culture, theology and life.

As a matter of fact, evaluations of this kind concerning the Jewish Bible and the Jewish way of life may be seen in many Christian documents, Catholic as well as Protestant; and quite frequently the point is made that when Jesus referred to Holy Scripture, the reference of course was to the Jewish Bible – the so-called Old Testament – a source of profound inspiration for Jesus himself, as for so many from that day to this.

Some Christian writers have noted, moreover, that the Jewish Bible has often been maligned, in Christian writings and preachings, as being characterized by anger and vengefulness, rather than love, grace and forgiveness – and that, in actual fact, this is a perversion of the truth. In a book entitled *Bound for Freedom: The Book of Exodus in Jewish and Christian Traditions* (Hendrickson, 1999), the author, Dr. Göran Larsson, a director at the Jerusalem Center for Biblical Study and Research, and visiting scholar at the University of California, San Diego, goes to great lengths, on the basis of a wide-ranging study of the sources, to debunk the notion of a kind of "schizophrenic deity": the "vengeful God of the Old Testament" vs. "the loving God of the New Testament." In discussing the well-known

biblical injunction, "an eye for an eye," for example, Larsson intro-
duces his subject thus:

> ...The next principle of penalty is the most well-known, discussed
> and misunderstood in the whole Bible. It is sometimes called "the
> law of revenge," or, in judicial terms, *ius* (or *lex*) *talionis*, from the
> Latin word for "law" plus *talio*, which means retaliation. "Eye for
> eye, tooth for tooth" is to many the epitome of the so-called Old
> Testament God and one of the reasons for characterizing the Old
> Testament and Jewish ethics as harsh, brutal and inhuman. It has
> sparked endless anti-Jewish outbursts from pulpits and in theo-
> logical literature....[Yet] mutilation is a virtually unknown pun-
> ishment in the Bible....In Jewish tradition, "eye for eye, tooth for
> tooth" exclusively dealt with monetary compensation and nothing
> else....Rabbinic commentaries provide biblical as well as humani-
> tarian arguments to prove the literal application of this law to be
> unbiblical, unjust, absurd and impossible.

1981: Dutch Council of Churches – On Persistent Antisemitism

Antisemitism and the need to fight against this social scourge is the
one single subject that probably is encountered more often than any
other in the many Church statements that have been issued in recent
decades in the realm of Christian-Jewish relations. In many cases,
however, the treatment of the subject is fleeting and superficial. On
the other hand, the Declaration "On Persistent Antisemitism" issued
by the Council of Churches in The Netherlands at Amersfoort in
1981 is of a different order. In the Introduction to the Declaration,
the subject is tackled in some detail and on the premise that "a special tie exists between the Jewish people and the Church" and that
therefore the Church "can and should speak about antisemitism in
a special way." (Full text of Introduction in Appendix K.)

1983/1984: Lutheran World Federation – On Luther's Role

The position adopted by the Lutheran Church has already been
alluded to, earlier in this chapter (see pp. 75–76), with particular reference to the role played by the pronouncements of that Church's

16th century founder, Martin Luther. Since, however, that earlier discussion was based mainly on the American branch of the Lutheran
Church, and since its umbrella organization, the Lutheran World
Federation (LWF), is also on record in this regard, we felt it would
be appropriate to cite that record in a separate section.

Between the years 1981 and 1983, the LWF's Committee on the
Church and the Jewish People held a series of consultations with
the International Jewish Committee for Interreligious Consultations
(IJCIC), culminating in a conference, in Stockholm in 1983, on the
theme: Luther, Lutheranism and the Jews. At its conclusion, three
declarations were adopted representing, respectively, the Lutheran
participants, the Jewish ones and the gathering as a whole. At a plenary meeting of the LWF that was held in Budapest from July 22
to August 5, 1984, these declarations were "gratefully received," with
the recommendation that they be studied and noted by the LWF's
member-churches.

The following are excerpts from the first declaration mentioned
above – that representing the Lutheran participants at the 1983 conference:

> We Lutherans take our name from Martin Luther, whose under
> standing of Christianity also largely constitutes the foundation of
> our teachings. However, we can neither acquiesce in nor excuse
> the repulsive anti-Jewish writings of this reformer. While it is true
> that Lutherans and Jews interpret the Hebrew Bible in differing
> ways, we believe that a Christological construction of Scripture
> must not be allowed to lead to anti-Judaism, and certainly not
> to antisemitism....
>
> We must here determine, with deep regret, that Luther's name
> was used, during the Nazi era, to justify antisemitism, and indeed
> his writings lend themselves to such abuse.... The sins of Luther's
> anti-Jewish pronouncements and the vehemence of his attacks
> on the Jews are, to our great sorrow, things that cannot be denied.
> We must see to it that such a sin can no longer be committed in
> our churches – not today, nor in the future....
>
> We hope that we have learned something from the tragic events

of the recent past. We must see to it that, today and in the future,
there will be no question or doubt concerning our attitude to
racial and religious prejudice, and that we show ourselves ready
to offer the totality of the human race the dignity, the freedom
and the friendship that are the right of all God's children.

(Full text of 1984 LWF Statement in Appendix E.)

1985: The Notes – Deepening the Groove

Coming back now, once more, to the Catholic side, let us consider
the next major document published by that Church following its 1974
Guidelines (see p. 74). Issued in June 1985, it is known as "Notes on
the Correct Way to Present Jews and Judaism in Preaching and Catechesis in the Roman Catholic Church" (or "Notes," for short), and
it is addressed specifically to "preachers and teachers" in churches,
colleges and schools.

Dr. Geoffrey Wigoder, who for many years and until his death
in 1999 was one of the leading Jewish figures in the Jewish-Catholic
dialogue, wrote a critique, shortly after the publication of the Notes,
in which he enumerated what he considered to be the document's
positive and negative aspects. On the positive side of the ledger,
Wigoder cited the following features:

- Affirmation of "the remarkable theological formula" coined by
  Pope John Paul II on November 17, 1980, in Mainz, Germany, concerning *the people of God of the Old Covenant, which has never
  been revoked.*" The incorporation of this statement in an official
  Vatican document, writes Wigoder, "constitutes an important step
  forward, whose full implications remain to be explored."

- The warning of *the care to be taken in reading certain New Testament texts.* In Section IV, 21A, the Notes state: "It cannot be
  ruled out that some references hostile or less than favourable to
  the Jews have their historical context in conflicts between the
  nascent Church and the Jewish community...[reflecting] Christian-Jewish relations long after the time of Jesus." The translation of this acknowledgment into practical terms today could,

in Wigoder's words, "lead to the elimination of the sources of many historical frictions between Catholic and Jew." The Notes "lay down clear guidelines for the study and teaching of the text in a manner designed to eliminate expositions likely to lead to anti-Jewish prejudice."

- The call to *work together for social justice, based on "a common hope for the Kingdom of God."* Here is the quotation of that passage from the Notes (Sec. 11, Par. 11) in full:

> Attentive to the same God who has spoken, hanging on the same word, we have to witness to one same memory and one common hope in him who is the master of history. We must also accept our responsibility to prepare the world for the coming of the Messiah by working together for social justice, respect for the rights of persons and nations and for social and international reconciliation. To this we are driven, Jews and Christians, by the command to love our neighbor, by a common hope for the kingdom of God and by the great heritage of the Prophets. Transmitted soon enough by catechesis, such a conception would teach young Christians in a practical way to cooperate with Jews, going beyond simple dialogue.

- *The reappraisal of Jewish life in New Testament times,* including emphasis of *the Jewishness of Jesus* and what Wigoder calls "a long-overdue rehabilitation" of the much-maligned Pharisees. These, Wigoder suggests, constitute "historic advances" in Christian thought.

- Acknowledgment that *Judaism is a contemporary and not only a historical reality* and the Notes' reference to *the continuing fecundity of the Jews down the ages* – refuting the earlier Christian view of Judaism as fossilized and ossified. Pope John Paul 11 was to do some singular "dotting of the i's and crossing of the t's" on this subject, some years later (see pp. 79–80).

- *The expansion of earlier findings,* in Nostra Aetate and the Guidelines, *on the subject of deicide and the condemnation of antisemi-*

tism. These, too, are major contributions to Christian-Jewish reconciliation.

As stated, Wigoder also expounds, in his response to the Notes, on a number of perceived shortcomings characterizing this document. If we do not dwell on these at length here, it is not because Wigoder's criticisms are not important, or not of interest; they are. However, we do not wish to digress unduly from the central theme of this book: the changes that are taking place in Christian thought and theology with respect to Church attitudes towards Judaism and the Jewish people. A brief recapitulation – in Wigoder's own words – of his critical remarks will suffice for our purposes. Here is how he summarizes these remarks:

> ....The Hebrew Bible is denied to us, in its essence, [in the Notes] as incomplete in itself and to be read exclusively through Christian eyes. Our early history and traditions are appropriated as merely a preparation for the Church. Our post-Biblical religious development and history are largely ignored or, where acknowledged, seen for their implications for the Church, rather than having absolute values in themselves. There is inadequate attempt to understand the Jewish people today in all its complexity, including its attachment to the State of Israel which is not only religious, as the Notes acknowledge – but based on a variety of factors, not least of which has been the lessons of living as a persecuted minority for too long a time. Many basic aspects of Jewish self-understanding have got lost.

Returning to the positive aspect of his assessment of this document, and with reference to the ongoing Catholic-Jewish dialogue, Wigoder then delineates –

> clear areas where we can work together – in the words of the Notes – "for social justice, respect for the rights of persons and nations, and for social and international reconciliation." Dialogue could also be employed fruitfully towards filling the *lacunae* of the Notes – the teaching of Jewish history, the lessons of Christian antisemitism and the Holocaust, the understanding of the nature of Judaism and the Jewish people today – and, conversely,

it should be added, for the better understanding, among Jews, of Christianity today.

1987: Presbyterian Church (USA) – 'A Theological Understanding'

One of the most articulate and incisive documents to be produced by any Christian Church during the period in question is undoubtedly the 13-page Study Document issued in June 1987 by the Presbyterian Church (USA). Entitled "A Theological Understanding of the Relationship Between Christians and Jews," it is an eloquent and wide-ranging analysis of the history – as well as the present state – of that relationship. The reader, be he layman or theologian, cannot but be struck by the manifest honesty of this document as it comes to grips with some of the most difficult, sensitive and complex issues ever discussed in the domain of interreligious relations.

Like the Vatican's Notes, which preceded it, and other Church documents that have preceded or followed it, it is far from being a perfect instrument – certainly from the Jewish point of view. Yet it is at times so brutally honest and uninhibited, and so painstakingly detailed in the treatment of its subject, that the reader stands in awe and admiration. What we undoubtedly have here is a sound and solid building-block in the growing edifice of Christian-Jewish reconciliation. For this reason, it is one of the documents to be published in this book in its full, unabridged text (see Appendix L).

In order, however, to give the reader a "taste" of this remarkable paper, and a sampling of the qualities we have described, we shall quote here from what is perhaps the most penetrating, the most powerful, segment of this document of seven theological affirmations and their explications.

Affirmation No. 5 reads as follows:

> 5. We acknowledge in repentance the Church's long and deep complicity in the proliferation of anti-Jewish attitudes and actions through its "teaching of contempt" for the Jews. Such teaching we now repudiate, together with the acts and attitudes which it generates.

EXPLICATION

...For many centuries, it was the Church's teaching to label Jews as "Christ-killers" and a "deicide race." This is known as the "teaching of contempt." Persecution of Jews was at times officially sanctioned and at other times indirectly encouraged or at least tolerated. Holy Week became a time of terror for Jews. To this day, the Church's worship, preaching and teaching often lend themselves, at times unwittingly, to a perpetuation of the "teaching of contempt."...

It is agonizing to discover that the Church's "teaching of contempt" was a major ingredient that made possible the monstrous policy of annihilation of Jews by Nazi Germany. It is disturbing to have to admit that the Churches of the West did little to challenge the policies of their governments, even in the face of the growing certainty that the Holocaust was taking place. Though many Christians in Europe acted heroically to shelter Jews, the record reveals that most Churches as well as governments the world over largely ignored the pleas for sanctuary for Jews.

As the very embodiment of anti-Jewish attitudes and actions, the Holocaust is a sober reminder that such horrors are actually possible in this world, and that they begin with seemingly small acts of disdain or expedience. Hence, we pledge to be alert for all such acts of denigration from now on, so that they may be resisted.... The Church's attitudes must be reviewed and changed as necessary, so that they never again fuel the fires of hatred....

Again, we must note here that the Jewish dialogue-partner (and others perhaps too) will find things to criticize in this paper. However, as in the case of the Catholic Church's "Notes," we do not wish to delve too deeply into this negative aspect of our presentation, except to make one point, and that is that Affirmation No. 6, concerning "the continuity of God's promise of land," appears somewhat one-sided. In the opening portion of the Explication for Affirmation No. 6, there is an effort to "put on the table" different views, on the Jewish as well as the Christian side, of the modern-day implications of the biblical "promise of land to Abraham and his and Sarah's descendants."

Later, however, it avers that "we...dare not fail to uphold the divine right of the dispossessed....In particular, we confess our complicity in the loss of land by Palestinians as they cry for justice as the dispossessed...."

Judith H. Banki, of the American Jewish Committee, in a response to this document entitled "A Jewish Perspective on a Presbyterian Document," wrote the following observation:

> What disturbs me most about these formulations are the unspoken political presuppositions. It is assumed that it is Israel's fault that the Palestinians do not have a homeland. This assumption is never made explicit and is never tested. It ignores a forty-year history of persistent and vehement rejection, by those who claim to speak for the Palestinians, of Israel's existence or right to exist; it ignores the refusal of neighboring Arab states, with the notable exception of Egypt, to come to grips with the reality of Israel, to end the state of war against her and to sit down across the table to make peace. It ignores a record of terrorism...Despite the document's endorsement of non-violent solutions, this history cannot be lightly dismissed. Theology based on poor history is poor theology.

The issue of the national rebirth of Israel in 1948 in its ancestral homeland is the one issue, perhaps, which most of the Church documents that form the backbone of this book and its central thesis treat most gingerly and hesitatingly, if they treat it at all. We shall have more to say on this important subject in the last chapter. For now, suffice it to say that the Presbyterian paper we have been discussing here, so remarkable and noteworthy in so many respects, is by no means the only one of these documents to relate to the modern State of Israel – to the phenomenon of Israel Reborn – with great circumspection. (See, for example, the 1974 Statement of the American Lutheran Church: Appendix D.)

1993: Holy See / State of Israel – Fundamental Agreement
A landmark document in the relations between the Catholic Church, on the one hand, and the State of Israel and the Jewish people, on

the other, is the Fundamental Agreement between the Holy See and Israel, signed in Jerusalem on December 30, 1993. The event took place at Israel's Foreign Ministry, and the signatories were Dr. Yossi Beilin, then Deputy Foreign Minister of Israel, and Msgr. Claudio M. Celli, the Vatican's Under-Secretary for Relations with the States.

The Agreement, which had been hammered out by a joint working commission set up in Rome on July 29, 1992, marked a turning point after 45 years of cool and sometimes troubled contacts between the Vatican and Israel (see also Chapter 5). It was at once welcomed, in both the Catholic and the Jewish worlds, as a long-overdue development bound to have a positive impact not only in the political-diplomatic realm but in the religious-spiritual one as well.

The language of the Agreement itself reflects the religious element as an integral part of the accord. The preamble refers to "the singular character and universal significance of the Holy Land," to "the unique nature of the relationship between the Catholic Church and the Jewish people" and to "the historic process of reconciliation and growth in mutual understanding and friendship between Catholics and Jews." Article 1 cites Nostra Aetate as the document that gave expression to the Church's "respect for other religions and their followers," and Article 2 contains a strong, unequivocal condemnation, by the Holy See, of "hatred, persecution and all other manifestations of antisemitism directed against the Jewish people and individual Jews…" In Article 3, Israel "recognizes the right of the Catholic Church to carry out its religious, moral, educational and charitable functions and to have its own institutions…"

Incidentally, the leaders of the other Christian communities in Israel were given solemn assurances by Israeli officials, following the signing of the Fundamental Agreement with the Holy See, that their own rights would in no way be infringed by this Agreement. And, indeed, Article 4 of the Agreement affirmed Israel's "continuing commitment to maintain and respect the status quo in the Christian Holy Places to which it applies and the respective rights of the Christian communities thereunder." A parallel commitment is recorded in the name of the Catholic Church.

Finally, under the terms of Article 14, full diplomatic relations were to be established (as indeed they were), "not later than four months after the coming into force of this Agreement," between the Holy See and Israel, on the level of Apostolic Nunciature and Embassy, respectively.

Msgr. Celli, in his opening statement before the signing, voiced the expectation of the Holy See "that the dialogue and respectful cooperation between Catholics and Jews will now be given new impetus and energy, both in Israel and throughout the world." Dr. Beilin, in similar vein, expressed his confidence that the Agreement's impact extended beyond the geographical boundaries of the states involved, and that it would "touch the hearts of millions of Jews and more than a billion Christians throughout the world…"

(Full text of Agreement in Appendix M.)

1993/1995: The Orthodox Churches – A Different Approach

The Orthodox Churches, centered in Greece, Russia and other eastern European nations, are late arrivals in the ongoing Christian-Jewish dialogue. Moreover, the dialogue with these Churches is of a somewhat different nature from that involving Catholics and Protestants. Dr. Geoffrey Wigoder, who represented the Israel Jewish Council for Interreligious Relations at the Third Academic Meeting Between Orthodoxy and Judaism in Athens in March 1993, explained it this way:

> For one thing, there is not the same depth of feeling of guilt concerning the Holocaust that prevailed among the Western Churches. The Orthodox Churches feel strongly that they themselves had been among the victims; and the Greek Church in particular is proud of its efforts in rescuing Greek Jews during World War II. [Another difference is] the absence of hostility to Israel…

The dialogue between the Jewish community and the Orthodox Churches really began in earnest only at that Athens meeting in 1993, when leaders of these two faith communities met, in what one observer described as "a potentially historic encounter," to recall more than 2,000 years of shared history and to discuss the relevant problems and challenges of the 1990s.

Hosted by the Greek Government, the Athens conference was co-sponsored by the Orthodox Center of the Ecumenical Patriarchate in Geneva and the International Jewish Committee for Interreligious Consultations (IJCIC), which for many years was under the chairmanship of Dr. Geoffrey Wigoder.

The central theme of the conference was sounded by His All Holiness the Ecumenical Patriarch Bartholomew when he said:

> The common spiritual origin of Christians and Jews seems today, more than ever, to offer a fruitful ground for the rejection of the consequences of mutually prevailing hostility in the past, and the establishment of a new relationship, genuine and authentic, rooted in the willingness to work towards mutual understanding and improved knowledge of each other.

Two years later, the Ecumenical Patriarch was to visit Israel, where he met with the President, the Prime Minister and other government and religious leaders. During his stay in Jerusalem, the Patriarch was hosted, at a reception in his honor at Ratisbonne Monastery, by the Ecumenical Theological Research Fraternity in Israel. This event also marked the launching of Issue No. 26/27 of *Immanuel*, a journal edited by Malcolm Lowe and published by the Fraternity. The issue in question was devoted mainly to the proceedings of the 1993 Athens meeting, in addition to surveys of the history and theology of dialogue between Orthodox Christians and Jews. In his remarks on this occasion, the Ecumenical Patriarch Bartholomew hailed this issue of *Immanuel* as having accomplished "its goal of promoting a more positive understanding among theologians and scholars and, in general, among lay-believers of Judaism and Orthodox Christianity – in a major effort to bring about a re-focusing of attitudes towards each other." The Patriarch praised the Fraternity for having "succeeded in deepening the relationship between Orthodox Christians and Jews."

Since 1972, the Patriarch noted, the Orthodox Churches "have been engaged in an academic dialogue of the highest level with Judaism," with neither side seeking to convert the other to its beliefs. Rather, he noted,

> there is a genuine interest – even an obligation – to open our minds and hearts to a fuller and more edifying understanding of man: his existence, his religion, his relationship with God and with his neighbor...The time has come, however, to put academic study into layman's language. It is time for the good will among theologians and scholars to be shared with the faithful of both the Jewish and the Christian traditions.

We might mention, in passing, that the need to broaden the scope of the Christian-Jewish dialogue, noted here by the Ecumenical Patriarch, has been articulated with growing frequency in recent years by religious thinkers and "dialoguers" in a number of countries. On this important point, too, we shall have more to say in Chapter 8.

1995: The Baptist Churches – Mixed Signals

What stand have the Baptist Churches taken vis-à-vis Judaism and the Jewish people? More than with any of the other Christian Churches, what we appear to be receiving from the Baptist Churches is, at best, a series of mixed signals: a readiness, on the part of the American, or Northern, Baptists, to acknowledge past Church sins, including the Christian role in helping to pave the way for the horrors of the Shoah in central Europe – and, in the case of the Southern Baptist Convention (SBC), a seemingly unrelenting persistence in pursuing a policy of proselytism with regard to the Jews.

This internal conflict – which must of course be seen also against the background of the long-standing split between Northern and Southern Baptists – finds expression in the introduction to a statement adopted by the Alliance of Baptists on March 4, 1995, on Jewish-Christian relations. The introduction reads as follows:

> Thirty years ago the Vatican document, Nostra Aetate, was adopted by the Second Vatican Council. This statement heralded a significant change in Jewish-Christian relations, first among the Roman

Catholics and soon thereafter among Protestant Christian bodies. As Baptists, we too have been influenced by this invitation to dialogue begun by Vatican II. Certain Baptists ... modeled out for a brief moment in time a different way to relate to the Jewish people and the Jewish faith. Regrettably, in recent years this effort at Jewish-Baptist dialogue has been reduced to a theology of conversion.

The statement itself (reproduced in full in Appendix N) is as forthright, in its language, as any similar Church document in dealing with an unsavory past – and, in particular, with the events surrounding the Shoah. It pointedly characterizes the Shoah as "the culmination of centuries of Christian teaching and Church-sanctioned action directed against the Jews simply because they were Jews." After listing in some detail the Church's theological distortions down the ages, the statement goes on to declare that "we, the Alliance of Baptists...confess our sin of complicity; confess our sin of silence; confess our sin of interpreting our sacred writings in such a way that we have created enemies of the Jewish people; confess our sin of indifference and inaction to the horrors of the Holocaust; confess our sins against the Jewish people; offer this confession with humility and with hope for reconciliation between Christians and Jews."

Among five action calls that conclude the statement is one that speaks of "seeking genuine dialogue with the broader Jewish community, a dialogue built on mutual respect and the integrity of each other's faith." Clearly, such an undertaking would preclude attempts to induce the Jewish dialogue-partner to abandon his own faith and adopt Christianity in its stead.

Yet only one year later, on June 14, 1996, the US Southern Baptist Convention, convening in New Orleans, Louisiana, adopted a resolution pledging to "direct our energies and resources toward the proclamation of the Gospel to the Jews." The Baptist Home Mission Board appointed a missionary to work among Jews in the United States. We will enter into a more detailed discussion of this development, and of other aspects of the way in which evangelism has impacted the process of reconciliation between Christians and Jews, in Chapter 8 – which deals with this subject. For the moment, suffice it to say that this direct advocacy of proselytism in the Southern Baptist Church runs counter to the Baptist Alliance's call, quoted above, for "genuine dialogue…built on mutual respect and the integrity of each other's faith."

One must bear in mind, of course, in this context, that the SBC is a separate entity, with governing bodies and policy lines of its own. It is a fact, however, that the wish to evangelize the Jews, as a matter of Church policy, is not confined to the SBC alone – witness the closing words of the above-cited introduction to the 1995 statement of the Alliance of Baptists: "Regrettably, in recent years this effort at Jewish-Baptist dialogue has been reduced to a theology of conversion."

1995/1996: Canadian Churches – "A Call to Do Something"

Canada's Churches have also played their role in the move towards reconciliation with Judaism and the Jewish people. Thus the Evangelical Lutheran Church in Canada, for example, at its 5th Biannual Convention in 1995, adopted a statement addressed to the Jewish people which was modeled very closely after the statement released a year earlier by the Evangelical Lutheran Church in America (Appendix G).

A year later, the United Church of Canada, at its British Columbia Conference on May 4, 1996, passed a resolution based on a prior resolution submitted to the Conference by the Vancouver South Presbytery. Entitled "A Call to Do Something About Possible Anti-Jewish Feelings Within the Church," it acknowledged that "the Holocaust…continues to haunt us as a vision of the dark side of Western culture"; that "anti-Jewish feeling and teaching in the Church has contributed to and is in large measure responsible for anti-Jewish atrocities through the ages"; and that "we as Christians can no longer deny nor avoid our responsibility in this matter…"

There follows a list of four "suggestions," the last of which encourages local – mostly Protestant – Churches to use a prayer, during Holy Week, ascribed to Pope John XXIII. The prayer ends with the words:

"Forgive the curse that we unjustly pronounced over the name of the Jews. Forgive that we crucified You again in their flesh."

1995/1997: European and US Catholic Bishops – On the Shoah

The 50th anniversary of the end of World War II and the liberation of Auschwitz and other Nazi concentration camps served as the occasion for a series of statements on these events issued by the Catholic Bishops of Germany, France, Poland, Hungary, Holland, Switzerland and the United States. (Excerpts from the German and French Bishops' Statements – in Appendixes P and Q.)

A careful reading of these statements will reveal a good deal of soul-searching and an apparently genuine effort to come to grips with one of the most shocking and horrendous series of events in the annals of humankind. It is noteworthy, too, that in several instances the language used by the bishops in confessing their collective responsibility for the silence of the Church in those dark days goes beyond what we find in the documents of the Vatican itself on this subject (see, for example, the Vatican document on the Shoah, "We Remember" – pp. 98–100).

1996: United Methodist Church – "New Bridges in Hope"

In April 1996, the General Conference of the United Methodist Church in the United States adopted a statement on Christian-Jewish relations entitled "Building New Bridges in Hope." Like several of its forerunners among the Protestant Churches, this document too opens with an introduction tracing the background of this "quest for new understanding," and then proceeds to postulate a number of propositions, some of these being theological principles, while others are more in the nature of calls for action. (The document in its entirety is reproduced in Appendix R.) Here, for the reader's convenience, we shall present the statement's nine propositions:

1. There is one living God in whom both Jews and Christians believe.
2. Jesus was a devout Jew, as were many of his first followers.
3. Judaism and Christianity are living and dynamic religious move-

ments that have continued to evolve since the time of Jesus, often in interaction with each other and with God's continual self-disclosure in the world.

4. Christians and Jews are bound to God through Biblical covenants that are eternally valid.

5. As Christians, we are clearly called to witness to the gospel of Jesus Christ in every age and place. At the same time, we believe that God has continued, and continues today, to work through Judaism and the Jewish people.

6. As Christians, we are called to dialogue with our Jewish neighbors.

7. As followers of Jesus Christ, we deeply repent the complicity of the Church and the participation of many Christians in the long history of persecution of the Jewish people. The Christian Church has a profound obligation to correct historical and theological teachings that have led to false and pejorative perceptions of Judaism and contributed to persecution and hatred of Jews. It is our responsibility as Christians to oppose antisemitism whenever and wherever it occurs.

8. As Christians, we share a call with Jews to work for justice, compassion and peace in the world, in anticipation of the fulfillment of God's reign.

9. As United Methodist Christians, we are deeply affected by the anguish and suffering that continue for many people who live in the Middle East region which includes modern Israel. We commit ourselves, through prayer and advocacy, to bring about justice and peace for those of every faith.

Some of these, of course, are reiterations of propositions and principles that have been stated in other Church documents, some of which have been quoted in this chapter. The reader is invited, however, to note in particular the striking difference between Propositions No. 3, 4 and 5 of the United Methodist statement and the strident call of the Southern Baptist Convention (see pp. 94, 130) for mission to the Jews. Proposition No. 5 lays it down very clearly that the Methodists have by no means set aside the traditional Christian call to preach the gospel; but, at the same time, they acknowledge that Judaism has its own role to play in God's plan – and that acknowledgment makes all the difference.

1998: The Vatican Remembers the Shoah

On March 16, 1998, the Vatican's Commission for Religious Relations with the Jews published a 14-page document entitled "We Remember: A Reflection on the Shoah." In an introduction to the paper addressed to "my Venerable Brother Cardinal Edward Idris Cassidy" (at that time President of the Commission, and a signatory of the document), Pope John Paul II wrote:

> It is my fervent hope that [this] document, which the Commission for Religious Relations with the Jews has prepared under your direction, will indeed help to heal the wounds of past misunderstandings and injustices. May it enable memory to play its necessary part in the process of shaping a future in which the unspeakable iniquity of the Shoah will never again be possible. May the Lord of history guide the efforts of Catholics and Jews, and all men of good will, as they work together for a world of true respect for the life and dignity of every human being, for all have been created in the image and likeness of God.

In the words of Rabbi Leon Klenicki of the Anti-Defamation League, who wrote a commentary on *We Remember*, "The document reflects partially the hopeful thought of Pope John Paul II, though some sections express concepts that are of serious concern to the Jewish reader." Rabbi Klenicki's distinctly mixed response to this paper reflects the general Jewish reaction as this found expression at the time in various published responses. Thus Rabbi A. James Rudin, then National Interreligious Affairs Director of the American Jewish Committee, while commending the document's reference to the uniqueness of the Shoah and its expression of "deep sorrow for the failures of the Church's sons and daughters," criticizes "the overly cautious and often disappointing document…"

The Jerusalem Post, in a March 18, 1998, editorial, draws an interesting comparison between this Vatican document and the statements made earlier by the French and German Bishops (see page 96), finding that *We Remember* is "not as bold as statements made by Pope John Paul ii [or] statements made by the French and German bishops..." The Vatican document, the *Post* contends, "seems more focused on documenting Christian resistance to Nazism than grappling with the wrenching issues of Christian complicity and passivity." Incidentally, Rabbi Klenicki, in his commentary cited above, makes a similar comparison between this document and the French and German statements – and also finds the Vatican paper wanting.

To conclude this discussion of *We Remember* on a positive note, however, let us quote two passages from the document that do give rather poignant expression to the Church's acknowledgment of the enormity of the events of those days and to its determination not to allow such horrors ever to happen again:

> This century has witnessed an unspeakable tragedy, which can never be forgotten: the attempt by the Nazi regime to exterminate the Jewish people, with the consequent killing of millions of Jews. Women and men, old and young, children and infants, for the sole reason of their Jewish origin, were persecuted and deported. Some were killed immediately, while others were degraded, ill-treated, tortured and utterly robbed of their human dignity, and then murdered. Very few of those who entered the camps survived, and those who did remained scarred for life. This was the Shoah. It is a major fact of the history of this century – a fact which still concerns us today.

And here is the second passage:

> At the end of this millennium, the Catholic Church desires to express her deep sorrow for the failures of her sons and daughters in every age. This is an act of repentance (*teshuva*), since, as members of the Church, we are linked to the sins as well as the merits of all her children. The Church approaches with deep respect and great compassion the experience of extermination, the Shoah, suffered by the Jewish people during World War ii. It is not a matter of mere words, but indeed of binding commitment. "We would risk causing the victims of the most atrocious deaths to die again if we do not have an ardent desire for justice, if we

do not commit ourselves to ensure that evil does not prevail over good as it did for millions of the children of the Jewish people… Humanity cannot permit all that to happen again."

The last two sentences were quoted from an address by Pope John Paul II on April 7, 1994. But, of course, the commitment the Pope articulated in his first sentence becomes, by virtue of its being incorporated in this statement, an integral part of the Vatican statement as well.

1999: House of Lords, Westminster – "The Time to Heal"

In the nature of things, this book in general – and the present chapter of documents in particular – deals mainly with statements produced by the world's major Christian Churches, Catholic, Protestant and Orthodox. It is important, however, to keep in mind that significant segments of Christendom are not necessarily attached to these "established" Churches but, in many cases, belong to non-denominational churches – or to Orders that may be affiliated in some way with an established Church but nevertheless lead an existence of their own. Also, there are Christian umbrella organizations and coalitions of like-minded believers which, all together, make up a not insignificant part of the Christian world. We feel that these voices need to be heard too if we are to obtain a nuanced overall impression of what Christians the world over are thinking and saying about the subjects at hand.

To give due representation, therefore, to these voices, we have elected to open here a small window on the deliberations of a gathering of Christians from Britain and other European countries that took place on November 1, 1999, at the House of Lords in Westminster.

Convened by a coalition that included such organizations as the Evangelical Sisters of Mary, the International Christian Embassy Jerusalem, City and Westminster PrayerNet, Christian Friends of Israel, Christian Action for Israel, the Centre for Biblical and Hebraic Studies and others, the meeting was timed to mark the anniversary of the banishment of the Jews of England, on November 1, 1290, by order of King Edward I at Westminster. Among those participating were Canon Andrew White, Director of the International Ministry at Coventry Cathedral; Father Peter Hocken, Adviser to the Roman Catholic Bishop of Northampton; Rt. Rev. John Taylor, former Bishop of St. Albans; Rev. R.M. Kingsbury, of the Ebenezer Emergency Fund (helping to bring many thousands of Jews from the former Soviet Union to Israel); Simon Rufus Isaacs, Marquess of Reading; and Sister Pista, of the Evangelical Sisterhood of Mary, headquartered in Darmstadt, Germany.

A highpoint of this very impressive gathering in the heart of London was the following Solemn Declaration:

> We come humbly before Almighty G-d this day to remember nearly 2,000 years of antisemitism perpetrated by the Christian Church. We acknowledge that from the first century of the Common Era through to this day, the common preaching of the Church has often claimed that G-d has finished with His covenant people, the Jews, despite the clear evidence of Scripture to the contrary, thus perpetuating a misunderstanding of the Scriptures.
>
> We confess that the Jewish people have often been accused of deicide and have been the object of blood libel, by those acting in the name of Jesus. We recognize that many persecutions, including the Holocaust, which we remember especially on this day, had their origins within the Christian Church.
>
> We therefore plead with Almighty G-d that He might have mercy upon us for the many sins of the Church and her children. We repent of our wrongdoing towards the Jewish people, and pledge ourselves to work tirelessly against antisemitism in all its forms, and especially within the Church.
>
> In praying for G-d's forgiveness for the Church and her members, we seek His blessing upon His covenant people, the Jews, both in Israel and in the Diaspora.

Sister Pista, of the Evangelical Sisterhood of Mary in Darmstadt, spoke not only as a Christian, but also as a German. Her obviously heartfelt words, therefore, carried special weight. Here is a small portion of her remarks at Westminster:

History has proven the truth of G-d's words regarding Israel: "I will bless those who bless you; and whoever curses you I will curse" (Gen. 12:3 NIV). Nowhere has this verse been demonstrated so plainly as in Germany. We burned and looted, maimed and killed. And as divine retribution caught up with us, we reaped what we had sown....

For centuries G-d has been grieving because of our attitude as Christians towards our older brother Israel. What it would mean to G-d the Father if we were to regard His people with His eyes and to love what He loves! As we approach the millennium, may our hearts be turned to His people. G-d has been waiting for this moment for nearly two thousand years. May He not have to wait any longer!

2000: A Jewish Response – *Dabru Emet* ("Speak Truth")

What more fitting way to close out this chapter (and the second millennium!) than by means of a wide-ranging, collective Jewish response – the first of its kind on record – to a half-century of Christian effort at reconciliation?

If something has been missing in this Christian-Jewish "peace process" (aside from lingering doubts and hesitations on the part of some Churches and Christian leaders), it surely has been a significant Jewish response in terms of a candid, unbegrudging acknowledgment by Jewish leaders and scholars that an important beginning has been made, on the Christian side, in righting the wrongs of the past and charting a new course for the future. Let us take heart, therefore, in the knowledge that, at the turn of the millennium, in September 2000, "a significant Jewish response" did come at last. It took the form of a full-page message, published simultaneously in *The New York Times* and *The Baltimore Sun* on September 11, 2000, and headlined:

DABRU EMET (Hebrew for "Speak Truth")
A JEWISH STATEMENT ON CHRISTIANS AND CHRISTIANITY

The message, released by the Institute for Christian and Jewish Studies in Baltimore, was signed by some 170 leading American rabbis and scholars belonging to the four Jewish denominations: Conservative, Reform, Orthodox and Reconstructionist.

Following a brief review of a number of aspects and ramifications of what the message calls the "dramatic and unprecedented shift in Jewish-Christian relations," based on the fact that, after nearly two millennia in which "Christians have tended to characterize Judaism as a failed religion or, at best, as a religion that prepared the way for and is completed in Christianity," in the decades since the Shoah "Christianity has changed dramatically."

"We believe," the statement continues, "these changes merit a thoughtful Jewish response. Speaking only for ourselves – an inter-denominational group of Jewish scholars – we believe it is time for Jews to learn about the efforts of Christians to honor Judaism. We believe it is time for Jews to reflect on what Judaism may now say about Christianity."

In the style of documents of this kind, the statement goes on to lay down eight propositions, each one followed by a brief explanation. We shall here quote the propositions themselves; their explanations, together with the remaining text of the message, may be found in Appendix S.

A prior word of caution: Proposition No. 5, if read without the accompanying explanatory text, is easily misunderstood – and, in point of fact, has caused some raising of eyebrows. In order to clear up any such misunderstanding, we present the reader with the statement's explanatory text relating to Proposition No. 5 – at the end of the list of propositions. Here, then, is the list:

1. Jews and Christians worship the same God.

2. Jews and Christians seek authority from the same book – the Bible (what Jews call *Tanakh* and Christians call the "Old Testament").

3. Christians can respect the claim of the Jewish people upon the land of Israel.

4. Jews and Christians accept the moral principles of Torah.

5. Nazism was not a Christian phenomenon.

6. The humanly irreconcilable difference between Jews and Christians will not be settled until God redeems the entire world, as promised in Scripture.

7. A new relationship between Jews and Christians will not weaken Jewish practice.

8. Jews and Christians must work together for justice and peace.

As promised above, here is the explanatory text for Proposition No. 5:

> Without the long history of Christian anti-Judaism and Christian violence against Jews, Nazi ideology could not have taken hold, nor could it have been carried out. Too many Christians participated in or were sympathetic to Nazi atrocities against Jews. Other Christians did not protest sufficiently against these atrocities. But Nazism itself was not an inevitable outcome of Christianity. If the Nazi extermination of the Jews had been fully successful, it would have turned its murderous rage more directly to Christians. We recognize with gratitude those Christians who risked or sacrificed their lives to save Jews during the Nazi regime. With that in mind, we encourage the continuation of recent efforts in Christian theology to repudiate unequivocally contempt of Judaism and the Jewish people. We applaud those Christians who reject this teaching of contempt, and we do not blame them for the sins committed by their ancestors.

The first authoritative Christian comment on the *Dabru Emet* message came from Dr. Eugene J. Fisher, Associate Director of Ecumenical and Interreligious Affairs in America's National Conference of Catholic Bishops:

> This is truly historic. I salute the courage and wisdom of the drafters and signers of this pioneering document. This is a major step forward in Jewish-Christian relations.

Amen!

Part Three

Problem Areas

Chapter 7

Baseless Hatred

*Therefore be it resolved that the General Council hereby
declare its opposition to antisemitism, and that it
disapprove of the ministers of the Assemblies of God
identifying themselves with those who are engaged in this
propaganda.... Should we, as children of God, hate those
whom God our Father loves?*
(From resolution adopted by
Assemblies of God General Council, 1945)

*The Church, moreover, rejects every persecution against any
person. For this reason, and for the sake of the patrimony
she shares with the Jews, the Church decries hatreds,
persecutions and manifestations of antisemitism against
Jews at any time and by anyone.*
(Nostra Aetate, Second Vatican Council, 1965)

*We pledge, God helping us, never again to participate in,
to contribute to or (insofar as we are able) to allow
the persecution or denigration of Jews or the
belittling of Judaism.*
(From Study Paper of Presbyterian Church – usa, 1987)

THE WORD "ANTISEMITISM," it needs to be said at the outset, is
a misnomer. It is even more of a misnomer when, as so often is the
case, it is spelled "anti-Semitism." The etymological implication of this

word – that the reference is to a doctrine directed against Semites – has frequently been exploited by Arab spokesmen to refute the charge of antisemitism on the grounds that Arabs, being Semites themselves, cannot be "anti-Semites" – a patently specious argument.

Christian leaders and theologians (e.g., Pope Pius XI in September 1938) have pointed out that members of the Christian community, too, may be considered Semites in the spiritual sense, since Christianity is an outgrowth of Judaism. Some have therefore suggested the substitution of the term "anti-Judaism" when the reference is to words and acts directed against Jews or the Jewish people and its faith. In popular parlance, this is what is known as calling a spade a spade; and there is much good logic in that approach.

However, in view of the fact that the term "antisemitism" has become so deeply imbedded in our language and culture as denoting what is actually anti-Judaism, and appears in numerous documents on the subject, some of which will be cited in this chapter, we really have no choice but to employ this word, at least part of the time. An alternative expression we will be using in this context is "baseless hatred," in line with the terms in which anti-Judaism has been defined in some of these documents.

Baseless hatred (*sin'at hinnam* in Hebrew) is cited, by the Jewish Sages, as the chief reason for the downfall of the Second Jewish Commonwealth two thousand years ago. Could it be that another form of punishment meted out to the Jewish people for having engaged in this reprehensible practice was that this weapon of baseless hatred was later to be turned against them, as a people, and given the name "antisemitism"?

The Church's Role

Historians and New Testament scholars are divided over the question of whether the early roots of antisemitism are to be found in the New Testament or whether they are to be traced, rather, to the later pronouncements of the Church Fathers. Historically speaking, of course, it may be argued that there were manifestations of Jew-hatred long before the time of Jesus: The Egyptians' oppression of the Israelites (Exodus, Chapter 1) and Haman's plot against the Jews of Persia (Esther 3:6,8,9) are merely two instances that come readily to mind. Antisemitism may thus not be a Christian "invention." Since, however, our subject in this book is the history and development of Christian-Jewish relations, it is the Christians' adoption – or adaptation – of anti-Judaism that will concern us here.

David G. Burke, of the Department of Translation and Scripture Resources at the American Bible Society, maintains that the question of whether such New Testament books as Acts and the Gospel of St. John can be considered antisemitic, or anti-Jewish, depends on how the phrase *hoi Ioudiaioi* and related expressions are translated (viz., *Explorations*, Vol. 9, No. 2, American Interfaith Institute, 1995). This question becomes critical, Burke writes, "because the New Testament passages provide fuel for expressions of anti-Jewish hatred today."

Burke and others seem to feel that the problem lies not so much in the writings themselves as in the way these writings were later translated, edited and transmitted. Also, as Burke points out, "Few modern readers are equipped to sort out that 'the Jews' opposing Jesus and the Jesus movement are in many cases just other Jews who happen not to have accepted Jesus's identity as Messiah…it is difficult for the modern reader to think this through in terms of real-life ambiguities that would have applied then as now; that is, to consider that many of these 'enemies' may have been acting, in the events of the early (pre-synagogue expulsion) years, in order to be responsible and faithful to the tradition as they understood it…"

A different approach to this problem is suggested by Malcolm Lowe, a Christian writer, editor and lecturer residing in Jerusalem. Writing in *Christians and Israel* (Vol. 5, Nos. 1 & 2), the Jerusalem quarterly of the Association of Christians and Jews in Israel, with reference to John's Gospel, Lowe makes this point:

> By listening to what the evangelist is really saying, instead of focusing on one particular phrase, we shall find that he has no hostility to Jews as such. Quite the contrary. What concerns him is a human predicament of which both *hoi Ioudiaioi* and the apostles of Jesus are examples.

Citing an earlier article of his (in *Novum Testamentum*, 1976), Lowe argues that –

> the best translation of *hoi Ioudiaioi* in John's Gospel is usually "the Judeans," or people coming from *Ioudiaia* – Judea. But "Judea" had two meanings. Jews living in the Land of Israel would talk of Judea in its strict sense: the area around Jerusalem. But foreigners called the whole Land of Israel "Judea."... In John's Gospel – and in the other ones too – "Judea" is almost always used in the strict sense. Also the encounters with *hoi Ioudiaioi* are almost always situated in Judea. On the other hand, Nathanel the Galilean is called an "Israelite." So Jesus had his main confrontations not with "the Jews" but with the Judeans.

Moreover, argues Lowe, the Judeans' attitude towards Jesus was not uniformly negative or hostile but, like that of the apostles, often wavered between belief and disbelief. His conclusion:

> When the Gospel is read carefully, therefore, one sees that it is not hostile to the Jewish people at all. What troubles John is a general human weakness, of which both *hoi Ioudiaioi* and the apostles are examples.

Be that as it may – that is, whether the roots of Christian anti-semitism are to be found in the New Testament or in the manner in which some New Testament writings were exploited or recast by the Church Fathers – the fact remains that, down the centuries from that time to this, the Church formulated, developed and acted out a series of theological doctrines that, in effect, gave Christian believers a license to kill Jews. The "triumphalist" doctrines of supersessionism (or replacement theory), the teaching of contempt and others are discussed in an earlier chapter, and there is therefore no need to deal with them here again. Suffice it to say that these doctrines and dogmas set the tone for Christian teachings and behavior for many generations. Moreover, they furnished theological justification for countless acts and campaigns of oppression and persecution, mass-slander and mass-slaughter, perpetrated not only by adherents of the various Churches, but also by the leaders and members of other faiths. Secular movements, too, that were intent on inflicting harm on their Jewish neighbors were thus able to take advantage of the prevailing anti-Jewish mindset in the countries of Europe and parts of the Middle East.

The situation reached its nadir in the middle of the 20th century, with the meticulously planned, organized and executed Nazi campaign of genocide against the Jews of Europe that took the lives of more than six million men, women and children. The Nazi movement was not a Christian phenomenon; but its satanic genocidal campaign took place in the heart of what may quite accurately be called Christian Europe, having imbibed the regurgitated antisemitic poison of Martin Luther, together with such classical instruments of anti-Jewish Church doctrine as the teaching of contempt and related dogmas.

A Jewish View

Social scientists have long grappled with the question of what it is that fuels antisemitism (or anti-Judaism). A variety of reasons or causes have been suggested – as well as the proposition that, whatever the *cause*, there really is no *reason* for this phenomenon. Thus the 16th century Jewish philosopher, Judah Loewe, better known as Maharal, maintained that human beings have a tendency to hate and reject those who are different, presumably because they do not understand them, which in turn breeds fear, suspicion and hatred, with consequences that cannot always be calculated. Maharal puts it this way: "Jacob had a spiritual, near-divine quality about him that made him different from others, and that is why they wanted to kill him: because when someone is different, others will wish to kill him…" Then he adds the following:

> The Jewish people inherited this spiritual characteristic of Jacob's, and it is this that produced the hatred of the nations towards the Jewish people. In point of fact, the opponents of the Jewish people do not act against the Jews for a given reason, as is generally the case. The enemies of the Jewish people exercise their hostility without a reason, without the Jews having harmed them in any way…

Maharal, in other words, perceived antisemitism as a condition of hostility on the unconscious level, a hostility "without a reason," a baseless hostility. Antisemitism, in this conception, is not a reaction to specific Jewish actions or behavior but, rather, a kind of resistance, at the unconscious or subconscious level, to the Jewish ethos, to what the Jew represents.

Those who practice antisemitism will generally try to justify their words or actions by ascribing these to Jewish attributes or deeds, real or imagined. With antisemitism becoming less "fashionable" or acceptable, in most societies, since the European Holocaust, a new tendency has developed to disguise or mask it – notably, in recent decades, by peddling it as anti-Zionism or anti-Israelism. This is not to say, of course, that all criticism of Israel or Israeli policies is necessarily a form of antisemitism; but quite often it is exactly that. Dr. Martin Luther King, Jr. addressed this issue in a "Letter to an Anti-Zionist Friend" (*Saturday Review* XLVII, August 1967), with characteristic eloquence and simplicity:

> ....You declare, my friend, that you do not hate the Jews, you are merely "anti-Zionist." And I say, let the truth ring from the high mountain tops, let it echo through the valleys of God's green earth: When people criticize Zionism, they mean Jews – this is God's own truth.

No less an authority than the Vatican has reached much the same conclusion: Anti-Zionism, it avers, "serves at times as a screen for anti-Semitism" (Vatican's statement on "The Church and Racism," 1988).

Awakening

The theological revolution in the Catholic and Protestant Churches, in the wake of the Shoah/Holocaust and the revival of the Jewish nation in its land that came hard on its heels, is the principal subject of this book. Systematically documented in Chapter 6 and the Appendixes, it includes a concerted, systematic and persistent campaign, by the leading Churches in Christendom, to stamp out the scourge of antisemitism. Concerted – in that it is inspired and directed from the highest echelons in these Churches, and finds its echo in the various denominations' officialdom and in their literature, resolutions, curricula, etc. Systematic – in that it is not limited to high-sounding general pronouncements but often descends to the minutest, at times painful, details. And persistent – in that it is a phenomenon dating back to before World War II and continuing, virtually without letup, to this day. A few random examples follow (taken mostly from the closing decades of the 20th century):

- In 1937, Pope Pius XI issued an Encyclical Letter, entitled *Mit Brennender Sorge* ("With Burning Concern"), in which he excoriated the widespread repressive measures the Nazi regime, under Hitler, had begun to institute against the Jews.

- In 1945, the General Council of the Assemblies of God in the USA published the statement in condemnation of antisemitism that is quoted briefly at the start of this chapter and, at much greater length, in the previous chapter (see p. 71).

- In 1965, the Second Vatican Council, in its Nostra Aetate declaration, "decried" manifestations of antisemitism (see Chapter 6, p. 73, and Appendix B).

- In 1974, the Vatican published the first of what was to become a series of documents elucidating Nostra Aetate. Known as the "Guidelines," this document in fact went a step further than Nostra Aetate by "condemning" antisemitism (see Chapter 6, p. 74), where the earlier declaration had only "decried" it.

- In 1981, the Council of Churches in The Netherlands issued a Declaration "On Persistent Antisemitism," in which the subject is treated in considerable detail (see Chapter 6, p. 82, and Appendix K) and the assertion is made that, since "a special tie exists between the Jewish people and the Church," the latter "can and should speak about antisemitism in a special way."

- In 1987, the Presbyterian Church (USA) published one of the most detailed and thoroughgoing analyses of antisemitism ever produced in an official Christian document (see Chapter 6, p. 87, and Appendix L: Affirmation No. 5 and its Explication).

- In 1988, the Pontifical Commission for Justice and Peace issued the landmark document entitled "The Church and Racism: Towards a More Fraternal Society." In Paragraph 15 of this document, anti-Semitism [thus in the official English text] is described as "the most tragic form that racist ideology has assumed in our century, with the horrors of the Jewish 'holocaust'..." The document goes on to declare that "Anti-Zionism...serves at times as a screen for anti-Semitism, feeding on it and leading to it."

- In 1989, Pope John Paul II, who condemned antisemitism on many occasions, had this to say about it in his Apostolic Letter on the occasion of the 50th anniversary of the outbreak of World War II: "I wish to repeat here in the strongest possible terms that hostility and hatred against Judaism are in complete contradiction to the Christian vision of human dignity."

- In 1991, during a visit to Hungary – which, like other countries in central and eastern Europe in the post-Communist era, was experiencing a revival of antisemitism – Pope John Paul II said: "In the face of a risk of a resurgence and spread of antisemitic feelings, attitudes and initiatives, of which certain disquieting signs are to be seen today, and of which we have experienced the most frightful results in the past, we must teach consciences to consider antisemitism and all forms of racism as sins against God and humanity."

- In Dececmber 1993, a Fundamental Agreement Between the Holy See and Israel was signed in Jerusalem (see Chapter 6, p. 89, and Appendix M), Article 2 of which contains a strong and unequivocal condemnation by the Holy See of "hatred, persecution and all manifestations of antisemitism directed against the Jewish people and individual Jews..."

- In the mid-1990s, a series of statements marking the 50th anniversary of the liberation of Auschwitz and other Nazi death camps were issued by the Catholic Bishops of Germany, France, Poland, Hungary, The Netherlands, Switzerland and the United States. The statements reflect the contrition felt by these religious leaders for the silence of the Church in that dark era. (Excerpts from the German and French Bishops' Statements – in Appendixes P and Q.)

- In 1996, the General Conference of the United Methodist Church in the United States adopted a statement on Christian-Jewish relations (see Chapter 6, p. 96, and Appendix R) that included an acceptance of "our responsibility as Christians to oppose antisemitism whenever and wherever it occurs."

- In 1997, an international symposium in Vatican City on "The Christian Roots of Anti-Judaism" issued a communique that said, among other things: "The errors and omissions of the past must not be repeated in the future....Christians who succumb to anti-Judaism offend God and the Church itself." All countries represented undertook a commitment to work to eliminate all traces of Christian anti-Judaism. Addressing the symposium, Pope John Paul II strongly condemned antisemitism as "totally unjustifiable" and linked what happened in the Holocaust to centuries of Christian anti-Jewish teachings, a theme that was echoed by Father Georges Cottier, sometimes referred to as "the Pope's theologian." Here is what the Pope said on this subject:

> In the Christian world – I am not saying on the part of the Church as such – the wrong and unjust interpretations of the New Testament relating to the Jewish people and their supposed guilt [in Christ's death] circulated for too long, engendering sentiments of hostility toward this people. This contributed to a lulling of consciences, so that when Europe was engulfed by a wave of persecutions inspired by a pagan antisemitism...the spiritual resistance of many was

not what humanity had a right to expect from the disciples
of Christ.

- In 1998, during the traditional Good Friday procession in Rome,
Pope John Paul II made the unprecedented statement that the
Jewish people "has been crucified by us for too long," and that
"not they, but we, each and every one of us" are responsible for
Christ's crucifixion, "because we are all murderers of love." On
the same occasion, Father Cantalamessa, addressing the Pope and
the entire Roman Curia, cited the Church Fathers of the second
century who "sowed the seeds" of anti-Judaism and "indirectly
favored the Shoah." Moreover, he said, "antisemitism is born not
of fidelity to the Scriptures, but of infidelity to them."

- In 1999, in an address hailed by Christian and Jewish observers
as remarkable in its bluntness and its candidness, Milwaukee
Archbishop Rembert Weakland said: "I acknowledge that we
Catholics, by preaching a doctrine that the Jewish people were
unfaithful, hypocritical and God-killers, reduced the human
dignity of our Jewish brothers and sisters, and created attitudes
that made reprisals against them seem like acts of conformity to
God's will. By doing so, I confess that we Catholics contributed
to the attitudes that made the Holocaust possible."

- In August 2000, the leaders of Poland's Roman Catholic Church
placed their stamp of approval on a letter of apology for failings
in its 2,000-year history, asking forgiveness "for those among us
who show disdain for people of other denominations or toler-
ate antisemitism....Antisemitism, just like anti-Christianism, is
a sin." The letter called for greater Christian solidarity with "the
people of Israel, to prevent such a tragedy [as the Holocaust]
from ever happening again, anywhere."

- In April 2001, more than 1,000 Christians from various countries
gathered in Jerusalem for an unprecedented three-day repentance conference, under the motto, "Changing the Future by

Confronting the Past," to confess before the Jewish people, and repent before God, two millennia of antisemitism in the name of Christianity. "Six million Jews perished," said Sister Pista of the Evangelical Sisterhood of Mary, headquartered in Germany, which sponsored the conference, "because of thousands of Bible-believing Christians like me who had been deceived and went along with the flow....We are not coming to ask for forgiveness.... We really wish to say we have greatly sinned – and to say it here, that you may understand that we wish to turn over a new leaf."

- On April 13, 2002, unidentified assailants attacked the Brodsky Central Synagogue in Kiev. Two days later, the attack was denounced in the strongest terms by Lubomyr Cardinal Husar, head of the Ukrainian Greek Catholic Church, in a message addressed to "the citizens of Ukraine." The message reads, in part:

> Even though the perpetrators of this heinous act have not been identified as yet..., we feel a strong need to denounce the desecration of a sacred place.... Our intensive activities...should be based on deep respect for the human being, on equality of rights for all, without dividing people into "us" and "them," and on justice..., because as Christians, we believe that all people are the children of God. Only on the basis of such principles can we find our true identity and the hope for a better future.

Anti-Jewish Concepts in Scripture

Confrontation and change are two themes receiving major attention in *Constantine's Sword: The Church and the Jews*, a book by James Carroll published early in 2001. *The Jerusalem Post* (March 9, 2001) calls it a "provocative and exhaustive study"; and Rabbi A. James Rudin, the senior interreligious adviser of the American Jewish Committee, describes the book as "extraordinary and painfully honest." In a

Jerusalem Post interview, Carroll was asked what the Church needs to do now. Here is his reply:

> ...we have to revisit the way we read and think of Scripture – in particular, how we preach the anti-Jewish concepts of Scripture. We have to ask ourselves if Jesus Christ is the only way to God and, if so, what about the Covenant of Israel? Is it still to be honored as sacred? The Church has not only to recover the respect of the Jewish people, but to develop a profound appreciation of its own Jewish roots and its own character as a religion of Israel. The Catholic Church is an institution that changes slowly... But we are now in the middle of a profound confrontation with history that is going to lead to very deep changes.

Cardinal Bernardin: "The Continuing Challenge"

The late Joseph Cardinal Bernardin of Chicago, USA, on March 23, 1995, addressed the Hebrew University of Jerusalem on the subject of "Antisemitism: The Historical Legacy and the Continuing Challenge for Christians." To this day, this document stands out as one of the most thoughtful and comprehensive treatments of this subject ever to be presented. For this reason, we believe it deserves separate and detailed consideration.

Extensive excerpts from Cardinal Bernardin's speech may be found in Appendix O. Here is a small selection:

> In recent years the Catholic Church has undertaken important efforts to acknowledge guilt for the legacy of antisemitism and to repudiate as *sinful* any remaining vestiges of that legacy in its contemporary teaching and practice....antisemitism has deep roots in Christian history, which go back to the earliest days of the Church.... Inclusion of this history, as painful as it is for us to hear today, is a necessary requirement for authentic reconciliation between Christians and Jews in our time....

> The Holy See's action in formally recognizing Israel through the [Holy See-Israel] Accords represents a final seal on the process begun at the Second Vatican Council to rid Catholicism of all vestiges of "displacement theology" and the implied notion of perpetual Jewish homelessness. The Accords represent the Catholic

Church's full and final acknowledgment of Jews as a *people*, not merely as individuals....

For many baptized Christians, traditional Christian beliefs about Jews and Judaism constituted the primary motivation for their support, active or tacit, of the Nazi movement....In the Church today, we must not minimize the extent of Christian collaboration with Hitler and his associates. It remains a profound moral challenge that we must continue to confront for our own integrity as a religious community....

The Orthodox Churches

In assessing the role of the Orthodox Churches* in the Christian campaign against antisemitism, we must keep in mind that their responsibility in this domain is of a different order from that of the Catholics and the Protestants. Ask a priest of the Greek Orthodox Church about the Nazi era, for example, and he is more than likely to deny any kind of culpability as far as his Church is concerned. In fact, he may go so far as to maintain that his co-religionists were themselves victims of the Nazi regime and its persecutions.

While, historically, there probably would be some truth in such an approach, this does not mean that the Orthodox Churches are free of the antisemitic taint. Nor does it mean that they should be exempt from the overall Christian obligation to fight antisemitism and its consequences. It may explain, however, why the Orthodox voice on this subject is somewhat muted. Every once in a while, we do hear an Orthodox leader speak out on the theme of Christian-Jewish relations, and on antisemitism in particular, and it would be only fitting and proper, in a discussion of this kind, to include such a pronouncement.

In October 1997, the Eastern Orthodox Ecumenical Patriarch Bartholomew visited the United States and, at the US Holocaust

---

* They are to be found principally in Greece, Russia, Ukraine, Georgia, Armenia, Romania, Bulgaria, Serbia, Yugoslavia and in several countries of the Middle East, including Cyprus, Lebanon and Israel. There are nearly three million Orthodox Christians living in the USA.

Memorial Museum, held a major address in which he vigorously denounced antisemitism and described the State of Israel as a "guarantor" of the Jewish people's survival. He acknowledged the "bitter truth" that during that "icon of evil," the Holocaust, "many Christians of that terrible time…did not connect the message of their faith to their actions in the world" – a somewhat roundabout way of stating this obvious truth. The point, nevertheless, is clear enough.

Rabbi A. James Rudin, at that time National Interreligious Affairs Director of the American Jewish Committee, in his weekly column for the Religion News Service, on June 11, 1998, wrote the following:

> In late May, two prominent leaders of the Old Calendarist Church of Greece, who live in the Astoria section of New York City – Metropolitan Paisios and Bishop Vikentios of the St. Irene Chrysovalantou Monastery – publicly acknowledged that, as recently as 1993 and 1994, their church's newspaper "perpetuated some antisemitic myths whose origins extend back into the medieval period."

> The Paisios declared: "I categorically reject all forms of antisemitism and categorically deny these lies. We genuinely seek forgiveness for having communicated such un-Christian sentiments."

> Added the Bishop: "We not only repent of these statements, but we understand the true nature of our relationship to Jews and people of other faiths." He also said the group had expressed views about Jews and Judaism "which we now know to be false."…

> Sadly, the ugly pathology of religious antisemitism still persists as we near the end of this troubled century. But it is encouraging that Orthodox Christian officials like Metropolitan Paisios and Bishop Vikentios are following the teachings of Bartholomew and Archbishop Spyridon, the Primate of the Greek Orthodox Church of America, in the essential task of eradicating the hatred of Jews and Judaism from all areas of Christian life. In this effort, they join many Roman Catholic and Protestant leaders as well.

> What is critically needed now is the speedy practical implementation of the positive statements that continue to emerge from Church authorities. Christian leaders agree this campaign must start with nursery school and extend through high school, col-

lege and seminary training. Sermons, hymns, Bible study, adult education including Church history, and especially liturgies need to reflect the incompatibility of authentic Christian belief with antisemitism.

A Losing Battle?

Considering, then, that this widespread effort to wipe out antisemitism has been moving forward for over half a century – and with particular intensity since the groundbreaking Nostra Aetate declaration of the Second Vatican Council in 1965 – it might have been expected that this destructive social phenomenon had by now been removed from the earth. However, that is not the case.

Not only has antisemitism not vanished; it is, unfortunately, alive and well. The number of antisemitic incidents (attacks on Jewish institutions, personal assaults, antisemitic epithets, acts of vandalism and the like) has fluctuated, over the years, but so far has not been reduced even to what one might call "a manageable minimum." On the contrary, statistics furnished by organizations monitoring such incidents show a palpable increase in the waning years of the 20th century. And the question is: Why is that?

The answer is probably to be found on a number of different levels:

First and foremost, there is the lapse of time. The revelations that gradually came to light after World War II, concerning the unspeakable horrors – and the magnitude – of the Nazi Shoah, produced a "shame (or guilt) factor," in Europe and beyond, that served to put a significant, if temporary, damper on antisemitism, or at least on public displays of antisemitism. In many people, to be sure, it generated a process of soul-searching that ultimately led, among other things, to the changes in Church doctrine that are discussed in this book. Others never really abandoned their anti-Jewish feelings and prejudices, but merely relegated these to the subliminal domain.

With the passage of time, however, the shame factor began to fade, as memory faded, and thoughts and feelings that had been pushed into the subconscious began to re-emerge. Moreover, a generation has grown to adulthood that had not yet been born when these events occurred, and whose knowledge of them must rely on information that is often scanty, biased or not forthcoming at all. It is a generation that provides an easy target for the neo-Nazi propagandists and the Holocaust deniers.

It has been suggested, too, that the recent increase in antisemitic incidents in Europe, more than anywhere else, and the repeated and persistent displays of hostility, by some European statesmen and governments, towards Israel reflect a kind of delayed-action subconscious attempt to transfer their Shoah-related guilt feelings to the Jews themselves – and to the national manifestation of Jewish peoplehood: the State of Israel.

The growth of the Internet and a burgeoning hi-tech industry in recent decades have also contributed to the revival of antisemitism, through the proliferation of websites peddling racist, neo-Nazi and totalitarian doctrines. Meanwhile, the emergence of a new social and political order in central and eastern Europe, as a result of the collapse of the Soviet Empire, has seen the release of nationalist, ethnic and ultra-rightist elements previously held in check by a Soviet regime that, for reasons of its own, wished to keep a lid on antisemitic outbreaks (though not on antisemitic sentiments).

As for the Churches' message on the need to combat antisemitism, this has indeed been articulated firmly and boldly – but largely at the highest levels of ecclesiastic authority. Unless and until that message is effectively disseminated among the rank-and-file membership of these Churches, the so-called grassroots, it will remain a dead letter and not much more than that. Clearly, the antisemitic virus has been raging in the collective body of the human race for too long a time to be quickly or easily eradicated.

Is it, then, a losing battle that the Christian Churches have undertaken against the antisemitic scourge? The answer to that question is that what the Churches are waging here is not merely a battle, but a war. The forces arrayed against antisemitism may, at this stage, and for the reasons cited above, be at the losing end of this initial battle. But the war against baseless hatred goes on. It must go on. And, if it is conducted vigorously and wisely, and with the cooperation of both the Christian and the Jewish communities, this war will end in the triumph of the forces of human dignity and respect over the evils of prejudice and blind hate.

The element, mentioned here, of Christian-Jewish cooperation in this struggle is a very important one. It found eloquent expression in a *Jerusalem Post* editorial published on November 3, 1997, on the occasion of a symposium held at the Vatican on the roots of anti-semitism. The editorial ended with the following words:

> Israel clearly cannot be the driving force behind a process of repentance that must come mainly from within. But it would be a tremendous shame if, through sheer lethargy and negligence, Israel were to show indifference to the positive steps that have been taken and squander the opportunity to help the Church confront elements of its past in preparation for its new millennium.

You must, they say, fight fire with fire. A major factor in the current spread of antisemitic poison has been the Internet. Surely, that vehicle can be used with equal efficacy to propagate the truth! To cite just one example, the website known as Virtual Holy Land (VHL) has been running a powerful, thought-provoking series on the way Christians have treated Jews down the ages. Says VHL about its series: "Until we confront and come to terms with the history of Jewish-Christian relations, we can never make meaningful moves toward building positive relationships based on unconditional love and trust in the future."

Unconditional love! Is that not the obvious answer to the evils of baseless hatred? The Second Jewish Commonwealth, as we mentioned on the opening page of this chapter, is said to have been destroyed by baseless hatred; the Third will come into its own, in the words of the late Chief Rabbi Abraham Isaac Hacohen Kook, when there is unconditional love (*Orot Hakodesh* III, 324):

> If we were destroyed, and the world together with us, by baseless hatred, we will be restored, and the world will be restored with us, by unconditional love.

Chapter 8

Mission / Witness / Dialogue

*Preaching the Gospel is not a reason for me to boast – it is a
necessity laid on me: Woe to me if I do not preach the Gospel!*
(1 Corinthians 9:16)

The term mission, *in its proper sense, refers to conversion
from false gods and idols to the true and one God, who
revealed Himself in the salvation history with His elected
people. Thus* mission, *in this strict sense, cannot be used
with regard to Jews, who believe in the true and one God.*
(Walter Cardinal Kasper, New York City, May 2001)

*Some of us believe that we have to bear witness also to
the Jews; some of us are convinced, however, that Jews
are faithful and obedient to God even though they do not
accept Jesus Christ as Lord and Savior. Many maintain
that, as a separate and specific people, the Jews are an
instrument of God with a specific God-given task – and, as
such, a sign of God's faithfulness to all humankind...*
(From paper adopted by the Jerusalem Conference of
World Council of Churches Consultation on the Church
and the Jewish People, June 20–23, 1977)

MORE THAN ANY OTHER ASPECT of the Christian-Jewish relationship, the subject of evangelization (proselytization? mission? witness? What indeed should we call it?) exercises the minds and souls

of the protagonists on both sides of the divide. The three quotations that open this chapter epitomize the tension that characterizes the Christian mindset when it comes to witnessing to the Jews. The reader will note three distinct approaches to the subject: from the evangelizing imperative expressed so powerfully, yet so simply, in the New Testament – to an entirely new interpretation of this imperative, as enunciated by a leading Vatican figure nearly two thousand years later – and, in between, the cautious and somewhat hesitant stance so typical of today's "mainline" Protestant Churches (here represented by the Protestants' umbrella organization, the World Council of Churches), still groping for that golden path.

For Christians, the call to proclaim the Gospel to an unbelieving world is a religious obligation of the highest order. Indeed, it is the very heart and essence of the Christian faith. As stated in a 1982 document of the World Council of Churches, "Christians are called to witness to their faith in word and deed. The Church has a mission and it cannot be otherwise. This mission is not one of choice." There is no need to drive this point home to the Christian reader; he or she will be acutely aware of it. It is the Jewish reader who needs to internalize this basic fact before we go any further in the discussion of mission and evangelism. In all fairness, this is something we can ask of the Jewish partner in the relationship, seeing that the Jewish partner would like his Christian counterpart to do some internalizing of his own, after listening to the Jewish side of this story. And, needless to say, there is a Jewish side to this story. But, before we present it, we would do well to try to sort out the confusion, in the minds of many, concerning the terminology one encounters on this subject – a confusion briefly and parenthetically alluded to above.

Witness and Proselytism
Christian writers and theologians distinguish, basically, between "mission" and "witness," on the one hand, and "proselytism," on the other.

The Catholic theologian Prof. Tommaso Federici, a consultant member of the Commission for Religious Relations with the Jews,

discussed this distinction at some length in a study paper he prepared for the sixth meeting of the Liaison Committee between the
Roman Catholic Church and the International Committee for Interreligious Consultations (IJCIC), held in Venice in March 1977. Here
is how he defined "witness":

> By this [witness] is understood the permanent action in which
> a Christian or the Christian community proclaims the action of
> God in history, and tries to show how with Christ has come the
> "true light that enlightens every man" (Jn 1:9).

As for the term "proselytism," Professor Federici acknowledges that
"in certain linguistic, cultural or denominational contexts" this term
has assumed "a pejorative sense." In other contexts, however, he writes,
the word "has kept its original meaning of zeal for the propagation
of the faith…" When used in the unacceptable sense, therefore, it
should be qualified "with expressions such as 'unwarranted proselytism'…that indicate clearly reprehensible attitudes and ways of
acting that are to be rejected." The writer then proceeds to define
"unwarranted proselytism:"

> Here by "unwarranted proselytism" we understand an attitude
> and action that stands outside Christian witness. It includes, in
> fact, anything that forces and violates the right of every person
> or human community to be free from external and internal con-
> strictions in matters of religion… Therefore, the Church clearly
> rejects every form of unwarranted proselytism. Excluded, then, is
> every kind of testimony and preaching that in any way becomes a
> physical, moral, psychological or cultural constraint on the Jews,
> as individuals or as a community…

> We are reminded also of the rejection of any action that aims
> at changing the religious faith of the Jews, whether in groups,
> minorities or individual persons, by making more or less open
> offers of protection, legal, material, cultural, political and other
> advantages, using educational or social assistance pretexts…. Still
> more is excluded every kind of threat and coercion, even when
> it is indirect or concealed.

The World Council of Churches has taken a similar stand. The following discussion of proselytism is taken from a conference paper on Christian-Jewish relations adopted by the Jerusalem Conference of the World Council of Churches Consultation on the Church and the Jewish People that met June 20–23, 1977:

> Proselytism, as distinct from Mission or Witness, is rejected in the strongest terms by the WCC: "Proselytism embraces whatever violates the right of the human person, Christian or non-Christian, to be free from external coercion in religious matters..." (*Ecumenical Review*, 1/1971, p. 11)
>
> This rejection of proselytism and our advocacy of respect for the integrity and the identity of all peoples and faith communities is the more urgent where Jews are concerned. For our relationship to the Jews is of a unique and very close character. Moreover, the history of "Christian" anti-Semitism and forced baptisms of Jews in the past makes it understandable that Jews are rightly sensitive towards all religious pressures from outside and all attempts at proselytizing.
>
> We reject proselytism both in its gross and in its more refined forms. This implies that all triumphalism and every kind of manipulation are to be abrogated. We are called upon to minimize the power dimension in our encounter with the Jews, and to speak at every level from equal to equal. We have to be conscious of the pain and the perception of the others and have to respect their right to define themselves.
>
> We are called upon to witness to God's love for and claim upon the whole of humankind. Our witness to Christ as Lord and Savior, however, is challenged in a special way where Jews are concerned. It has become discredited as a result of bad behavior on the part of Christians. We therefore are seeking authentic and proper forms of Christian witness in our relations with the Jews....

The paper goes on to discuss what constitutes such "authentic and proper forms of Christian witness" to the Jews. (The various options are cited in the third quotation appearing at the start of this chapter.)

Clearly, then, Christians for their part generally distinguish between "mission," "witness," "evangelism," on the one hand, and "proselytism" or "unwarranted proselytism," on the other. The former set of terms denotes, from their point of view, a positive – indeed essential – aspect of Christianity. The latter is widely recognized today as theologically wrong and thence to be shunned. The American fundamentalist writer, lecturer and Bible prophecy expert, Dr. Hal Lindsay (*The Late Great Planet Earth; The Late Great 20th Century: Prelude to Catastrophe*), has advanced the view that evangelization should be regarded as a perfectly acceptable Christian practice – so long as it is carried out in an open and aboveboard fashion.

A number of Christian theologians and groups, moreover, have made the point that a further distinction needs to be drawn between mission "to the nations" (*ad gentes*) and the approach to Jews. Both for historical and for theological reasons, it is felt that there is a "special relationship" between Christians and Jews, which "calls for dialogue and shared witness, rather than unwarranted proselytism" (footnote to Statement on Jewish-Christian Relations approved unanimously by the Texas Conference of Churches in 1982).

This point was underscored in a 1995 document entitled "Renunciation of Mission to the Jews," issued by the Society for Jewish-Christian Cooperation in Hamburg, Germany:

> Jews experience [Christian] mission to Jews as a brusque threat to their existence. That is only too understandable after the experiences of the past centuries, and especially the Shoah. Only if the Churches clearly refuse to missionize Jews, is their fight against anti-Judaism within the Church and against every form of antisemitism in society really plausible.

The statement maintains, furthermore, that mission to the Jews is devoid even of *theological* foundation:

> It is not only that mission to Jews has become historically obsolete; it is also in conflict with Biblical findings. The mission command (Mt 28:19 f.) says that the disciples are sent out to bring the teaching of Jesus, his interpretation of the Torah, to the gentile nations

of the world – that is, not to the Jews, who already have and guard the Torah. Out of theological, historical as well as political reasons arises the demand for the Church's decision against mission to the Jews that leaves no one in doubt: Mission to the Jews – that is, the methodic, organized and intentional effort of Christians to dissuade Jews from the Jewish religion – shall not be!

The Jewish View

We shall have more to say on the subject of dialogue towards the end of this chapter. But, first, let us turn the page, as it were, to the Jewish view of these things – a view, let it be noted at once, that some Christian groups and Churches have learned to recognize and respect, leading to such pronouncements, for example, as the footnote quoted on page 128 and the 1977 WCC paper cited on page 127 ("...Jews are rightly sensitive towards all religious pressures from outside...").

The history of Christian persecution of the Jewish people, through the ages, is primarily a history of enforced conversions to Christianity – or of often unsuccessful attempts at such conversions. "Be baptized or die!" was the Church's only too frequent battle-cry. At other times, it was "Be baptized or get out of the country!" Thus, mass-slaughter and mass-expulsion alternated, in the countries of medieval Europe, as their Christian rulers went about the business of "promoting Christianity." (That this work of mission was to be carried out among the heathen, and not among God-fearing people like the Jews, somehow escaped most of the Christian powers-that-be in those days.)

It should not be too difficult, therefore, to understand why and how, in many Jewish eyes to this day, the words *Christianity, mission, conversion* and *persecution* have become, in a manner of speaking, synonymous. In the Jewish mind, over the centuries, the boundaries between these concepts have been blurred to the point where they have nearly disappeared. As in the game of "Association," the mention of any one of these words was likely to elicit, in a kind of knee-jerk response, any one of the others on the list.

Nor should it come as a surprise that, among Jewish communities today, in Israel and elsewhere, the threshold of tolerance for Christian missionary activity in their midst is extremely low. Thus, when in June 1996 the US Southern Baptist Convention (SBC), the largest of America's Protestant denominations, adopted a resolution calling on its members to "direct our energies and resources toward the proclamation of the Gospel to the Jews," there were sharp negative reactions on the Jewish side. The World Jewish Congress issued a statement saying that the SBC resolution "represents an unacceptable religious triumphalism, weakening the underpinning of harmonious coexistence among different faiths. As such, it directly threatens the rapprochement between Jews and Christians."

The Israel Colloquium, an interfaith group operating out of Jerusalem and Washington, DC, took particular exception to the notion, expressed in the Baptists' resolution, that "repentance and remission of sins should be preached in his [Jesus's] name among all nations, *beginning at Jerusalem*" (emphasis ours). In a statement by the founder of the Colloquium, Dr. Kitty O. Cohen, we read:

> It would seem that, almost 2,000 years after the founding of Christianity by the Apostles, after a thousand years of Christian domination of the Western world, and barely fifty years after the Holocaust, it is hardly an appropriate time to evangelize among the Jews in their land.

Considering the size and prominence of this Protestant Church, its evangelizing fervor, in the face of Jewish repugnance and opposition, cannot be dismissed out of hand. However, it must be noted that most major Christian Churches today have taken a quite different position on the subject – a position more in line with the new thinking of the Church in relation to its history and to developments in the 20th century in the domain of Christian-Jewish relations.

"Converging Verticality"

Father Marcel Dubois, a Dominican priest long resident in Jerusalem, and Professor Emeritus of Philosophy at the Hebrew University, has expounded a rather intriguing thesis concerning the true meaning of the word "witness." He calls his concept "converging verticality" –

seemingly an oxymoron, yet not really that, when one stops to think about it – philosophically.

Men and women everywhere – Father Dubois explains – regardless of background and religious affiliation, instinctively desire to attain a more perfect knowledge of God. They do so, however, from different starting points, different faith systems. Since we all strive for the sublime goal, our hope and prayer is to meet one day in that perfect recognition, that perfect knowledge, which is the ultimate objective of our quest. Meanwhile, our best course is not to seek to impose on others the image of our own particular faith community. Instead, Father Dubois urges, let us live exemplary lives, as individuals and as a community, so that others may approve and emulate us.

Not to seek to impose on others the image of our own particular faith community – but to live exemplary lives: There you have a subtle, elegant, persuasive rejection of the notion of proselytization – and, at the same time, a definition of "witness" that comes very close to meriting the adjective "sublime." Note, too, how closely Father Dubois' thesis is echoed – this time together with an explicit rejection of proselytism – in a paper on "Mission and Witness of the Church," presented by Prof. Tommaso Federici at a conference on "Fifteen Years of Catholic-Jewish Dialogue, 1970–1985," held at the Lateran University in Rome in 1988:

> The best documented missionary experience in the New Testament is that of Paul....[A] renewed examination of Paul's text allows the conclusion that the Church's mission to Israel consists rather in living a Christian life in total fidelity to the One God and His revealed Word. This should lead to a competitiveness having saving value between Jews and Christians in relation to God (cf., e.g., Rom. 11:1–14)....It may be stated further that the Church recognizes that, in God's revealed plan, Israel plays a prominent fundamental role of her own: the "sanctification of the Name" [*kiddush Hashem*] in the world....
>
> It should be just as carefully realized and remembered today, and continually brought to the mind of all Christians, that precisely believing Jews, as such, who "sanctify the Name of God" in the world by a life of justice and holiness in which God's gifts bear

fruit, are a real witness before the whole world to the Jewish people's destiny....

The Church thus rejects in a clear way every form of undue prose-lytism. This means the exclusion of any sort of witness and preaching which in any way constitutes a physical, moral, psychological or cultural constraint on the Jews... Also excluded is every sort of judgment expressive of discrimination, contempt or restriction against the Jewish people as such and against individual Jews as such or against their faith, their worship, their general – and, in particular, their religious – culture, their past and present history, their existence and its meaning....

Consequently, attempts to set up organizations of any sort...for the "conversion" of Jews must be rejected.

The Swedish theologian Krister Stendahl, Professor Emeritus at Harvard Divinity School, once expressed a similar notion and called it "holy envy":

The real trick [in attaining religious understanding] is what I call Holy Envy. There is something in the other that is beautiful, that even tells you something about God. But it ain't yours – it's different.... We are different, and we should celebrate that diversity. (*Sojourners*, Sept.–Oct. 2001)

Writing in *Method in Theology*, the Catholic theologian Bernard Lonergan put it this way: "Just as it is one's own self-transcendance that enables one to know others accurately and to judge them fairly, so – inversely – it is through knowledge and appreciation of others that we come to know ourselves and to fill out and refine our appreciation of values."

And it is all, you might say, variations on a theme – the theme being Father Marcel Dubois' "converging verticality."

The Hyperbola Curve

As another variation on that theme, we might consider the hyperbola curve in mathematics. The two ends of that curve, placed in the area between the horizontal (x) axis and the vertical (y) axis, crossing each other at right angles, will approach each of these axes *ad infinitum* – drawing constantly nearer to it, without ever quite reaching it.

What we have here is a graphic illustration of the aforementioned human striving for God – and its built-in limitation. It is this combination of humankind's insatiable aspiration for perfect knowledge, truth, peace and an understanding of the Divine essence – and the realization that we humans, in the nature of things, are incapable of ever actually attaining that perfection – that is the very essence of the human condition. Living that kind of life, performing life's tasks and responding to its challenges in that spirit, will produce in us that "right" combination of ambition and humility that will enable us to function as God would, as it were, expect His creatures to function in this world.

The difference, of course, between the hyperbola curve and Father Dubois' model is that, in the latter, everything merges in the end; whereas our aspiring curve keeps aspiring... but never quite gets there.

Religious Self-Determination

Moving on now to the Protestant Churches, we find, as mentioned at the start of this chapter, a somewhat more hesitant attitude to the question of evangelism where Jews are concerned. The Protestant Churches' umbrella organization, the World Council of Churches (wcc), alluded to the subject in 1977, in the text adopted by the British Working Group for wcc Consultation on the Church and the Jewish People (ccjp). It begins by noting, in some detail, "the vibrant and continuing development of Judaism in post-biblical times" and "the emergence of the State of Israel which, by restoring the *Land* to its relationship with *People* and *Religion*, has made it possible for Judaism to regain its wholeness." It then goes on to suggest "the necessity for a review, on the part of the Church, of its traditional attitude of proselytism." Christians, it says, "have been facing the challenge and demands of religious pluralism by a new way of relating to other faiths, epitomized by dialogue" (about which more later). "Meeting in dialogue...demands respect at a deeper level and acceptance of the integrity of the faith of the other. We allow others to define their religious identity in terms of their own self-understanding, and expect that our own Christian commitment and identity are similarly respected."

This recognition of the right of others "to define their religious identity in terms of their own self-understanding" – a kind of religious self-determination – has become one of the pillars of interfaith dialogue and, as such, will be encountered frequently in the dialogue literature – Catholic, Protestant as well as Jewish. It is, of course, basically anti-evangelistic, implicitly if not explicitly.

The Sigtuna Statement

If explicit renunciation is what we are looking for, we find that too – in a document produced eleven years later by the same WCC, whose Consultation on Church and the Jewish People, meeting in Sigtuna, Sweden, in 1988, adopted a statement that included the following two propositions:

- that proselytism is incompatible with Christian faith, and that claims of faith, when used as weapons against anyone, are against the spirit of Christ;

- that Jews and Christians...have a common responsibility as witnesses in the world to God's righteousness and peace, and that, as God's partners, they must work in mutual respect and cooperation for justice, reconciliation and the integrity of creation.

Enter: The State of Israel

Where and how does the State of Israel come into the picture here? What is its attitude to the issue of Christian missionary activity? The answer to these questions may be found at three levels: (a) the legislature; (b) the courts; and (c) the general public.

Israel does not have a written constitution. However, its respect for and guarantee of basic human rights, including the freedom of religion, are anchored in its Declaration of Independence (1948), as well as in the International Covenant on Civil and Political Rights, to which Israel acceded in 1991. Moreover, the laws of the Knesset protect the adherents of all religions in Israel and their institutions and houses of worship, as well as their religious practices and observances, from violations of any kind.

The Knesset, Israel's parliament, has been sparing in its legislation on the subject. There is no law against engaging in missionary activity as such. Whenever legislative proposals with this objective have been advanced, they have been defeated. There are, however, two laws on the books regarding missionary activity. The first outlaws the use of material enticements to cause a person to change his or her religion; it states:

PENAL LAW AMENDMENT
Enticement to Change Religion Law, 5738 / 1977

1. Whosoever gives or promises to a person money, money's worth or some other material benefit in order to induce him to change his religion, or in order that he may induce another person to change his religion, is liable to imprisonment for a term of five years or a fine of 50,000 pounds.

2. Whosoever receives or agrees to receive money, money's worth or some other material benefit in return for a promise to change his religion, or to cause another person to change his religion, is liable to imprisonment for a term of three years or a fine of 30,000 pounds.

3. As from the time of this Law coming into force, Paragraphs 1 and 2 shall form Paragraphs 174(a) and 174(b) of the Law.

The second law prohibits the conversion of a minor under the age of 14, or inducement to such conversion, without the knowledge of the parents or guardian.

The courts of the land, for their part, have on a number of occasions issued rulings on the subject. In 1967, for example, in the case of Rufeisen (Brother Daniel) vs. The Minister of the Interior (103/67, p. 333), the Supreme Court held that –

> ...indeed there is no doubt that, just as any person in Israel has the right to change his/her religion, so any person in Israel has the right, regardless of what his/her religion may be, to preach that religion and to disseminate it through all the legal means that may be chosen for this purpose....

The principle underscored in this judgment was reiterated in another case (2266/93, p. 257) that came before the Court in 1993:

> Undoubtedly an important aspect of freedom of religion is the freedom of conversion to another religion. Is this freedom, however, to be granted, in its full scope, to a child? The answer is No.

A ruling handed down by the Supreme Court in 1972 (312/72, p. 764), in a case involving a local council's opposition to a plot of land in the center of town being sold to a German woman, it being feared that she intended to make use of this purchase to engage in missionary activity. We shall quote here from the opinions of two of the justices.

Justice Etzioni:

> Is there, anywhere in our body of laws, a legal prohibition against the acquisition of land by a German subject or by the subjects of other countries? Is there a legal prohibition against missionary activity in our country? Let us not forget that we are part of the family of nations, and that the relations between nations are based on reciprocity.

Justice Berenson:

> ...and with the renewal of our independence in the State of Israel, we must be extremely careful to refrain from even a hint of discrimination or double standards towards any lawful gentile person residing in our midst and who wishes to live with us in his/her own way, in accordance with his/her religion and faith.

The point that Israel does not have a "state religion" was made in a judgment issued in 1977 (563/77, p. 97):

> In the State of Israel – unlike most of its neighbors – there is no religion that is defined in its laws as the religion of the State. Everyone is entitled to live here and to practice his/her faith and to serve God in his/her own way. The judicial authorities in Israel see to it that no one is persecuted for his/her religious faith – or lack of such...

The principle of religious liberty is discussed likewise in a judgment handed down in 1971 (175/71, p. 821), in the case of the Abu Ghosh Music Festival vs. The Minister of Education, but the Court goes out of its way here to add a note of caution on the subject of evangelization:

> The basis for the prohibition against religious discrimination is to be found in two principles: religious tolerance and religious equality... The principle of tolerance demands that citizens and society as a whole not only tolerate the existence of a given religion, though they do not believe in its tenets, but that they relate to it with courtesy and respect, that they not harm it or treat it with contempt, and that they not hurt the feelings of its adherents....

> Furthermore, of a religious community that wishes to win others over to its faith, it may be expected that it do this with a certain degree of self-restraint... It goes without saying that, in the conduct of missionary activities, it is incumbent upon those engaging in such activities to be careful not to hurt the feelings or the dignity of the members of other faiths...

In introducing the latter proviso, the Court here reflected the strongly held feeling, among the Israeli public-at-large (see also page 146), that there is no room for overt or aggressive evangelizing among Jews wherever they may be – and especially not in the Jewish homeland, Israel. (See Dr. Kitty Cohen's comment in this regard, on p. 130.)

Latter-day Saints

By and large, the Churches – and individual Christians in Israel – have respected these legislative and judicial guidelines, and the two laws cited above have rarely had to be invoked. An interesting case, in this context, is that of the Church of Jesus Christ of Latter-day Saints (also known as the Mormon Church), which in the early 1980s erected the Brigham Young University, architecturally one of the finest buildings in Jerusalem, on the western slopes of Mount Scopus.

When the public at large became aware of the Mormons' plans to build their university on this choice spot in the Holy City, there was considerable alarm – particularly in Jewish religious circles, though not only there. The Mormon community is known for its evangelizing zeal, and the fear was expressed that its institution in Jerusalem would soon become a hotbed of missionary activity. Attempts, however, to have the project halted at this point, through government intervention, were of no avail. It transpired that all of the requisite permits for the project had been duly obtained. Even the customary legal notice in the newspapers had been published – but apparently no one had "noticed" until it was too late.

The story, in any event, has a happy ending. The government, essentially left with no choice in the matter, gave its blessings to the project, on one condition: that the Mormons solemnly pledge not to use the building to engage in missionary activity. The undertaking was given, and the university was built.

Since, in point of fact, the Mormons have honored their commitment, it may be said that everybody is happy: The Mormons got their university; the fears and forebodings of many Israelis were laid to rest; and visitors of all faiths and persuasions can admire this handsome edifice and enjoy the concerts regularly performed there.

Essence and Impact of Dialogue

One of the most important and effective tools in the ongoing promotion of greater understanding and respect between the Christian and Jewish communities has been the dialogue between the two. Without it, it is doubtful that the bold initial steps taken by the Church in the 1960s, in generating the re-thinking of Church doctrines and dogmas concerning Judaism and the Jewish people, could have been sustained and, indeed, advanced to the point where we are now.

How is the Christian-Jewish dialogue viewed by those engaged in it?

First of all, it needs to be stated that there is a palpable imbalance or lopsidedness here: Christians have shown a far greater readiness to engage in such dialogue than have Jews. The reason should not be difficult to fathom, considering what we know about the traumatic nature of the relationship, over the centuries, and the deep-seated feelings of resentment and suspicion that this has created among Jews. Many Jewish religious leaders, particularly in the Orthodox (i.e., strictly observant) camp – precisely those whom Christian theologians would like to see joining these meetings – tend to view dialogue simply as yet another vehicle for the conversion of Jews to Christianity; and so they will have nothing to do with it. But there have been some exceptions.

The late Rabbi Joseph B. Soloveitchick, a widely respected scholar, teacher and writer, lent his approval to Jewish-Christian dialogue and cooperation *in the field of social and humanitarian issues* – though he made it very plain that under no circumstances was this to be allowed to "spill over" into the religious or theological domain. Here is what Rabbi Soloveitchick wrote on this subject in a 1964 article (*Studies in Judaica*, edited by Leon D. Stitskin, Ktav Publishing House / Yeshiva University Press, 1974):

> ...it is important that the religious or theological *logos* should not be employed as the medium of communication between two faith communities whose modes of expression are as unique as their apocalyptic experiences. The confrontation should occur not at a theological but at a mundane human level. There, all of us speak the universal language of modern man. As a matter of fact, our common interests lie not in the realm of faith, but in that of the secular orders. There, we all face a powerful antagonist; we all have to contend with a considerable number of matters of great concern. The relationship between two communities must be

outer-directed and related to the secular orders with which men of faith come face to face. In the secular sphere, we may discuss positions to be taken, ideas to be evolved and plans to be formulated. In these matters, religious communities may together recommend action to be developed and may seize the initiative to be implemented later by general society.

Rabbi Soloveitchick's "liberalism" here should be appreciated all the more in view of the fact that his comments were made in the early 1960s – at a time when the positive change in Church attitudes towards Judaism had not yet taken hold (Nostra Aetate, which signaled the big breakthrough, was not to be published until 1965).

Be that as it may, the Orthodox Rabbinate, on the whole, has tended to stay away from these interfaith discussions. The actual conduct of the dialogue, therefore, on the Jewish side, has been left to the lay leadership and some religious leaders belonging mostly to the Reform, Reconstructionist and Conservative denominations. Among the institutions involved, mention must be made, first of all, of the International Jewish Committee for Interreligious Consultations (IJCIC), which was established for this specific purpose and, for most of its existence, was headed by the late Dr. Geoffrey Wigoder; its present Chairman is Mr. Seymour Reich. Composed of representatives of 11 major Jewish organizations, IJCIC has devoted most of its time and energy to meetings and discussions with the Pontifical Commission for Relations with the Jews and other relevant bodies in the Catholic Church – which, from the start, has led the way in the Christian-Jewish dialogue. The fact, moreover, that the Roman Catholic Church is probably the most highly structured and disciplined of all the Christian Churches has facilitated the carrying on of a fairly systematic and orderly dialogue involving that Church and its institutions.

Once launched at the Catholic-Jewish level, the dialogue branched out to the World Council of Churches and to some of its Protestant constituent Churches as well. Much later, and to a more limited extent, contacts were initiated also with the Eastern Orthodox Churches. The Jewish side has been represented, in addition to IJCIC, by some of IJCIC's constituent organizations, acting independently, such as the World Jewish Congress, the American Jewish Congress, the American Jewish Committee and the B'nai B'rith Anti-Defamation League. Also involved are such interfaith-oriented associations as the International Council of Christians and Jews, the American Christian Trust, the Ecumenical Theological Research Fraternity in Israel, the Interreligious Coordinating Council in Israel, the Israel Interfaith Association, the Service International de Documentation Judéo-Chrétienne (SIDIC), headquartered in Rome, Christians and Jews for the Teaching of Esteem (CJE) in Brussels, and many others. A recent development has been the official recognition by the Vatican, in early 2002, of the new Pontifical Institute for the Study of Religions and Cultures at the Gregorian University in Rome. The Institute includes the Cardinal Bea Center for Judaic Studies that offers a degree program in Judaic Studies.

Let us return now to the question we posed earlier: How is the dialogue viewed by its two partners?

Jewish Assessments

The fact is, it needs to be stated at the outset, that there is no authoritative personality or organization that could speak on this subject on behalf of collective Jewry. Nevertheless, there have been pronouncements by a number of leading Jewish figures that will give us a fairly good idea where the Jewish community stands.

As already noted, many rabbis and lay leaders, particularly in the Orthodox (strictly observant) sector of the community, shy away from interfaith contacts of any kind, whether for practical reasons (lack of opportunity or interest) or for ideological/religious ones. There have been some prominent exceptions; but, on the whole, the conduct of the dialogue, on the Jewish side, has been left to the non-Orthodox elements in the community.

If the Orthodox Jewish voices in this domain have been few in number, however, it may be said that they "make up in quality for what they lack in quantity." Israel Chief Rabbi Israel Meir Lau, echoing the position taken by Rabbi Soloveitchick thirty years earlier (see

p. 139), speaks of the necessity of "finding a common language" with our Christian brothers and sisters, in order to be able, together, to do battle against "the common enemies threatening mankind and the whole world...hunger, privation, cancer, AIDS, the atom and hydrogen bombs, ignorance and the rejection of religious faith...." Speaking at the San Egidio Conference in Milan, Italy, in September 1993, Rabbi Lau said:

> ...a call must issue from the depths of our hearts, all of us here assembled, to all who dwell on this earth: All mankind are the children of one Father, all of us are made by the Creator. As our ancient Jewish teaching reminds us, God Himself rebuked His angels who sang in glee when the waters of the Red Sea engulfed Pharaoh's troops who were pursuing the Children of Israel in their flight from Egypt. God scolded the erring angels: "My creatures are drowning in the sea, and you celebrate?!"...

> If we have not, so far, been blessed with the peace of Isaiah's vision, we must adopt the conclusion emerging from the account of Noah and the deluge – namely, that it is incumbent upon us to find a common language and a life together in brotherhood, embracing all the peoples of the world, in view of the dangers facing us all and the shadow of two world wars that brought upon us untold horrors and devastation.... Let us unite in mobilizing mankind's resources for a common war against...hunger and drugs and disease and all the other afflictions that put the world in jeopardy.

> The Ten Commandments...open with the words, "I am the Lord your God" – to emphasize man's obligations to his Creator. They conclude with the words,"...and anything that is your neighbor's" – to emphasize man's obligations to his fellow-man.

Rabbi David Rosen, formerly Chief Rabbi of Ireland and now Director of the American Jewish Committee's Interfaith Department and President of the International Council of Christians and Jews, cites the words of a 17th century rabbi as his own signpost to Jewish-Christian dialogue. Writing in the Tenth Anniversary Zeitschrift of the Caspari Center for Biblical Studies in Jerusalem in 1993, Rabbi

Rosen reminds his readers of "the tragic history of Jewish suffering in the Christian world and the use of religious rationales to justify such," which meant that "in the main, there was little inclination, let alone opportunity, for positive Jewish-Christian engagement." And yet, he adds, "there were exceptions, and many Jewish religious authorities referred to those positive values that Christianity brought to the world at large." Rabbi Rosen continues:

> Amongst Rabbinic authorities in Christian lands, there were a number who, despite their overwhelmingly negative experience of Christianity, recognized a particular, special relationship with Christianity, born out of history and faith.

> Rabbi Moses Rivkes, author of a major commentary on the *Shulhan Aruch*, the code of Jewish law, was one of them. He writes of the obligation of Jews to show moral responsibility towards Christians who "believe in the Creator, the Exodus and the Revelation at Sinai, and whose whole intent is to serve their Maker." Herein is the root of our special relationship, which is affirmed by Christianity's view of itself, in Paul's metaphor, as being grafted onto the original olive tree.

Rabbi Rosen concludes that "if we acknowledge that Christianity shares with us values rooted in a history and revelation, then, despite our fundamental differences, we have an obligation to work together as far as all that binds us together is concerned."

Rabbi Rosen's predecessor in the post of interfaith director at the American Jewish Committee was Rabbi A. James Rudin, of the Reform movement. In an article entitled "Into the Twenty-First Century: A Jewish View of the Dialogue," published in the December 1992 issue of the Fordham University Quarterly, *Thought*, Rabbi Rudin, addressing himself to the challenges facing the Jewish-Catholic dialogue, had some practical suggestions for making that dialogue more effective:

> Hopefully in the new century, Catholics and Jews will intensify their studies of each other's religious beliefs. I dream that rabbinical students of the future will receive part of their training at

Catholic seminaries. And likewise, candidates for the priesthood, and those who aspire to be sisters and brothers in the Church, will study also at rabbinical schools. I am convinced that such studies will deepen the religious commitments of our future leaders. And Catholics and Jews will need that commitment to face together the threats and challenges that await us all.

As has been noted, the Orthodox branch of Judaism has not, on the whole, been very receptive – to put it mildly – to the idea of Jewish-Christian dialogue. And yet there have been voices in that camp that have spoken out, with varying degrees of fervor, in support of that notion. To the rabbinical figures already cited in this context, we want to add two other voices: that of Marcie Lenk Yarden, a teacher of Bible and Talmud at the Pardes Institute, the Ecce Homo Convent, the Swedish Theological Institute and other Jewish and Christian seminaries in Jerusalem – and that of Israel's Minister for Religious Affairs in the 1999–2001 Ehud Barak government, Rabbi Yitzhak Cohen.

Writing in a 1999 compendium of articles on "Pilgrimage in a New Millennium," published by the Interreligious Coordinating Council in Israel and the Israel Ministry of Tourism, Ms. Yarden made the following observations on the subject under discussion:

> I believe that only through dialogue and an open exchange of ideas between Jews and Christians can we grow to truly understand, forgive and respect one another. Many groups around the world have already come together to engage in such dialogue. Most Jews and Christians, however, are still wary. Some feel threatened, others don't believe that there is any need to respect the other. I look forward to a time in the future when the traditions that we share, as well as those that we do not, will bring us closer together in peace and a recognition that all human beings were created in the image of God.

The approach of Rabbi Yitzhak Cohen to the subject (and, incidentally, he is a member of the strictly Orthodox Shas party) is somewhat different, mainly in that his call for joint action is coupled with an earnest plea for non-evangelization. Here is what Rabbi Cohen said, in his greetings delivered at the President's 2000 New Year's reception for the heads and representatives of Churches and Christian organizations in Israel:

> We must take hold of ourselves and renew the faith in God and go forth into the streets and call humanity to bring God back into their lives and homes, so that a new and better future may rise upon the horizon of mankind. In order to reach this stage, we must emphasize that every religion must have the right to preach to its followers. Let us agree that each religion – Judaism and Christianity – will preach to its own members and not try to convince members of the other religion to join theirs. In doing so, we can move forward together to promulgate faith and spirituality.

This notion that dialogue and evangelization are mutually antithetical is heavily underscored in the statement released in February 1995 by the Society for Christian-Jewish Cooperation, meeting in Hamburg, Germany. In an outspoken criticism of the Church on this subject, it maintains that –

> The positive encounters between Jews and Christians still experience one obstacle in particular: The Churches have not yet expressed a clear, unambiguous, authoritative renunciation of mission to Jews.

Whether this is really so or not, there is no doubt about the fact that this is exactly how most Jews appear to perceive the situation.

The Society's statement does cite some earlier attempts by various Church bodies, mainly in Germany, to come to grips with this challenge, but maintains that these attempts all reflect one degree or another of "hesitation and ambiguity," constituting "an extraordinary burden on the Christian-Jewish partnership." The dialogue, it says, can continue to be trusting and fruitful "only if every intention – however concealed – of missionizing Jews is completely rejected....Only if the Churches clearly refuse to missionize Jews, is their fight against anti-Judaism within the Church and against every form of antisemitism in society really plausible."

The Grassroots

What of "the man and woman in the street"? How do Jews at the grassroots level feel? As already stated, there is strong popular mistrust of Christian motives when it comes to assessing any kind of Christian approach to Jews – as individuals or as a community. However, one also hears voices in this community that reflect a more open-minded attitude. In Israel, for example, attempts to legislate harsh anti-missionary measures in the Knesset (parliament) have regularly been defeated. On one such occasion, in 1998, a letter to the editor of *The Jerusalem Post* made the case for openness and dialogue – while, at the same time, stressing the need to keep the missionaries at arm's length:

> Similarly, in the fight against missionaries – who most certainly do constitute a threat to the Jewish religion – we cannot curtail freedom of speech, for that would severely threaten the Western democratic foundations on which our country was built. In addition, how does one determine what speech is intended to convert Jews? Does such speech include, for example, conversations between Jews and Christians about the theologies of their respective religions?

> Personally, I have found such interfaith dialogue to be a spiritually uplifting way to enhance my faith as a Jew. Were such dialogue to be banned under Pinhasi's proposed law, I and many others would be deprived of a wonderful opportunity to learn and grow....

The best way, perhaps, to sum up the Jewish approach to Christian mission is to cite the scripture from the Book of Micah (4:5) that is so often referred to by Jewish speakers and writers when dealing with this subject:

"For all the nations walk each in the name of its god, and we will walk in the name of the Lord our God for ever and ever."

We had some difficulty deciding whether or not to capitalize the first mention of the word *God* in this verse. The Hebrew text is not helpful in this sense, since the Hebrew language is devoid of capital letters altogether. The translations we have consulted (including the New International Version of the Holy Bible) all render the word with a small *g*, in the word's first appearance in the verse, implying an across-the-board idolatry. Would, then, the capitalization of the word imply an across-the-board *recognition* of the true God? And is that the intent of this scripture?

The answer to this last question is probably No. The whole point here, clearly, is to posit the *faith* of the people of Israel as a contrast to what Cardinal Ratzinger would call the *beliefs* of the other peoples of the world. On the other hand, if we were to adopt – for the moment, at least – Father Marcel Dubois' intriguing "converging verticality" concept (see p. 130), a case could be made for the proposition that, since virtually all human beings on this earth are instinctively reaching out, as Father Dubois says, for a more perfect knowledge of God (regardless of what name they may assign to Him) the capitalization of the name, in its first as well as its second appearance in the verse, would be very much in place.

Christian Assessments

Christian approaches to the subject of Christian-Jewish dialogue are many and varied. As on the Jewish side, so on the Christian, one cannot speak of a single authoritative voice on the nature – or, for that matter, the very need or desirability – of Christian-Jewish dialogue.

(a) The Lutheran Church

A kind of "mirror-image," on the Christian side, to Rabbi Soloveitchick's advocacy of cooperation and dialogue on social issues (see p. 139) may be seen in the Lutherans' call "to take the initiative in promoting friendly relationships and in making common cause with Jews in matters of civil and social concern.... Jews and Lutherans need not share a common creed in order to cooperate to the fullest extent in fostering human rights ("The American Lutheran Church and the Jewish Community," 1974).

There is a very important difference, however, between this document and the Soloveitchick thesis. Whereas Rabbi Soloveitchick felt that Jewish-Christian cooperation and dialogue should be *restricted* to the social domain, the above-cited statement by the Lutheran Church posits this as only *one* of the areas in which such dialogue should be undertaken. Thus, in the document cited above, we also read the following:

> Within a context of respect and cooperation, Lutherans should invite Jews to engage in a mutual sharing of convictions....not only for the sake of greater maturity, but also because Christian faith is marked by the impulse to bear witness, through word and deed, to the grace of God in Jesus Christ.

Reference has been made to the contrast between the notion of *mission*, on the one hand, and that of *dialogue*, on the other. The Lutheran document we have cited posits the concept of *witness* as a bridge between these two notions:

> Witness, whether it be called "mission" or "dialogue," includes a desire both to know and to be known more fully. Such witness is intended as a positive, not a negative, act. When we speak of a mutual sharing of faith, we are not endorsing a religious syncretism. But...there will be an exchange that calls for openness, honesty and mutual respect.

(b) The World Council of Churches

On January 2, 1982, following several years of discussion on the subject, the World Council of Churches Consultation on the Church and the Jewish People (ccjp) adopted a series of "Ecumenical Considerations on Jewish-Christian Dialogue" which were "received and commended to the churches for study and action" by the wcc's Executive Committee in Geneva on July 16, 1982.

The paper adopted laid down several basic principles that were considered necessary for effective dialogue. The first of these was the principle of *spiritual self-determination* – i.e., "to allow participants to describe and witness to their faith in their own terms" so as to avoid the pitfalls of "prejudice, stereotyping and condescension."

Significant dialogue, we are told, grows "out of a reciprocal willingness to listen and learn."

Another principle mentioned in the statement is recognition
of the existing *asymmetry* between the Christian and Jewish faith
communities:

> In the case of Jewish-Christian dialogue, a specific historical and
> theological asymmetry is obvious. While an understanding of
> Judaism in New Testament times becomes an integral and indis-
> pensable part of any Christian theology – for Jews, a "theological"
> understanding of Christianity is of a less essential or integral sig-
> nificance. Yet, neither community of faith has developed without
> awareness of the other.

The *avoidance of stereotyping* has already been alluded to, but is
then given special emphasis:

> Both Judaism and Christianity comprise a wide spectrum of opin-
> ions, options, theologies and styles of life and service. Since gener-
> alizations often produce stereotyping, Jewish-Christian dialogue
> becomes the more significant by aiming at as full a representation
> of views as possible within the two communities of faith.

Appreciation of "the *richness and vitality of Jewish faith and life* in
the covenant" is next. "Through dialogue with Jews," the paper states,
"many Christians have...been enriched in their own understandings
of God and the divine will for all creatures." The paper goes on to
describe, in some detail, the powerful revival of the Jewish people,
"which gave them the vitality capable of surviving the catastrophe
of the loss of the Temple. It gave birth to Rabbinic Judaism, which
produced the Mishnah and Talmud and built the structures for a
strong and creative life through the centuries."

Finally, for Jews, there is "the memory of *the Land of Israel and
of Zion, the city of Jerusalem*," which have at all times been "central
in the worship and hope of the Jewish people....And the continued
presence of Jews in the Land and in Jerusalem was always more than
just one place of residence among all the others."

"Dialogue," the WCC paper concludes, "can rightly be described
as a *mutual witness* – but only when the intention is to hear the

others in order better to understand their faith, hopes, insights and concerns, and to give, to the best of one's ability, one's own understanding of one's own faith...."

(For more extensive extracts from this document, see Appendix J.)

(c) The Presbyterian Church

In its 1987 Study Paper on Christian-Jewish Relations (for full text, see Appendix L), the Presbyterian Church (USA) deals with the subject of dialogue, in both its positive and its negative aspects – defining it, in other words, not only in terms of what it is, but also in terms of what it is not. The Study Paper consists of seven theolgical affirmations and their respective "explications." The fourth affirmation refers to God's reign being attested to "both by the continuing existence of the Jewish people and by the Church's proclamation of the gospel of Jesus Christ" and asserts that "when speaking with Jews about matters of faith, we must always acknowledge that Jews are already in a covenantal relationship with God."

The explication of this affirmation deals with the dilemma that confronts Christians in considering "the very sensitive issue" of evangelism, concluding that, for Christians, "there is no easy answer to this matter." Moving on to the subject of dialogue, the paper then states the following:

> Dialogue is the appropriate form of faithful conversation between Christians and Jews. Dialogue is not a cover for proselytism. Rather, as trust is established, not only questions and concerns can be shared, but faith and commitments as well.... Dialogue, especially in light of our shared history, should be entered into with a spirit of humility and a commitment to reconciliation. Such dialogue can be a witness that seeks also to heal that which has been broken. It is out of a mutual willingness to listen and to learn that faith deepens and a new and better relationship between Christians and Jews is enabled to grow.

(d) The Catholic Church

When we speak of Christian-Jewish dialogue, what we are talking about, first and foremost, is an ongoing dialogue between the Jewish community and the Catholic Church. The dialogue began with this Church, in the wake of its 1965 Nostra Aetate declaration, and it is between Jews and Catholics that most of the dialogue-hours have been recorded. Following are three pronouncements that have been made by members of that Church on the subject of dialogue. The first – by the Latin Auxiliary Bishop and Vicar General of Jerusalem, Kamal-Hanna Bathish – is taken from a 1999 message "toward the third millennium" and lists "some of the basic conditions necessary for truly constructive dialogue":

> The first condition is that each side eliminate previous prejudices about the other....The parties must recognize each other's existence as partners in dialogue.... To dialogue means to accept one another as we are and as equal human beings... Each side must be ready to accept and respect the other's equal rights, obligations and freedoms... Dialogue requires us to be understanding and courageous enough to sacrifice when necessary... Sincere inter-religious dialogue means remaining open to believers of other religions while maintaining full fidelity to one's own faith.

Joseph Cardinal Ratzinger, Prefect of the Pontifical Congregation for the Doctrine of the Faith, is the author of one of the most controversial documents to be issued by the Catholic Church on this subject in recent history: the "Declaration *Dominus Iesus* on the Unicity and Salvific Universality of Jesus Christ and the Church." Paragraph 22 of this document (published in September 2000) deals with the tension between the concepts of "dialogue" and "mission," which has been examined, in various ways, earlier in this chapter. Here is what it says:

> In interreligious dialogue, the mission *ad gentes* "today as always retains its full force and necessity" (Second Vatican Council)....
> "Because she believes in God's universal plan of salvation, the Church must be missionary" (Catechism of the Catholic Church). Interreligious dialogue, therefore, as part of her evangelizing mission, is just one of the actions of the Church in her mission *ad gentes*. Equality, which is a presupposition of interreligious dialogue, refers to the general personal dignity of the persons in dialogue, not to doctrinal content...

Indeed, the Church, guided by charity and respect for freedom, must be primarily committed to proclaiming to all people the truth definitively revealed by the Lord, and to announcing the necessity of conversion to Jesus Christ and of adherence to the Church...

Two rather disturbing questions (from the Jewish point of view) present themselves as we read this text:

1. If this indeed is the way in which the Catholic Church views the function of dialogue, i.e., that it is "part of her evangelizing mission," can a Jew participate in good conscience in dialogue with Catholics without having to fear that he is being evangelized in the process?
2. In expressing the Church's commitment "to proclaiming to all people the truth...revealed by the Lord, and...announcing the necessity of conversion...," does this commitment not embrace the Jews as well? And, if it does, what of the Catholic Church's avowed renunciation of mission to the Jews?

There have been subsequent efforts, by Cardinal Ratzinger himself and by other representatives of the Vatican, to set these fears at rest by explaining (as others have done in this context in the past) that "mission to the nations" is *not* intended to embrace the Jewish people: that Judaism is recognized to be the "mother religion" from which Christianity itself sprang, and the Jews "a covenant community"; that the Jews are thus not included in the "mission *ad gentes*" concept; and that, therefore, there is no essential contradiction between the general theological determinations of *Dominus Iesus* and the renunciation of mission to the Jews.

Walter Cardinal Kasper, in a statement on this subject delivered at the International Catholic-Jewish Committee meeting in New York (May 1–4, 2001), related to both of the questions posed above. "It is evident," says Cardinal Kasper, quoting directly from an article written by Cardinal Ratzinger himself (*L'Osservatore Romano*, Dec. 29, 2000: "The Heritage of Abraham"), "that dialogue of us Christians with the Jews stands on a different level from the dialogue with the other religions. The faith witnessed in the Bible of the Jews, the Old Testament of Christians, is for us not a different religion but the foundation of our own faith." Developing this theme further, Cardinal Kasper, among other things, makes this point:

> ...Dominus Iesus does not state that everybody need become a Catholic in order to be saved by God. On the contrary, it declares that God's grace, which is the grace of Jesus Christ according to our faith, is available to all. Therefore, the Church believes that Judaism, i.e., the faithful response of the Jewish people to God's irrevocable covenant, is salvific for them, because God is faithful to His promises.

(See also Cardinal Kasper's remarks on mission, quoted at the start of this chapter, on p. 124.)

A book published by the Pontifical Biblical Commission that made its unobtrusive appearance in Rome bookstores towards the end of 2001 may shed further light on this issue. Entitled *The Jewish People and Their Sacred Scriptures in the Christian Bible*, and with a Preface by Cardinal Ratzinger, this scholarly work says, among other things, that "the Jewish interpretation of the Old Testament is a possible reading that stands in continuity with Jewish sacred writings of the Second Temple period, and is analogous to the Christian reading that developed parallel to it." Cardinal Ratzinger, in his Preface, notes that "Christians can learn a great deal from the [subsequent] 2,000 years of further Jewish exegesis."

On the subject of messianism, the document offers a rather innovative approach to the difference between the way Jews and Christians relate to this issue. "The Jewish wait for the Messiah," it avers, "is not in vain." It goes on to advance the proposition that Jews and Christians in fact share the expectation of the Messiah – though Jews are waiting for the first coming, and Christians for the second.

Neil Rubin, Senior Editor of the *Baltimore Jewish Times*, greeted the publication of the document's English edition with these words (May 17, 2002):

> Can Catholics validate – albeit disagree with – a "Jewish under-

standing" of the messiah, acknowledge a "Jewish reading" of the Torah and accept that for Jews the sacred text does *not* predict Jesus's life? Not long ago, even the questions were heretical. But the latest work of this Vatican commission responds with a resounding "yes" to such questions, a reply that is sparking vigorous, albeit respectful, debate among veterans of the Catholic and Jewish dialogue.

One cannot escape the thought that this new Vatican document may have been intended to correct the impression, created by Dominus Iesus, that the latter reflects an exclusivist theological approach. The fact that publication of the document was not accompanied by publicity or fanfare may indicate that its authors are aware of a certain opposition, in Catholic theological circles, to some of the ideas expressed there and preferred therefore to adopt a low profile at this stage. Even if this is so, however, it does not detract from the intrinsic importance of the document, particularly in view of the fact that the man behind it is no less a personage than the Prefect of the Vatican's Congregation for the Doctrine of the Faith.

Israel's Ambassador to the Holy See, Joseph Lamdan, hailed this document as yet another milestone on the road to better Christian-Jewish relations. Addressing a meeting of European and African members of the Catholic Integrated Community and members of Israel's kibbutz movements (pioneering communities), in January 2002, Ambassador Lamdan suggested to the kibbutzniks: "If you thought you were pioneers – *halutzim* – in a different area, in the area of rebuilding Eretz Israel, you are also pioneers in the important area of rebuilding a relationship that went wrong for 1,500 years, and slowly, slowly is changing. Let's hope we can open that door!"

Over the years, no doubt, the Christian-Jewish dialogue has produced some very positive and beneficial results in terms of improving the atmosphere and generating a better overall relationship between the two faith communities. The results are to be seen, if nowhere else, in the steadily growing number of Church documents reflecting this improvement.

"Mainstreaming" the Dialogue

If the dialogue has had a downside, it is that it has remained, so far, almost exclusively in the rarefied sphere of the upper echelons of the two communities. In the words of another prominent Catholic figure, Prof. John T. Pawlikowski, of the Catholic Theological Union of Social Ethics in Chicago, "a critical need remains to mainstream the results of the dialogue if it is not to remain an isolated experience limited to a select number of Christians and Jews. The potential exists for a major transformation in mutual understanding, but it is a potential far from realized in the Christian and Jewish communities at large."

That this view is held outside Catholic circles as well is illustrated by the following quotation from an article by Alice L. Eckardt, a Protestant, and Professor Emerita of Religion Studies at Lehigh University (in *More Stepping Stones to Jewish-Christian Relations*, Paulist Press, 1985):

> To what extent do the thinking and the implications of the contents [of the church statements cited] permeate the regular preaching, teaching and life of the denominations and individual congregations? The answer so far appears to be: very little. Unless the wider Christian community enters into the process of critical reexamination, and does so with a sense of urgency, the most ideal reformulation of Christian beliefs must remain a buried treasure, an unused resource for a transformation that could be spiritually liberating and genuinely redemptive for both parties.

Glorifying "The Name"

We are not here to pass judgment on the manner in which Christians feel called upon to practice their religion. Still, in light of the evidence presented in this chapter, it may be possible to suggest certain parameters in defining the meeting point between Christianity and Judaism – and what might be considered, by both communities, to be acceptable terms for such a meeting. To be sure, no conceivable formula will gain across-the-board acceptance in either community. But there is enough common ground to make it possible for the main body of both faith communities to build an edifice that will be acceptable to both.

As we have seen, the widespread Jewish fear of Christian missionary activity finds its echo, today, in a general acknowledgment on the Christian side that what Christian theologians term "proselytism" (or, in some Churches, "undue" or "unwarranted proselytism") is to be shunned. And if this is so in relation to other faith communities in general, it applies especially in relation to the Jewish people, with whom Christendom, as is now widely recognized in the Church, enjoys a "special relationship."

What, then, about "mission"?

Again drawing upon the material, from Christian and Jewish sources, brought forward in these pages, one must conclude that this term lies in a gray area that is likely to defy all attempts to bring about a common Christian-Jewish denominator. Even when one focuses on the Christian side alone, one will find different shades and nuances of meaning and purpose in how people relate to the word and what it implies. In general, it is probably accurate to say that, while many Christians will want to insist on their right and duty to engage in mission (to Jews as to others), the vast majority of Jews will continue to view any Christian missionary activity in their midst as totally unacceptable.

When, on the other hand, we speak of "witness" – that is a different story. Here we have a way in which the two narratives can meet and play themselves out in harmony. Here, as has been suggested by some thinkers on both sides of the divide, we have an instrument that is to be found in the spiritual tool-kits of both faith communities and may thus be utilized by both without arousing suspicion or fear. Christians call it witness; Jews – the sanctification, or glorification, of The Name.

Let every man and woman in both communities – and, for that matter, let both communities as such – practice and live out their respective religions, in word and deed, in such manner as to earn the admiration and respect of the other.

This, in itself, would make the world a better place.

Chapter 9

The Missing Link

*The most remarkable of all such resurgence is the emergence of the State of Israel, which, by restoring the **Land** to its relationship with **People** and **Religion**, has made it possible for Judaism to regain its wholeness.*

(From Guidelines adopted in 1977 by British Working Group for World Council of Churches Consultation on the Church and the Jewish People)

THE JEWISH-CHRISTIAN-ISRAEL TRIANGLE – that is the subtitle of this book. In the nature of things, our theme being the sea-change that is taking place in the relationship between the first two dimensions, it is these two dimensions, or legs of the triangle, that have occupied center stage in our discussion. What of the third leg – the State of Israel?

It has already been suggested (see p. 52) that the rebirth of national Israel in 1948, three years after the end of World War II and the Shoah, probably served as the catalyst in bringing about the above-mentioned sea-change. One would have thought, therefore, that the change in Christian attitudes towards Judaism and the Jewish people would, as a matter of course, be applied also to *national* Israel, the political manifestation of Jewish peoplehood, whose re-emergence in the mid-20th century had triggered the change in the first place! Yet this has by no means always been the case.

"Rebirth" vs. "Creation"

The words "rebirth" and "re-emergence" are used here advisedly. Contrary to the mindless – yet, unfortunately, ubiquitous – use of the phrase "the creation of Israel," the State of Israel was not "created" in 1948. "Creation" (as in *In the beginning God created the heavens and the earth*") implies putting something into existence where nothing had existed before: a totally absurd notion where Israel is concerned!

Of all the institutions in the world, the Churches should have been the first to appreciate the profound significance of the rebirth of Israel in our day, from the biblical/religious point of view. Is it only a fundamentalist who can experience a tingle of excitement and a feeling of awe at the spectacle of biblical prophecy being realized in our generation? Does one have to be an evangelical Christian to be able to relate to the return of Israel's young pioneers to the long-neglected soil of their ancient patrimony – the heartland of Judea and Samaria? Is it necessary to be "born again" to shout "Hallelujah!" at the sight of the desert being made to bloom (as God said it would), or "the waste cities" being rebuilt (as God said they would be), or the children of Israel coming back to their land and becoming one nation again on the mountains of Israel (as God said would happen)? Would a Presbyterian or an Episcopalian be any less Christian in his soul or his spirit if he opened his eyes and ears wide enough to see and hear these things – and praised the Lord for them?

Yes, Israel was reborn – born again, if you will – after a national existence in the land for some one thousand years, followed by many centuries of political dormancy and eclipse. Other tribes, clans and groups of adventurers came to the Holy Land, over those centuries, and tried to "make something" of the land. None succeeded. On the contrary, they denuded the land of its trees and forests, an act that in itself over time caused still greater desolation, because the sparser the vegetation, the less rain fell on the land… and the less receptive it became to cultivation and production. What little cultivation there was – as often as not was plundered or destroyed by roving bands of nomads, the real rulers of the land. Again and again, the peasants, unable to feed their families, got up and left, to seek their fortunes elsewhere. Nearly always, there were Jews living in the land, side by side with the others, but, until late in the 19th century, they were few in number, unable to take matters into their own hands, unable to make a difference. Here is just a small sampling of descriptions of the Holy Land, taken from various accounts published by travelers in the course of the 18th and 19th centuries:

British archaeologist Thomas Shaw, in his book, *Travels and Observations Relating to Several Parts of Barbary and the Levant* (London, 1767), referred to a visit to Palestine in 1738, at which time the country was "lacking in people to till its fertile soil." In 1785, the French historian and traveller, Count Constantine François Volney, described it as a "ruined" and "desolate" country (*Travels through Syria and Egypt in the Years 1783, 1784 and 1785*, London, 1787). Alphonse de Lamartine, in 1835: "A complete, eternal silence reigns in the town, on the highways, in the country...the tomb of a whole people" (*Recollections of the East*, London, 1845). H.B. Tristram, in 1865: "Both in the north and the south [of the Sharon Plain] land is going out of cultivation, and whole villages are rapidly disappearing from the face of the earth. Since the year 1838, no less than 20 villages have been thus erased from the map by the Bedouin and the stationary population extirpated" (*The Land of Israel: A Journal of Travels in Palestine*, London, 1865). Mark Twain, in 1867: "Of all the lands there are for dismal scenery, I think Palestine must be the prince. The hills are barren... The valleys are unsightly deserts... It is a hopeless, dreary, heartbroken land... Palestine is no more of this workday world. It is sacred to poetry and tradition – it is dreamland" (*The Innocents Abroad*, London, 1881).

Mark Twain had it right. He recognized the land for what it was: sacred to poetry and tradition, dreamland. But then, a short time after he wrote those things, the people for whom the land indeed was sacred began coming back to it in ever-growing numbers, joining their brethren who had been "holding the fort" over the centuries. And they did something no other tribe or people had succeeded in doing before them: They brought the land back to life. They for whom this land had always been part of their tradition, the soul and inspiration of their poetry and liturgy, the stuff of their dreams, now translated all these into hard, solid facts on the ground. It was as if the soil that had, all those dreary years, refused to respond to the efforts of a variety of interlopers now – and only now – allowed itself to be coaxed back to vibrant life and bloom: now that its sons and daughters of yore had returned to it, offering it the loving care only a son and a daughter can offer.

Arab Immigration

And – lo and behold! – after this miracle began to play itself out, at the end of the 19th century and the start of the 20th, a steady stream of folks from the neighboring lands began entering Palestine (as it was known then), eager to take advantage of the economic opportunities that were opening up as a result of this development. So, side by side with the influx of Jews from various European countries, there were Arabs coming in from the adjacent countries and further afield. According to a Yale University study published by the Esco Foundation for Palestine (*Palestine: A Study of Jewish, Arab and British Policies*, Yale University Press, New Haven, 1947), "the present-day inhabitants of Palestine are not in the main the descendants of the ancient inhabitants of the land, nor are they predominantly the descendants of the Arab conquerors of Palestine.... Authorities agree that the peasantry of Palestine who might be regarded as being most directly descended from the ancient inhabitants had, by the nineteenth century, greatly dwindled in numbers." The Study then goes on to bring us this revealing and highly significant finding:

> Of the Arabs living in Palestine at the beginning of the First World War, no small proportion had immigrated from neighboring countries since 1882. His [German jurist Ernst Frankenstein's] calculations led him to believe that only some 228,000 descendants of the 1882 Moslem settled population were living in Palestine at the outbreak of World War II. He thus comes to the conclusion: "In other words, 75 percent of the Arab population of Palestine are either immigrants themselves or descendants of persons who

immigrated into Palestine during the last hundred years, for the most part after 1882."

Statistics published in the Palestine Royal Commission Report of 1937 reflect a remarkable phenomenon: Palestine, traditionally a country of Arab *emigration*, became after World War I (according to Ernst Frankenstein, already some years before World War I) a country of Arab *immigration*. As already noted, the principal cause of this change of direction was Jewish development of the land, which had created new and attractive work opportunities and, in general, a standard of living previously unknown in the Middle East. The historian James Parkes, in his *A History of Palestine from 135 A.D. to Modern Times* (London, 1949), calls the reader's attention to this little-known – and certainly under-publicized – aspect of the history of Palestine between the two World Wars:

> The Arab population continued to grow at a phenomenal rate; there was a substantial illegal immigration of Arabs, especially from the Hauran, and Arab prosperity increased through the increased activity of the Jewish community and the many new openings for employment which it offered.

Ernst Frankenstein (*Justice for My People*, Dial Press, New York, 1944) sums up this phenomenon of Arab immigration and settlement in these words:

> This infiltration explains the otherwise inexplicable growth of the Moslem population of Palestine. It explains likewise why the genuine Arabs of Palestine are mostly newcomers. They were not interested in settling in a desolate land. Their immigration started only when Palestine became attractive, i.e., in 1882...

In the absence of hard statistical evidence dating back to that period, it is of course difficult to pinpoint 1882 as the actual date of the start of significant Arab net immigration into Palestine. Nor is it likely that the positive effects of Jewish settlement and development activities were felt in Palestine before the turn of the century. Two facts, however, emerge clearly from the sources we have cited:

1. Some time after 1882, the emigration trend was indeed trans-
   formed into an immigration trend – involving both Jews and
   Arabs.

2. The steady influx of non-Palestinian elements, Arab and non-
   Arab, even before 1882 and certainly after that date, puts an
   entirely different complexion on the alleged and largely assumed
   "antiquity" of the Arab element in the Palestinian population.

The reader may, at this point, be asking – and with some measure of justice – what all this has to do with the Church's attitude
towards the State of Israel. In point of fact, it has a great deal to do
with that attitude, as will presently become evident.

"Arab Land"?

Arab leaders and spokespersons have been at pains to depict the area
once known as Palestine as "Arab land," based on the claim that they
and their ancestors have inhabited this land "since time immemo-
rial." The Jewish presence in this area, and particularly in Judea and
Samaria (the "West Bank") and the Gaza Strip, is branded as an "illegal occupation" and an "act of aggression." Now, one can approach
this issue from two different angles: the biblical/historical and/or the
demographic/contemporary angle. Even, however, without going into
the long history of the area and evoking the authority of the Bible on
this question, the recent historical evidence of demographic movements there, as cited above, should be sufficient to show that the
Arabs' claim of antiquity in the land is totally unsubstantiated and
that, objectively speaking, the least that needs to be said, in describing this piece of real estate in the Middle East, is that it is disputed
territory, with its Jewish and Arab inhabitants both laying claim to it.
Certainly, the Jews of Israel cannot be faulted for residing in towns
and villages they have established and developed, over the years, in
Samaria, Judea and the Gaza area – as in other parts of the land.

In 1922, the League of Nations, recognizing "the historical connection of the Jewish people with Palestine" and "the grounds for

reconstituting their national home in that country," granted Britain a mandate over Palestine, pending the establishment there of such a national home. One of the rights granted the Jews, under the terms of the Mandate, was that of "close settlement" on the land. As for the ultimate political disposition of this territory, in terms of what the name "Palestine" really denotes, here is what Dr. Eugene V. Rostow, then Professor of Law and Public Affairs at Yale Universtiy and former US Under-Secretary of State (1966–69), wrote in *Yale Studies in World Public Order*, Vol. 5, 1979:

> The only possible geographic, demographic and political defini-tion of Palestine is that of the [League of Nations] Mandate, which included what are now Israel and Jordan as well as the West Bank and the Gaza Strip. The term "Palestine" applies to all the peoples who live or have a right to live in the territory – Jews, Christians and Moslems alike. Thus the West Bank and the Gaza Strip are not "Arab" in the legal sense, but territories of the Mandate which have been recognized as belonging to Israel or to Jordan.

A year earlier, William O'Brien, Professor of Government at Georgetown University in Washington, writing in *The Washington Star* (Nov. 26, 1978), had described the status of Judea-Samaria in similar terms:

> The West Bank is an integral part of the Palestine Mandate within which a Jewish national home was to be created. In this sense, the territory must be considered today to be unallocated territory.

Clearly, then, there is nothing "illegal" about Israeli Jews living in this unallocated territory, any more than it is illegal for Arabs to live there. The fact is that Israel had come into possession of Judea-Samaria and Gaza as the result of a war of self-defense against Arab aggression. In continuing, therefore, to exercise its right to live in those parts of the land that were under its control, Israel was well within its rights under international law. Nevertheless, Israel at no time adopted a doctrinaire position on this issue. Indeed, the record shows that, ever since 1967, it has always declared its readiness to give up some of the disputed territories it was holding – *if, on that basis, a compromise could be reached with Israel's Palestinian Arab neighbors leading to a genuine peace settlement.* The Arabs, on the other hand, have shown little if any inclination to arrive at a territorial compromise with Israel.

The Illusion of Peace

The so-called peace process launched at the Madrid Peace Conference in October 1991, and intensified in September 1993, with the signing of the first of a series of agreements between Israel and the Palestine Liberation Organization (PLO) that came to be known as the Oslo Accords, seemed to usher in a new era. But that turned out to be an "optical illusion." Israel, for its part, on several occasions in the course of the ensuing talks, gave up considerable parts of both the Judea-Samaria area and the Gaza Strip to the newly established Palestinian Authority (PA), until over 95 percent of the Arab population of these areas found themselves under the PA's jurisdiction. The Palestinian Arabs, on the other hand, under the leadership of Yasser Arafat, failed to keep their commitments under the Oslo Accords: They amassed an armed force about three times the size agreed upon; they did not confiscate illegal arms held by their population; they did not put a stop to the campaign of constant incitement and calls to acts of violence against Israel and the Jewish people, conducted in the schools, in the media, in the mosques and in the statements and speeches of Arafat and other PA leaders. Nor did they honor their undertaking to eschew violence in favor of negotiations to achieve their political objectives.

Matters came to a head in the autumn of the year 2000. In July of that year, Israel's then-Prime Minister Ehud Barak, in an obviously earnest effort to sew up a peace settlement, offered Arafat a series of far-reaching and unprecedented concessions that included the handing over of virtually the entire disputed area (actually including an area inside "hard-core" Israel to compensate the Arabs for a similar-sized area in Judea-Samaria where Israel would concentrate some of its settlements) plus half of Jerusalem, including effective control over the Temple Mount. These were concessions that no previous Israeli government had ever dreamed of offering its Arab neighbors; indeed, many Israelis were shocked to the core when they heard of them. *Yet they were turned down cold by Yasser Arafat – simply because they failed to fill one hundred percent of his demands and expectations.* Arafat did not even dignify the offer with a counter-offer of his own.

Instead, two months later he launched a war of attrition and terror against Israel that, as these lines are written, still has not come to an end. The evidence, moreover, is clear that Arafat's decision – to press Israel, by an ongoing campaign of violence and terror, into making the political concessions he wanted and could not get through negotiation – was *a strategic decision whose ultimate goal was not coexistence and peace with Israel, but the eradication of the Jewish state.*

The signs and indications that this is so are many; one of these is the June 1974 PLO decision to eliminate Israel in stages, the first stage being the retrieval of as much Palestinian territory as possible through diplomacy and negotiations – and the final stage, a concerted pan-Arab assault on a truncated and weakened Israel. But the plainest and most transparent proof of this proposition is the fact that *not a day goes by that the official Palestinian print and electronic media do not spread hate and incitement to acts of violence and terror against Israel and the Jews of Israel,* stressing again and again that *the Arabs' ultimate objective must be, as it always has been, to wipe Israel off the map* (the State of Israel already does not appear on the PA's official maps, nor in school textbooks!) *and to establish a Palestinian state "from the Jordan River to the Mediterranean Sea"* (e.g., PA Minister Feisal Husseini, in *Al-Arabi*, June 24, 2001). Arafat could put a halt to this daily incitement if he were of a mind to do it. Clearly, if he were sincere in his protestations that he wants peace ("the peace of the brave" he likes to call it), he would begin talking about this over the airwaves and instructing his people – in government, TV and radio, and in the schools – to do likewise. Not only has he done no such thing, but he continually speaks the language of war and hate and encourages those around him to do likewise.

Which brings us, finally, to our answer to the question: Where do the Christian Churches come in here?

What is "Occupation"?

One has to wonder about the rock-bottom sincerity of some of the Churches' assertions, discussed in earlier chapters of this book, on the need to combat antisemitism, to prevent a repetition of the kind of horror that engulfed Europe in the Holocaust years, etc. – when it is possible for the leaders of some of these very same Churches to observe the brutal assault on Israel in the years 2000–2002 and to react to it by deliberately shutting their eyes to the plain truth of this assault. The "mainline" Protestant Churches, in particular, and their umbrella organization, the World Council of Churches, have been guilty of treating the plainly evident fact of the Palestinian Arab assault on Israel as if it were somehow justified by Israel's very presence in the land. In doing so, they have elected to adopt the language of the Arab propaganda machine. In other words, what any truly unbiased observer of the scene would have to describe as "Israel's presence in the disputed areas of Judea, Samaria and Gaza" now becomes, in the jargon of the anti-Israel propagandists, "the Israeli occupation of Arab land." Regrettably, some major Christian Churches have bought into this propaganda jargon and, on its basis, have chosen to make Israel the villain of the piece.

From a purely pragmatic and factual point of view, moreover, the term "Israeli occupation" is really no more than an empty slogan. The fact is that, in the course of the implementation, over the years, of the 1993 Oslo Accords, Israel has ceded about 40 percent of the area of Judea/Samaria, and six Arab-inhabited towns and cities, to Arafat's Palestinian Authority. As a result, as we pointed out earlier in this chapter, *more than 95 percent of the Arab population of these "occupied" territories have long since been under Palestinian Arab – not Israeli – rule!* And yet, again and again, "mainline" Protestant Churches have taken up the cudgels against Israel, much in the spirit of that well-worn slogan: Don't confuse me with facts – my mind is made up! The following is just one example:

In a joint appeal to US Secretary of State Colin Powell in June 2001, leaders of the Episcopal Church, the Presbyterian Church, the United Methodist Church, the Evangelical Lutheran Church and others condemned Israel for taking actions (actually, measured surgical military strikes) in its own self-defense. Their appeal also contains this statement: "Few things have done more to destroy the hope and pursuit of peace through negotiations than Israel's unrelenting settlement policy."

It is difficult to understand how these men of the cloth could exhibit such extreme hostility towards a phenomenon having such deep, authentic historical and religious roots. Whether it is viewed from the legal angle or the moral one, this so-called issue of the Jewish presence in Judea-Samaria (the "West Bank") and the Gaza Strip is quickly exposed as a non-issue. The legal right of Israeli Jews to live in these areas has already been established in these pages. As for the moral aspect of the question, a succinct summary of this aspect is offered by an American Catholic writer, former Secretary of Education William J. Bennett. In his book, *Why We Fight: Moral Clarity and the War on Terrorism* (Barnes & Noble, 2002), Bennett writes:

> There is no reason Jews should not be able to live in the West Bank unless there is a reason Arabs should not be able to live in Tel Aviv – which is to say, there is no reason at all. The freedoms to travel and live are fundamental. To claim that certain lands should be free of Jews is to claim that the Third Reich had a moral point.

Conduct such as that of the Churches cited above is bound to raise questions in Jewish minds about the authenticity of the spirit that moved them when, years ago, they issued those very thoughtful and seemingly sincere declarations and statements concerning the need for a new approach to Judaism and the Jewish people. One resident of Jerusalem, for example, reacted to the mainliners' collective appeal to Secretary of State Powell in a letter to *The Jerusalem Post* (June 22, 2001) which reads in part:

> Arafat has done everything possible to involve the Arab countries

in the present dispute. An attack by them would not be restrained. It would know no limits. Where are these same Christian bodies who apologize for the past when the same danger exists in the present? How deep can such apologies be when they do not change behavior? Where are the lessons supposedly learned?

We do not wish to belabor the point, but when it comes to the World Council of Churches (WCC), and it transpires that it too has joined the fray, that is a factor we dare not ignore. Meeting in Geneva September 11–14, 2001, the WCC's Executive Committee adopted a resolution on the events taking place in the Middle East. We will not sully the pages of this book by quoting extensively from this shameful document; the WCC will no doubt be happy to provide the full text to any interested reader. It will be sufficient, for our purposes, to point out (1) that, while the one-page resolution repeats *six times* the factually, legally and historically flawed phrase, "the illegal occupation of Palestine" (or some variant of that phrase), there is not a single mention of the brutal attacks on Israelis – civilians and soldiers – by Arafat's militias; (2) that, while the resolution laments "the destruction of Palestinian properties," it is totally silent on the wanton slaughter of Israeli men, women and children and the wholesale destruction of Israeli families; and (3) that, while the resolution calls for "international prayer vigils to strengthen the Chain of Solidarity with the Palestinian people," no prayer vigils are evoked on behalf of the targets of these ongoing attacks – the people of Israel.

The American Jewish Committee's senior interreligious adviser, Rabbi A. James Rudin, alluded to this issue in a different way. In a column written for the Religion News Service (March 29, 2001) and headlined, "Why Are Christian Leaders Buying into Arafat's Lies?" Rudin said this:

> Adolf Hitler and Joseph Goebbels, his propaganda minister, clearly understood a tragic truth about human behavior. The Nazis knew if a big lie is repeated loudly and often enough, it becomes accepted as fact. They also knew the more outrageous the lie, the greater its chances for believability....

A few years ago…Yasser Arafat, the PLO leader, asserted that Jesus was "a Palestinian."… Of course, Arafat's big lie flies in the face of historical accuracy. While scholars may debate precisely when the term "Palestine" came into common usage, it is clear that Jesus was a Jew who lived under Roman occupation in the land called Judea….

At last summer's Camp David meetings with President Bill Clinton and Prime Minister Ehud Barak, Arafat pushed the big lie envelope even further with the wildly inaccurate and dishonest assertion that the two Holy Temples never existed in Jerusalem, and that the Jewish attachment to that city is a total fabrication used by Israel for political purposes….

Christian criticism of the PLO's absurdities has been almost non-existent. This is surprising since there are at least 117 specific references to the Temple in the New Testament. If Arafat and [Jerusalem mufti Sheikh Ikrema] Sabri are correct, and there never was a Holy Temple in Jerusalem, then which building was it where Jesus walked and taught? Why was he on a Passover pilgrimage to Jerusalem, along with his fellow-Jews, during the last week of his life?

Does 21st century political expediency and the need to appease Palestinian nationalism mean Christian leaders are willing to abandon Jesus's first century connection with the Jewish Temple in Jerusalem? Do the silent Christians naively believe that such absurdities do not register on people and create the climate for physical violence?

If there is no Jewish connection with the land of Israel and the city of Jerusalem, the very roots of Christianity are called into serious question. If that absurdity becomes accepted as fact, then maybe Bethlehem and Nazareth refer simply to cities in Pennsylvania and not to the ancient places that profoundly resonate with Christianity.

What, indeed, are the answers to the questions posed by Rabbi Rudin? Can these Church leaders really not see and honestly relate to what is going on in the Middle East today? Or are we to be forced to the conclusion that what we are dealing with here is a case of antisemitism being practiced in the guise of anti-Zionism? It sounds almost paranoid; but, then again, it was none other than the Vatican that, in its 1988 document, "The Church and Racism," raised this very point! (See p. 114.)

The Catholic Church: Trend-Setter?

The chronology of the theological revolution in Christian-Jewish relations that is the theme of this book reflects the leadership role played by the Catholic Church in bringing about this revolution and moving it along. It was not until some time *after* the promulgation, by the Second Vatican Council, of the ground-breaking Nostra Aetate declaration in 1965 that the "mainline" Protestant Churches followed suit and began producing declarations and statements of their own, at times even outdoing the Catholics in the scope and intensity of their assertions on the subject.

Now consider the fact that in those early years of the revolution Catholics as well as "mainline" Protestants still harbored deep reservations about the State of Israel and, in their policy statements on the Middle East, tended to favor the Arab side in the Arab-Israeli conflict. Then, beginning some time in the 'seventies, certain almost imperceptible changes began to make themselves felt in the Vatican's Middle East policies, beginning with a change in its stand on Jerusalem (see Chapter 5, p. 58). Also, as the years went by, there were more and more contacts between the Vatican and Israeli leaders and representatives. In 1985, an official Catholic document, the Notes (p. 84), for the first time mentioned the State of Israel in a positive way. And in 1993, full diplomatic relations were established.

Would it be far-fetched, one has to wonder, to contemplate the possibility that "mainline" Protestants may, one day soon, again follow the Catholics' lead in all that concerns attitudes and policies vis-à-vis the Jewish State?

Three Basic Attitudes

In a 1989 monograph by Petra Heldt and Malcolm Lowe, entitled *Theological Significance of the Rebirth of the State of Israel*, published by the American Jewish Committee, the authors (the Executive Secretary of the Ecumenical Theological Research Fraternity in Israel and a New Testament scholar from Wales living in Jerusalem, respectively) distinguish among three basic Christian attitudes to the State of Israel. While, presumably, there may have been some "fine-tuning" in these attitudes in the time that has elapsed since then, significant or far-reaching changes are not likely to have taken place. A brief look at some of the authors' findings and conclusions, therefore, may prove enlightening.

The three basic attitudes are described in the following terms:

> Some Christians see in it [the State of Israel] virtually no significance or, at any rate, no theological significance. Others, at the opposite extreme, see the hand of God in the state's creation and subsequent history. Others, again, take an intermediate position. They may say, for instance, that the return of the Jewish people to their biblical land testifies to God's faithfulness to His promises, but that this return does not necessarily have to take the form of a sovereign Jewish state, at least not from a theological viewpoint.

To the first category ("virtually no significance") belong mainly the indigenous non-Chalcedonian Churches of the East, notably the Syrian Orthodox, Coptic, Ethiopian and Armenian Churches.

The second group ("the hand of God") comprise basically "some 90 million Christians in the world [who] believe in various forms of Christian Zionism that claim their roots in the Bible..." These, say the authors, are "Christians who recognize the State of Israel politically on the basis of a fundamental theological understanding."

Under the intermediate heading "are included a variety of attitudes found in different churches. Sometimes all theological significance is explicitly denied to the State of Israel, sometimes merely its creation is mentioned, but in either case the return is the paramount concept." Among the examples cited for this category are the American Presbyterian Church, the Netherlands Reformed Church and the Protestant Churches in Germany.

Over the years, the Heldt-Lowe monograph asserts, some of the more negative of these attitudes have begun to gravitate towards a greater degree of acceptance of the Jewish state, a development that, in turn, has been challenged by individual Christians and, at times, groups of Christians, among them Franciscan Conservatives, Greek Orthodox Conservatives and advocates of a "Palestinian Theology."

In their conclusion, the authors note a phenomenon mentioned elsewhere in this volume: "the slow rate of change of Christian attitudes – and, in many quarters, the absence of change – regarding the very idea of renewed Jewish sovereignty in the biblical homeland. Christians have not yet appreciated the depth of the challenge…"

"A Different Spirit"

Thank God, the negative attitude displayed today by some churchmen towards Israel does not represent the whole picture as far as the totality of Christendom is concerned. As noted in the monograph cited above, there are many millions of Christians with "a different spirit," Christians who are sensitive to Israel's spiritual legacy, and understand that this is a very important part of their own legacy as well. These are men and women who are ready to stand up and be counted for Israel and the message inscribed on its banner. We are not talking about blind, unquestioning support of Israel. On the contrary, we expect people to keep their eyes and ears – and minds – wide open, to look the facts in the face – and then to render their judgment without fear or favor.

Nor would it be fair – or correct – to say that support for Israel and advocacy on Israel's behalf is limited to those in Christendom who call themselves Evangelicals. One of the leading Christian organizations supportive of Israel in the United States for many years has been the National Christian Leadership Conference for Israel (NCLCI), a body composed of representatives of nearly all of the major Christian denominations in the country: Chairman of the Board is Dr. David Allen Lewis, a Pentecostal Minister of the Assemblies of God (and, incidentally, a frequent visitor and tour leader to Israel, and a highly prolific writer on religious matters and on Israel); the President (formerly Executive Director) is David Blewett, a Lutheran – and the previous Executive Director was Sister Rose Thering, a Catholic from Seton Hall University. Dr. Franklin Littell, a Methodist Minister and Professor Emeritus at Temple University in Philadelphia, has been a staunch and constant supporter of Israel. He has written numerous articles and books on Christian antisemitism and on Christian culpability in the Holocaust, and has lectured widely, in the United States and Israel, on these subjects.

In Israel, too, Christian support for Israel crosses denominational lines. To cite just one example, Father Marcel Dubois, Professor Emeritus of Philosophy at the Hebrew University of Jerusalem and a former President of the Ecumenical Theological Research Fraternity in Israel, is a Dominican priest; and the Executive Secretary of the Fraternity is Rev. Petra Heldt, a Lutheran. Both have been dedicated friends of Israel, over the years, while at the same time maintaining excellent relations with all of the Churches in Jerusalem, most of which of course have largely Christian Arab constituencies.

(The foregoing, we must emphasize, is not meant, in any way, to be an exhaustive or even a representative list of Christian leaders who have been supportive of Israel. The intention was simply to illustrate the wide denominational range of that support.)

The Catholic Church in France in June 2001 provided us with an outstanding example of how Church doctrine – in this case, the new and revised Church doctrine that eschews all manifestations of antisemitism – can be put into vibrant practice in the face of today's often ugly political realities. President Bashar Assad of Syria has on a number of occasions uttered some of the vilest anti-Jewish calumnies and blood libels, and did so again when Pope John Paul II visited Damascus in June 2001. When, later, Assad came to Paris on a State visit, the French Jewish community was not the only group to register its stern protest; it was joined, in this regard, by the French Catholic Church, which, with the blessings of Cardinal Louis Marie Bille, organized a protest demonstration against Assad and issued a strongly-worded statement recalling the dark days of the Nazi era when Jews were sent to Hitler's death camps simply because they were Jews.

"We remember," the Bishops' statement went on, "all those occasions when use was made of ostensibly religious arguments, and in particular when the Jews were accused of having killed Jesus. We remember all the pogroms and all the acts of violence that were generated by utterances like this. We have come here in order to remind Mr. Bashar Assad that, if he thinks he is going to enlist the support of the Catholic Church by means of the things he said in Madrid and Damascus concerning the Jews and Jesus, he is mistaken. We wish to proclaim here today that we reject any use that is made of ostensibly Christian antisemitic slogans in the service of political objectives of one kind or another..."

Permit us to salute Cardinal Louis Marie Bille and his Bishops' Committee for the principled public stand they took on that memorable occasion in Paris.

Christians in Israel

Having discussed at some length the Jewish-Israeli presence in Judea and Samaria, we can now turn to another presence that is very much a part of our story: the Christian presence in Jerusalem and other parts of the country. Probably the best way to describe this presence is to list (in alphabetical order) some of the Christian and interfaith organizations and institutions that have become active in Israel over the years, with a brief description of each, and the contact numbers and addresses that will help the reader avail him- or herself of further information:

- **All Nations Convocations Jerusalem**. Annual All Nations Convocation in Jerusalem, with worldwide representation. Worship and prayer groups ("Gatekeepers") maintain round-the-clock "Wall of Worship" surrounding Jerusalem. Helps promote *aliya*. Outreach to Arab community, encouraging reconciliation with the Jewish people in God (Isa. 19:23–25). Director: Rev. Tom Hess, author and lecturer. POB 31393, Jerusalem 91313; Tel.: 972-2-627-4126; Fax: 972-2-626-4239; E-mail: jhopfan@jhopfan.org Website: www.jhopfan.org

- **Association of Christians and Jews in Israel.** Publishers of quarterly *Christians and Israel*, distributed in Israel and overseas. POB 13092, Jerusalem 91131; Tel.: 972-2-566-5312; Cell: 067-566-531; Fax: 972-2-530-3469; E-mail: mmaumann@netvision.net.il

- **Bat Kol Institute.** A not-for-profit agency that facilitates the study of Judaism and the Hebrew language by Christian scholars and students, funds scholarships and sponsors seminars. President: Prof. Maureena P. Fritz, NDS, PhD. 5 Otniel St., Jerusalem 93503; Tel.: 972-2-671-5057; Fax: 972-2-671-5056; E-mail: msfritz@mscc.huji.ac.il

- **Beth Abraham.** Founded 1961 by Mother Basilea Schlink of the Evangelical Sisterhood of Mary (headquartered in Germany – see page 45), it serves as a guest-house for Holocaust survivors in Israel. Sisters currently in charge: Sr. Irene Molineus and Sr. Gratia Britz. 10 Ein-Gedi St., POB 10073, Jerusalem 91100.

- **Bible Lands Museum Jerusalem.** Extensive collection of artifacts that chronicle development in the lands of the Bible during the biblical period, from earliest civilization through the early Christian era. Special exhibitions; weekly lectures, concerts and special events. Offices in Israel, USA and Canada. Director: Batya Borowski. Resp. for Interreligious/Intercultural Matters: Amanda Weiss. POB 4670, Jerusalem 91046; Tel.: 972-2-561-1066; Fax: 972-2-563-8228; E-mail: biblelnd@netvision.net.il Website: www.blmj.org

- **Bridges for Peace.** Founded 1976 by the late Dr. G. Douglas Young as a "ministry of hope and reconciliation." Interprets Israel to Christians worldwide, in light of the Bible and current events; sponsors Hebrew classes, film series, study seminars and assistance for Israel's needy. Offices in Jerusalem and worldwide. International Director: Clarence H. Wagner, Jr. Publishes bimonthly *Dispatch from Jerusalem*, produces video magazine *Jerusalem Mosaic* and runs weekly E-mail news and prayer update. POB 1093,

Jerusalem; Tel.: 972-2-624-5004; Fax: 972-2-624-6622; E-mail: BFPIsrael@compuserve.com Website: www.bridgesforpeace.com

• **Christian Friends of Israel**. Evangelical para-church ministry based in Jerusalem, with offices worldwide. Informational and educational programs; social assistance for the needy and new immigrants. Annual Shavuot/Pentecost Conference in Jerusalem. Directors: Ray and Sharon Sanders. Publishes *Watchman's Prayer Letter* and *Israel News Digest* (monthly); *For Zion's Sake, Open Gates, Roots of Our Faith* (quarterly). POB 1813, Jerusalem 91015; Tel.: 972-2-626-4172; Fax: 972-2-626-4955; E-mail: cfi@cfijerusalem.org Website: www.cfijerusalem.org

• **Christian Media Association KEP**. Contact: Johannes Gerloff. POB 23379, Jerusalem 91233; Tel.: 972-2-573-4018; Cell: 057-442-446; Fax: 972-2-573-4019; E-mail: kep@netvision.net.il

• **Ecumenical Theological Research Fraternity in Israel**. Founded 1966 by group of theologians and clergy living in Israel to help Christian Church understand itself in new situation created by rebirth of Israel, and to deepen Christian relationship with Jews, Judaism and Israel. Study programs, lectures and seminars. President: Sister Dr. Kirsten Stoffregen Pedersen (Sister Abraham). Executive Secretary: Rev. Petra Heldt. Publishes quarterly newsletter and annual journal, *Immanuel*. POB 249, Jerusalem 91002; Tel.: 972-2-625-4941; Fax: 972-2-672-4237; E-mail: ecu_frat@netvision.net.il

• **Home for Bible Translators and Scholars**. Provides board and lodging for Bible translators, consultants and scholars taking the Hebrew University's Special Program for Bible Translators. Directors: Halvor and Mirja Ronning. POB 34120, Jerusalem 91341; Tel.: 972-2-534-2524; Fax: 972-2-533-3793; E-mail: BibleTranslators@JerusalemSchool.org Website: www.bibletranslators.org

• **International Christian Embassy Jerusalem**. Founded 1980 to demonstrate Christian support for Israel and for Jerusalem as its eternal, undivided capital. Annual Christian Feast of Tabernacles brings thousands of Christians from all over the world to Jerusalem. In Summer 2000, ICEJ's co-founder and for 20 years its Executive Director, Dr. Johann Lückhoff, retired and was succeeded in this post by Rev. Malcolm Hedding. Publishes bi-monthly *A Word from Jerusalem*, monthly *Middle East Digest*; daily E-mail news and analysis service; ongoing interaction with church and government bodies and officials, in Israel and worldwide. POB 1192, Jerusalem 91010; Tel.: 972-2-566-9823; Fax: 972-2-566-9970; E-mail: icej@icej.org.il Website: www.icej.org.il

• **International Christian Zionist Center.** Informational / inspirational Christian ministry with aim of "assembling all true believers to come to the aid of the people of Israel." Founder and Director: Jan Willem van der Hoeven (co-founder of Int'l Christian Embassy, and for many years its able spokesperson), author and lecturer. Annual International Feast of Tabernacles. E-mail news and analysis service. POB 49063, Jerusalem 91490; Tel.: 972-2-540-0133; Fax: 972-2-581-9701; E-mail: iczc@iczc.org.il Website: www.israelmybeloved.com

• **International Fellowship of Christians and Jews.** Headquartered in Chicago, IFCJ Founder and President Rabbi Yechiel Eckstein in 2000 opened offices in Jerusalem under the name *Hakeren L'Yedidut* (The Friendship Fund). Helps finance projects in areas of immigration, absorption and welfare, through the support of mostly Christian donors in USA and other countries. 22 Hahistadrut St., Jerusalem; Tel.: 972-2-623-6515; Fax: 972-2-623-6522; E-mail: kyedidut@ifcj.org.il Website: www.ifcj.org

• **Interreligious Coordinating Council in Israel.** Umbrella organization of over 70 institutions and individuals seeking to promote interreligious understanding within Israeli society. Resource center and information clearing house. Seminars, lectures, conferences. Director: Rabbi Dr. Ron Kronish. Publishes *Trialogue* (an occasional newsletter) and the annually updated *Guide to Inter-religious and Intercultural Activities in Israel* (details on p. 181). POB 8771, Jerusalem 91086; Tel.: 972-2-561-1899; Fax: 972-2-563-4148; E-mail: iccijeru@icci.co.il Website: www.icci.co.il

• **Israel Interfaith Association.** Nonprofit organization established 1957 by Martin Buber and others, to promote understanding and mutual respect between members of all religious and ethnic groups in Israel and the Middle East, through educational, social and cultural activities. Lectures, study sessions, seminars and conferences around themes of interfaith understanding. Presidency: Haifa Chief Rabbi She'ar Yashuv Cohen; Vicar for Jerusalem (Melkite Patriarchate) Archbishop Lutfi Laham; Kadi Ahmed Natour, Head of Sharia Court of Appeals. POB 7739, Jerusalem 91077; Tel.: 972-2-620-3251; Fax: 972-2-620-3388; E-mail: msyuda@mscc.huji.ac.il or mskrupp@mscc.huji.ac.il

• **Melitz Center for Interfaith Encounter with Israel.** For exploration and better understanding of varied perspectives and implications of modern and historical Israel for Jews and Christians in Israel and throughout the world. Educational programs for visiting groups of professionals, academics, community/religious leaders, students and lay people. Offices in Israel and USA. Director: Ophir Yarden. 19 Yishai St., Abu Tor, Jerusalem 93544; Tel.: 972-2-673-4441; Fax: 972-2-673-3447; E-mail: oyarden@cc.huji.ac.il or overseas@melitz.org.il

• **Mercaz Ami: The Jerusalem Center for Biblical Studies and Research.** Short-term study programs designed to balance classroom and field study for both ministers and laymen. Tuition scholarships for ministers from Third World countries to acquire elementary understanding of Jewish thought, practice and interpretation of Scripture. Comprehensive discussion of Jewish-Christian relations. Extensive reference and theological library. Publishes *The Bulletin* – activities and program report – and *Inside Israel* – monthly newsletter in Dutch, English, French, German, Japanese and Swedish. President: Shlomo Hizak. Resp. for Interreligious / Intercultural Matters: Daniel Gwertzman. POB 8017, Jerusalem 91080; Tel.: 972-2-563-6375; Fax: 972-2-563-8426; E-mail: ami_jc@netvision.net.il

• **Nazareth Village.** Restoration of first-century Nazareth: a living presentation of the life, times and teaching of Jesus of Nazareth. Director: D. Michael Hostetler. POB 2066, Nazareth 16100. In USA: Miracle of Nazareth International Foundation, 550 South Union St., Mishawaka, in 46544. In Canada: Mennonite Church Canada, 600 Shaftesbury Blvd., Winnipeg, MB R3P 0M4. E-mail: nazvil@netvision.net.il Website: www.nazarethvillage.com

• **Nes Ammim Village.** Name means "Sign to/for the Nations" (Isaiah 11:10). Founded 1963 as ecumenical Christian settlement in western Galilee, where Jews and Christians meet and converse with one another, based on mutual respect for each other's identity and tradition. Study programs, seminars, excursions. Guest House, Library, Museum. Publishes quarterly *Nes Ammim Magazine* (in Dutch and German). Contact: Rev. Andréas Gefen. Mail: DN Western Galilee 25225, Israel; Tel.: 972-4-995-0060; Fax: 972-4-995-0067; E-mail: com_center@nesammim.com

• **Pontifical Biblical Institute.** With a library of some 27,000 volumes and over 100 periodicals, PBI functions primarily on the academic level, serving students from the Pontifical Biblical Institute in Rome who have been coming to Jerusalem for over 25 years to study at Hebrew University. Jesuits at PBI participate in local Jewish-Christian-Muslim dialogue, occasionally hosting meetings for such groups. PBI Library open to public. Archaeological Museum. Superior: Rev. Thomas J. Fitzpatrick, SJ. Resp. for Interreligious/Intercultural Matters: Rev. Donald J. Moore, SJ. POB 497, Jerusalem 91004; Tel.: 972-2-625-2843; Fax: 972-2-624-1203; E-mail: dmoore@netvision.net.il or pbijer@netvision.net.il

• **Sisters of Sion**. Aims at inculcating mutual respect and understanding between Christians and Jews, deepening the Jewish roots of Christianity through education within the Church and working towards elimination of antisemitism and all forms of racism. Guest houses for pilgrims of all faiths, at Ecce Homo and Ein Karem. Ecce Homo study program (two 15-week sessions, in English and French) includes Scripture study and biblical excursions. Branches worldwide. Director: Sr. Darlene DeMong, Provincial Coordinator. Resp. for Interreligious/Intercultural Matters: Sr. Trudy Nabuurs, Director, Ecce Homo Convent, Jerusalem. POB 19056, Jerusalem 91190; Tel.: 972-2-627-7292; Fax: 972-2-628-2224; E-mail: eccehomo@inter.net.il Website: www.sion.org

• **Tantur Ecumenical Institute for Theological Studies**. Interdisciplinary study of unity and divisions of Christian Churches; Christian/Jewish/Muslim relations; human rights and conflict resolution; promotion of interreligious harmony. Assistance to serious study groups (no pilgrim or tourist groups) interested in Christian and interreligious relations. Room and board facilities on campus. 3-month and 1-month sessions for scholars, parish clergy, teachers of religion and students of theology, with Christian, Jewish and Muslim teachers. Monthly public lectures. Library of 70,000 volumes and 400 periodicals open to the public. Rector: Fr. Michael McGarry, CSP. Vice Rector: Rev. Dr. Knud Jeppesen. POB 19556, Jerusalem 91194; Tel.: 972-2-676-0911; Fax: 972-2-676-0914; E-mail: tantur@netvision.net.il Website: www.come.to/tantur

• **United Christian Council in Israel**. Fellowship, founded 1956, of mainly evangelical Christian churches and ministries in Israel. Chairman: Rev. Ray Lockhart. Liaison and Public Relations: Rev. Charles Kopp. POB 116, Jerusalem 91000, Tel: 972-2-625-9012; Fax: 972-2-623-4804; E-mail: exec@ucci.net

For a more complete picture of the Christian scene in Israel, the reader is herewith referred to three excellent sources:

1. Christian Information Centre, Jaffa Gate, POB 14308, Jerusalem. Tel.: 972-2-627-2692. Fax: 972-2-628-6471. E-mail: cicts@netmedia.net.il Website: www.cicts.org Issues bi-monthly *Associated Christian Press Bulletin* that includes selected items from Vatican Information Service and from Israeli press. Also publishes listings of religious holy days, churches and church services, etc.

2. *Promotion Handbook for Pilgrims and Christian Tourists*, published by Ministry of Tourism, Pilgrimage Division, A comprehensive reference book on a wide variety of subjects. POB 1018, Jerusalem. Tel.: 972-2-567-8777. Fax: 972-2-625-9837; E-mail: hanai@tourism.gov.il Website: www.goisrael.com

3. *Guide to Interreligious and Intercultural Activities in Israel*, published annually by Interreligious Coordinating Council in Israel (ICCI), comprising more than 70 Christian, Jewish and interfaith institutions and *ad personam* members. The Guide contains detailed information about each of the constituent institutions and organizations. POB 8771, Jerusalem 91086. Tel.: 972-2-561-1899. Fax: 972-2-563-4148. E-mail: iccijeru@icci.co.il Website: www.icci.co.il

A Treasure Waiting to be Dug Up

The time has come to tie up the loose ends of our narrative, and to see whether we now have answers to some of the questions posed in earlier chapters of this book. Perhaps the best way to do this is, first of all, to channel all the questions that have been asked into three "big ones" that may be said to encapsulate our theme:

1. *Direction:* Have the Christian Churches, theologically speaking, really changed course?

2. *Education:* Is the message of change being effectively passed down to the rank-and-file?

3. *Response:* Do we have an appropriate response from the Jewish side?

Now, for some answers.

If there is one proposition that surely has been established by the evidence presented in this book, it is the proposition that the revision of Christian theology that has been documented here (particularly in Chapter 6) is real. It is genuine. The detailed and carefully crafted treatment of the subject, in most of these Church documents, and the very fact that the Churches involved have persisted in its pursuit over a period of several decades provide ample evidence that the process we are witnessing is not some fly-by-night operation, but apparently is here to stay. The answer, in other words, to Question No. 1 is a resounding YES.

As for Questions No. 2 and 3, our answers will have to be more qualified. Prof. Alice Eckardt, whom we had occasion to quote, on the subject of dialogue, in our previous chapter, offers at least part of the answer when she says (see p. 155 for the full quote) that "very little" appears to have been done to allow the contents of these Church statements to "permeate the regular preaching, teaching and life of the denominations..." That, perhaps, is why the gap is sometimes so wide between the positions taken by a given Church with regard to its attitude towards Judaism and the Jewish people, on the one hand, and those it later adopts with regard to the current situation in the Middle East. Moreover, the fact that manifestations of antisemitism in the world have not only not come to an end, but have actually been on the increase in recent years, seems to point to a definite shortcoming in effectively bringing the message of change down to the grassroots level of the Christian public.

That is not to say, however, that the effort is not being made. In the Roman Catholic Church, in particular, this process of education has been going forward ever since the promulgation of the 1974 Guidelines (see p. 74), which were to be reinforced by the 1985

Notes (p. 84) and a series of lesser documents, in between and in subsequent years. Also, the courageous demonstration carried out by the French Catholic bishops, in June 2001, against Syrian President Assad's antisemitic outbursts (described in greater detail earlier in this chapter) gives proof that, at least in this instance, representatives of the Church were able to translate the lofty principles the Church had enunciated into the language of everyday life.

On balance, then, one would have to say – in answer to Question No. 2 – that something is being done to "spread the good word" and to make the message meaningful, but that, as in other matters connected with religion, it is a slow process, and in many areas of life one is hard put to see or feel the change. This subject of education, incidentally, is one of the issues the Jewish partner in the Christian-Jewish dialogue has been bringing up from time to time – with particular emphasis on the need to expedite the process if it is to be truly effective within the foreseeable future. Professor Eckardt warns that unless the wider Christian community is drawn, urgently, into this process of "critical re-examination…the most ideal reformulation of Christian beliefs must remain a buried treasure…" What is needed here, it seems, is for a few good people to roll up their sleeves, pick up some shovels and start digging!

Question No. 3, for a change, is directed to the Jewish side of our connection. Actually, it may be broken down into a number of questions: Is there a need for a Jewish response to these developments in the Christian Church? If so, how important is it that such a response be forthcoming? What kind of response has there been to date – and what is to be expected in the future?

The reader will find these questions discussed in the Epilogue, where we have endeavored to treat the subject within the overall context of the book as a whole.

Epilogue

JUDAISM AND CHRISTIANITY: Two millennia of estrangement and hostility, rancor and hatred, persecution, conflict and strife may finally have come to an end. It has taken a human holocaust to accomplish that – a holocaust followed by a miraculous re-flowering of Jewish nationhood. But it appears to be happening now. Our generation is witnessing a swelling tide of new thinking and new speaking in Christendom. It began slowly, quietly, haltingly more than fifty years ago. But with every passing decade, every passing year, it gains momentum, spreading from Church to Church, from denomination to denomination, from country to country across the continents. It promises – yes, we refer to a promise, not an accomplished fact – to revolutionize the Christian-Jewish relationship, to transform a two-thousand-year legacy of bottomless animosity into a totally fresh era of mutual respect, harmony and fraternal cooperation.

And yet, among many of those taking part in this process, on the Christian as on the Jewish side, there persists a feeling of unease and concern about the future of this relationship. Simply put, the reason for this unease and this concern is that *the vast majority of Jews and Christians continue to be quite unaware of this ongoing theological revolution.*

The issues we have discussed in this book could be of tremendous historic importance. They have the potential of ushering in a truly new era in the relations between the Jewish and Christian worlds, with all that this may imply in terms of human relationships, international processes and the impact of religion on human affairs. *But this potential can be realized only if the movement for change that has been launched in the top echelons of the Christian Churches is willingly adopted and reinforced by the rank-and-file of the Christian community; and that can happen only if the Church leadership educates its faithful, with this end in mind.* Indeed, such a process of education has begun (particularly in the Roman Catholic Church), but – like so much else in the world of religion – it is proceeding at an agonizingly slow pace. It is not surprising, therefore, that antisemitism continues to rear its ugly head in various places throughout the globe.

Another thing needs to happen before the connection that has been made can be pronounced permanent – indeed, irreversible: *The theological revolution that has been set in motion in the Churches needs to find its appropriate echo on the Jewish side of the Jewish-Christian spectrum.* It needs to be acknowledged, so that the Jewish partner in this dialogue can bless the change and encourage those who have been instrumental, on the Christian side, in bringing it about. As on the Christian side, here too it is, first of all, a matter of education. People cannot be expected to relate to what they do not know; ignorance needs to be replaced by awareness and knowledge.

But that is only part of the battle, albeit an important part. The average Jewish man or woman is conditioned – by a legacy of countless generations – to be deeply suspicious of Christian actions and motives. A long history of persecution, fed by the perpetuation of ancient anti-Judaic dogmas and doctrines and forced conversions, has left its mark on the Jewish soul and will not be easy to erase. The effort, however, has to be made – because, if it is not made, there is no guarantee that the positive direction the Church has taken in its approach to Judaism and the Jewish people will continue into perpetuity. The suspicions of the Jewish "man and woman in the street" must be addressed, and they must be allayed, with the help of the facts: facts that have been accumulating relentlessly for half a century, starting out with a low, soul-searching whimper, and burgeoning into a growing chorus of Christian voices insisting on honesty, on genuine *teshuvah* and on a total reversal of the hateful notions, preachings and actions of an inglorious past.

Moreover, a hand – a Christian hand – has been extended in a bid for Jewish partnership in the fight against antisemitism, whenever and wherever it threatens to sprout, and in the concomitant determination to make it impossible for anything like the Shoah of the mid-20th century ever again to threaten the social fabric of this planet. A positive response to this invitation, a grasping of that outstretched hand, is in order. The reader may be surprised (or, then again, perhaps not) to learn that the Jewish response will not always be a positive one. More than one Jewish person I have challenged on this score has been quick to divest himself of all responsibility for the battle against antisemitism and for the prevention of another Shoah. These, I am told by such people, should be considered as solely Christian responsibilities. That proposition, I submit, is very far removed from the truth.

The duty to wipe out every last vestige of the "Amalek" (see pp. 31–32) of antisemitism and of the Shoah (and these two constitute the same Amalek) rests primarily upon the people of Israel as the people that received and accepted the Torah at Sinai. *"...you shall blot out the memory of Amalek from under the heavens..."* – the Bible tells *us*, the Jewish people first of all. *We* are called upon, in the first instance, to do the job. We are not free, therefore, to divest ourselves, as some of us tend to do, of this responsibility. Nor dare we turn our backs on those of our Christian friends who solemnly pledge, as they have now done, over and over again, to fight antisemitism and to forestall its terrible consequences. On the contrary, that outstretched hand must be grasped – firmly, warmly, convincingly. We must say, loud and clear: Yes, brothers and sisters, we will stand with you, shoulder to shoulder, on this! We are your partners in this.

This precisely is the message being beamed to the citizens of the United States by the American Alliance of Jews and Christians, operating under the co-chairmanship of Rabbi Daniel Lapin and Mr. Gary Bauer. The Alliance is a project initiated by an organization called Toward Tradition. Established in 1991 in Mercer Island, Washington, Toward Tradition (website: www.towardtradition.org) has been building, in Rabbi Lapin's words, a "Jewish-Christian coalition based on common traditional values derived from the Torah (Old Testament)." In particular, the group has called on the Jewish community in the United States "to embrace Christians, despite theological differences, as moral allies." In September 2000 a further major step in this direction was taken by the American community: 173 prominent Jewish scholars signed a declaration entitled, *Dabru Emet: A Jewish Statement on Christians and Christianity* (see page 102), recognizing the positive changes that have been taking place in the Churches and setting forth a number of propositions based on that recognition.

Surely there will be more such voices in the course of time – because the voices of change emanating from the Christian world must find their appropriate echo. The Christian hand stretched out in friendship, as well as in friendly challenge, must and will be grasped. There is no future for humankind in any other course of action. We must, all of us, Jews and Christians – and, ultimately, the members of all the other faith communities as well – join in the common quest for a better world, because this is the prime common interest of all humankind. Then, and only then, will we prove worthy of the Divine promise that He will "give them one heart and put a new spirit in them..." (Ezekiel 11:19)

Then, again, perhaps He has already begun to do so. Perhaps that is what this book is all about.

List of Appendixes

The Ten Points of Seelisberg

An Address to the Churches

Issued by the Christian participants in the Second
Conference of the International Council of Christians and
Jews at Seelisberg, Switzerland, on August 5, 1947

We have recently witnessed an outburst of antisemitism which has led to the persecution and extermination of millions of Jews. In spite of the catastrophe which has overtaken both the persecuted and the persecutors, and which has revealed the extent of the Jewish problem in all its alarming gravity and urgency, antisemitism has lost none of its force, but threatens to extend to other regions, to poison the minds of Christians and to involve humanity more and more in a grave guilt with disastrous consequences.

The Christian Churches have indeed always affirmed the un-Christian character of antisemitism, as of all forms of racial hatred, but this has not sufficed to prevent the manifestation among Christians, in various forms, of an undiscriminating racial hatred of the Jews as a people.

This would have been impossible if all Christians had been true to the teaching of Jesus Christ on the mercy of God and love of one's neighbour. But this faithfulness should also involve clear-sighted willingness to avoid any presentation and conception of the Christian message which would support antisemitism under whatever form. We must recognize, unfortunately, that this vigilant willingness has often been lacking.

We therefore address ourselves to the Churches to draw their attention to this alarming situation. We have the firm hope that they will be concerned to show their members how to prevent any animosity towards the Jews which might arise from false, inadequate or mistaken presentations or conceptions of the teaching and preaching of the Christian doctrine, and how on the other hand to promote brotherly love towards the sorely-tried people of the Old Covenant.

TEN POINTS

1. Remember that One God speaks to us all through the Old and the New Testaments.

2. Remember that Jesus was born of a Jewish mother of the seed of David and the people of Israel, and that His everlasting love and forgiveness embraces His own people and the whole world.

3. Remember that the first disciples, the apostles and the first martyrs were Jews.

4. Remember that the fundamental commandment of Christianity, to love God and one's neighbour, proclaimed already in the Old Testament and confirmed by Jesus, is binding upon both Christians and Jews in all human relationships, without any exception.

5. Avoid distorting or misrepresenting biblical or post-biblical Judaism with the object of extolling Christianity.

6. Avoid using the word "Jews" in the exclusive sense of the enemies of Jesus, and the words "the enemies of Jesus" to designate the whole Jewish people.

7. Avoid presenting the Passion in such a way as to bring the odium of the killing of Jesus upon all Jews or upon Jews alone. It was only a section of the Jews in Jerusalem who demanded the death of Jesus, and the Christian message has always been that it was the sins of mankind which were exemplified by those Jews and the sins in which all men share that brought Christ to the Cross.

8. Avoid referring to the scriptural curses, or the cry of a raging mob – "His blood be upon us and our children!" – without remembering that this cry should not count against the infinitely

more weighty words of our Lord: "Father, forgive them, for they know not what they do."

9. Avoid promoting the superstitious notion that the Jewish people are reprobate, accursed, reserved for a destiny of suffering.

10. Avoid speaking of the Jews as if the first members of the Church had not been Jews.

Nostra Aetate

Declaration on the Relation of the Church to Non-Christian Religions

Proclaimed by His Holiness Pope Paul VI
on October 28, 1965

(Excerpt in English translation)

The Jewish Religion

4. As the sacred synod searches into the mystery of the Church, it remembers the bond that spiritually ties the people of the New Covenant to Abraham's stock.

Thus the Church of Christ acknowledges that, according to God's saving design, the beginnings of her faith and her election are found already among the Patriarchs, Moses and the Prophets. She professes that all who believe in Christ – Abraham's sons according to faith – are included in the same Patriarch's call, and likewise that the salvation of the Church is mysteriously foreshadowed by the chosen people's exodus from the land of bondage. The Church, therefore, cannot forget that she received the revelation of the Old Testament through the people with whom God in His inexpressible mercy concluded the Ancient Covenant. Nor can she forget that she draws sustenance from the root of that well-cultivated olive tree onto which have been grafted the wild shoots, the Gentiles. Indeed, the Church believes that by His cross Christ, Our Peace, reconciled Jews and Gentiles, making both one in Himself.

The Church keeps ever in mind the words of the Apostle about his kinsmen: "Theirs is the sonship and the glory and the covenants and the law and the worship and the promises; theirs are the fathers and from them is the Christ according to the flesh" (Rom. 9:4–5), the Son of the Virgin Mary. She also recalls that the Apostles, the Church's mainstay and pillars, as well as most of the early disciples who proclaimed Christ's Gospel to the world, sprang from the Jewish people.

As Holy Scripture testifies, Jerusalem did not recognize the time of her visitation, nor did the Jews in large number accept the Gospel; indeed not a few opposed its spreading. Nevertheless, God holds the Jews most dear for the sake of their Fathers; He does not repent of the gifts He makes or of the calls He issues – such is the witness of the Apostle. In company with the Prophets and the same Apostle, the Church awaits that day, known to God alone, on which all peoples will address the Lord in a single voice and "serve him shoulder to shoulder" (Soph. 3:9).

Since the spiritual patrimony common to Christians and Jews is thus so great, this sacred synod wants to foster and recommend that mutual understanding and respect which is the fruit, above all, of biblical and theological studies as well as of fraternal dialogues.

True, the Jewish authorities and those who followed their lead pressed for the death of Christ; still, what happened in His passion cannot be charged against all the Jews, without distinction, then alive, nor against the Jews of today. Although the Church is the new people of God, the Jews should not be presented as rejected or accursed by God, as if this followed from the Holy Scriptures. All should see to it, then, that in catechetical work or in the preaching of the word of God they do not teach anything that does not conform to the truth of the Gospel and the spirit of Christ.

Furthermore, in her rejection of every persecution against any man, the Church, mindful of the patrimony she shares with the Jews, and moved not by political reasons but by the Gospel's spiritual love, decries hatred, persecutions, displays of antisemitism, directed against Jews at any time and by anyone.

Besides, as the Church has always held and holds now, Christ underwent His passion and death freely, because of the sins of men and out of infinite love, in order that all may reach salvation. It is, therefore, the burden of the Church's preaching to proclaim the cross of Christ as the sign of God's all-embracing love and as the fountain from which every grace flows.

We cannot truly call on God, the Father of all, if we refuse to treat in a brotherly way any man, created as he is in the image of God. Man's relation to God the Father and his relation to men his brothers are so linked together that Scripture says: "He who does not love does not know God" (1 John 4:8).

No foundation therefore remains for any theory or practice that leads to discrimination between man and man or people and people, so far as their human dignity and the rights flowing from it are concerned.

The Church reproves, as foreign to the mind of Christ, any discrimination against men or harassment of them because of their race, color, condition of life, or religion. On the contrary, following in the footsteps of the holy Apostles Peter and Paul, this sacred synod ardently implores the Christian faithful to "maintain good fellowship among the nations" (1 Peter 2:12), and, if possible, to live for their part in peace with all men, so that they may truly be sons of the Father who is in heaven.

Martin Luther on the Jews

Excerpts from Martin Luther's book,
"On the Jews and Their Lies" (1543)

...Therefore be on your guard against the Jews, knowing that wherever they have their synagogues, nothing is found but a den of devils in which sheer self-glory, conceit, lies, blasphemy and defaming of God and men are practiced most maliciously...

Moreover, they are nothing but thieves and robbers who daily eat no morsel and wear no thread of clothing that they have not stolen and pilfered from us by means of their accursed usury...

If I had to refute all the other articles of the Jewish faith, I should be obliged to write against them as much, and for as long a time, as they have used for inventing their lies – that is, longer than two thousand years....

Alas, it cannot be anything but the terrible wrath of God which permits anyone to sink into such abysmal, devilish, hellishly insane baseness, envy and arrogance....

Over and above that, we let them get rich on our sweat and blood, while we remain poor and they suck the marrow from our bones....

To save our souls from the Jews – that is, from the devil and from eternal death – my advice, as I said earlier, is:

First, that their synagogues be burned down,...

Second, that all their books – their prayer books, their Talmudic writings, also the entire Bible – be taken from them, not leaving them one leaf...

Third, that they be forbidden, on pain of death, to praise God, to pray and to teach among us...

Fourth, that they be forbidden to utter the name of God within our hearing...

They remain our daily murderers and bloodthirsty foes in their hearts. Their prayers and curses furnish evidence of that, as do the many stories that relate their torturing of children and all sorts of crimes for which they have often been burned at the stake or banished.

The American Lutheran Church and the Jewish Community

Excerpts from a Statement adopted by the Seventh General
Convention of the American Lutheran Church in October 1974

Preamble

There are many cogent reasons which urge us to reconsider the relationship of Lutherans, and indeed of all Christians, to Jews. Christians are not as aware as they should be of the common roots and
origin of the church and the Jewish tradition of faith and life. Both
Judaism and Christianity regard the Hebrew Bible – the Old Testament – as the document which bears witness to the beginning of
God's saving work in history. They worship the same God and hold
many ethical concerns in common, even though they are divided
with respect to faith in Jesus of Nazareth as the Messiah.

Christians must also become aware of that history in which they
have deeply alienated the Jews. It is undeniable that Christian people
have both initiated and acquiesced in persecution. Whole generations
of Christians have looked with contempt upon this people who were
condemned to remain wanderers on the earth on the false charge
of deicide. Christians ought to acknowledge with repentance and
sorrow their part in this tragic history of estrangement. Since anti-
Jewish prejudice is still alive in many parts of the world, Christians
need to develop a sympathetic understanding of the renewal among
Jews of the terror of the Holocaust. It is as if the numbness of the
injury has worn off, old wounds have been reopened, and Jews live
in dread of another disaster. Christians must join with Jews in the
effort to understand the theological and moral significance of what
happened in the Holocaust....

1. Solidarity

Our common humanity
Lutherans and Jews, indeed all mankind, are united by virtue of their humanity. Lutherans and Jews agree that all people, regardless of race, religion or nationality, are equally God's children, and equally precious in His sight. This conviction is based on a concept of God as Creator of the universe, Who continues to care for His creation, Whose mercies are over all His creatures.

Our common heritage
The existence of Jewish congregations today shows that a religious tradition which traces its ancestry back to the time of Abraham is still living and growing. It is a tradition that gave rise to Christianity; a tradition from which Christianity has borrowed much. But modern Judaism has grown, changed and developed considerably beyond the Judaism of biblical times, just as the modern Church has grown, changed and developed considerably beyond its New Testament beginnings.

It is unfortunate that so few Christians have studied Judaism as it grew and flowered in the centuries since the New Testament era. The first step for Lutherans, therefore, is to devote themselves to completing this long-neglected homework. It is strongly recommended that Lutherans ask the Jews themselves to teach them about this long and critically important period in Jewish history.

Our spiritual solidarity
Our solidarity is based on those ideas and themes held in common, most of which were inherited by Christianity from the Jewish tradition. It is important to note that the ministry of Jesus and the life of the early Christian community were thoroughly rooted in the Judaism of their day. To emphasize the Jewishness of Jesus and his disciples, and to stress all that binds Jews and Christians together in their mutual history, is also to attack one of the sources of anti-Jewish prejudice. We are, after all, brothers one to another. Judaism and Christianity both worship the one God. We both call Abraham

father. We both view ourselves as communities covenanted to God. We both feel called to serve in the world as God's witnesses and to be a blessing to mankind.

This emphasis on solidarity is not meant to ignore the many differences that exist between Lutherans and Jews. Rather it is through an understanding and appreciation of what we have in common that we can best discuss our differences. But for the moment, Lutherans have an obligation to fulfill – namely, to understand adequately and fairly the Jews and Judaism. This is the immediate purpose of Lutheran conversations with Jews.

It is hoped that as Lutherans better understand this similar yet different religious tradition, the wounds of the past will be healed, and Lutherans and Jews together will be able to face the future receptive to the direction of the Holy Spirit as he seeks to accomplish the will of the One in whom all men live and move and have their being.

11. Confrontation

The history of separation and persecution

American Lutherans are the heirs of a long history of prejudicial discrimination against Jews, going back to pre-Christian times. The beginnings of this history of hate are obscure, but gross superstition and the desire for a scapegoat were prominent aspects. The separation between Church and Synagogue became final by the end of the first century. When Christianity was made the official religion of the Roman Empire, a systematic degradation of Jews began in which both Church and Empire played their parts. Jews were regarded as enemies who were to be eliminated by defamation, extermination, prohibition of their writings, destruction of their synagogues and exclusion into ghettos and despised occupations. During these 19 centuries, Judaism and Christianity never talked as equals. Disputation and polemics were the media of expression. More recent developments reflect the continuation of patterns of ethnic behavior growing out of this heritage, by which Jews have been excluded by non-Jews, and have, in turn, themselves drawn together in separate communities.

No Christian can exempt himself from involvement in the guilt of Christendom. But Lutherans bear a special responsibility for this tragic history of persecution, because the Nazi movement found a climate of hatred already in existence. The kindness of Scandinavian Lutherans towards Jews cannot alter the ugly facts of forced labor and concentration camps in Hitler's Germany. That the Nazi period fostered a revival of Luther's own medieval hostility toward Jews, as expressed in pugnacious writings, is a special cause of regret. Those who study and admire Luther should acknowledge unequivocally that his anti-Jewish writings are beyond any defense.

In America, Lutherans have been late and lethargic in the struggle for minority rights in the face of inherited patterns of prejudice. We have also been characterized by an inadequate level of ethical sensitivity and action in social and political areas.

Distinctive ideas, doctrines, practices

Customarily, American Lutherans have increased misunderstanding by trying to picture Jews as a "denomination" or "faith-community" like themselves. Actually, Jewishness is both a religious phenomenon and a cultural phenomenon which is exceedingly hard to define. While for most Jews, ancient and modern, it is seen as a matter of physical descent, the aspects of religion and nationhood have at times occupied decisive positions, as is currently true in regard to Zionism. We create misunderstanding when we persist in speaking of "Jewish" creeds and "Jewish" theology, for not all Jews necessarily believe in Judaism, although that religion is their heritage.

Judaism, while it does indeed have teachings, differs markedly from Christian denominations in that its essence is best summed up not in a set of beliefs or creeds, but in a way of life. The distinctive characteristics of the words "Jew" and "Judaism" should neither be ignored nor should they be revised to fit better with Christian presuppositions. We must rather allow Jewishness to be defined by Jews, and content ourselves with the already tremendous difficulties of trying to keep aware of the complexities of this shifting and not uncontradictory self-understanding.

To the extent that both religious practices and theological reflection manifest themselves among Jews, some basic guidelines can be attempted. There is no reason why Jewish practices and beliefs should be understood or judged differently from those of any minority group. They ought, indeed, to be respected especially by Christians, since they flow from a tradition which served as the "mother" of Christianity. But even where they are in disagreement with the practices and beliefs of Christians, they still deserve the same full protection and support which are given to the religious convictions of any American citizen. While modern interest in ethnicity has furthered the appreciation of diversity of heritages, American Lutherans still need warnings against bigotry and urgings to work toward minority rights....

III. Respect and cooperation

In recognition of the solidarity that unites us and of the tensions and disagreements which have divided us, we affirm the desire of the American Lutheran Church to foster a relationship of respect and cooperation with our Jewish neighbors.

Cooperation in social concern
Jews and Lutherans live together in the same society. They have common problems and obligations. The bonds of common citizenship ought to impel Lutherans to take the initiative in promoting friendly relationships and in making common cause with Jews in matters of civic and social concern. It is of special importance that Lutherans demonstrate their commitment to the intrinsic worth of Jewish people by giving them all possible assistance in the struggle against prejudice, discrimination and persecution. Jews and Lutherans need not share a common creed in order to cooperate to the fullest extent in fostering human rights.

A mutual sharing of faith
It is unrealistic to expect that Lutherans will think alike or speak with one voice on the motive and method of bearing witness to their Jewish neighbors. Some Lutherans find in Scripture clear directives

to bear missionary witness in which conversion is hoped for. Others hold that when Scripture speaks about the relation between Jews and Christians, its central theme is that God's promises to Israel have not been abrogated. The one approach desires to bring Jews into the body of Christ, while the other tends to see the Church and the Jewish people as together forming the one people of God, separated from one another for the time being, yet with the promise that they will ultimately become one.

It would be too simple to apply the labels "mission" and "dialogue" to these points of view, although in practice some will want to bear explicit witness through individuals, special societies or ecclesiastical channels, while others will want to explore the new possibilities of interfaith dialogue. Witness, whether it be called "mission" or "dialogue," includes a desire both to know and to be known more fully. Such witness is intended as a positive, not a negative, act. When we speak of a mutual sharing of faith, we are not endorsing a religious syncretism. But we understand that when Lutherans and Jews speak to each other about matters of faith, there will be an exchange which calls for openness, honesty and mutual respect. One cannot reveal one's faith to another without recognizing the real differences that exist and being willing to take the risk of confronting these differences....

The State of Israel

The LCUSA "Guidelines" wisely suggest that "The State of Israel" be one of the topics for Jewish-Lutheran conversations. The tragic encounter of two peoples in the Middle East places a heavy responsibility upon Lutherans to be concerned about the legitimacy of the Jewish state, the rights of the Palestinians and the problems of all refugees.

The history and circumstances of the Israeli-Arab conflict are very complicated. It is understandable that Lutherans should be deeply divided in their evaluation of the situation in the Middle East. In Jewish opinion, Israel is more than another nation. It is a symbol of resurrection following upon the near-extinction of the Jewish people within living memory. There are also some Lutherans who find a religious significance in the State of Israel, seeing in recent events a fulfillment of biblical promises. Other Lutherans espouse not a "theology of the land," but a "theology of the poor," with special reference to the plight of the Palestinian refugees. Still other Lutherans endorse what might be called a "theology of human survival," believing that the validity of the State of Israel rests on juridical and moral grounds.

It seems clear that there is no consensus among Lutherans with respect to the relation between the "chosen people" and the territory comprising the present State of Israel. But there should be a consensus with respect to our obligation to appreciate, in a spirit of repentance for past misdeeds and silences, the factors which gave birth to the State of Israel and to give prayerful attention to the circumstances that bear on the search for Jewish and Arab security and dignity in the Middle East.

The Lutheran World Federation

Statement commended to member churches by the
Assembly of the LWF in 1984

We Lutherans take our name and much of our understanding of Christianity from Martin Luther. But we cannot accept or condone the violent verbal attacks that the reformer made against the Jews. Lutherans and Jews interpret the Hebrew Bible differently. But we believe that a Christological reading of the Scriptures does not lead to anti-Judaism, let alone anti-Semitism.

We hold that an honest, historical treatment of Luther's attacks on the Jews takes away from modern anti-Semites the assumption that they may legitimately call on the authority of Luther's name to bless their anti-Semitism. We insist that Luther does not support racial anti-Semitism, nationalistic anti-Semitism or political anti-Semitism. Even the deplorable religious anti-Semitism of the 16th century, to which Luther's attacks made an important contribution, is a horrible anachronism when translated to the conditions of the modern world. We recognize with deep regret, however, that Luther has been used to justify such anti-Semitism in the period of national socialism, and that his writings lent themselves to such abuse.

Although there remain conflicting assumptions, built into the beliefs of Judaism and Christianity, they need not and should not lead to the animosity and the violence of Luther's treatment of the Jews. Martin Luther opened up our eyes to a deeper understanding of the Old Testament and showed us the depth of our common inheritance and the roots of our faith. Many of the anti-Jewish utterances of Luther have to be explained in the light of his polemic against what he regarded as misinterpretations of the Scriptures. He attacked these interpretations, since for him everything now depended on a right understanding of the Word of God.

The sins of Luther's anti-Jewish remarks, the violence of his attacks on the Jews, must be acknowledged with deep distress. And all occasions for similar sin in the present or the future must be removed from our churches.

The Lutheran European Commission On the Church and the Jewish People

Statement adopted by the Commission at Driebergen,
The Netherlands, on May 8, 1990

At its meetings in Birmingham (1986), in Budapest (1987), in Vienna (1988), in Ustron (1989) and in Driebergen (1990), the Lutheran European Commission on the Church and the Jewish People – an association of Evangelical Lutheran churches and organizations from all parts of Europe – issued a joint statement about the attitude of Lutheran Christians from various European countries towards Jews and Judaism, on the basis of the present state of their knowledge and experience.

In this context, it became increasingly clear to what extent Christians, even after the Holocaust, have still to change their preaching and teaching and also their whole practice. The Churches as a whole, their organizations, their parishes and all their co-workers in the fields of preaching and teaching are facing great learning challenges.

Anew we have come to realize the extent to which theological assertions – then and now – have affected society and politics; and we have become aware of the great responsibility the Church has in this context. The reappraisal of history, and especially that of theology, is imperative, if we wish to attain credibility for the Church and to reform our living together in Europe.

The following assertions are addressed to the Evangelical Lutheran Christians within and outside the Churches represented here. It is our hope that they will help to renew the relationship between Christians and Jews.

(a) Fundamental Aspects

1. Since Jesus comes from the Jewish people and did not dissociate himself from them, and since the Old Testament was the Bible of Jesus and the early Church – Christians, by professing Jesus Christ, have a unique relationship with Jews and their faith, differing essentially from their relationship with other religions.

2. This relationship between Christians and Jews is rooted in the witness to the One God and His covenant, as handed down to us in the Scriptures of the Old Testament, which we have in common. In these Scriptures we read the same words, although we interpret and pass them on differently: Jews through the Talmud, and Christians through the New Testament.

3. God has chosen Israel as His people. This assertion has not been renounced. It has even been renewed and confirmed in the New Testament's confession of Jesus as the Messiah already come. Israel is not replaced by the Church.

4. We believe that God in His faithfulness has led His people of Israel through history and has preserved them as a people through the Jewish tradition of faith. We consider their return to the land of their fathers to be a sign of God's faithfulness to His covenant.

5. The Christian community originated within the Jewish people and needs, therefore, a relationship with Judaism for defining its own identity. Since its beginning, the Church has consisted of Jewish people as well as people of other nations. Messianic Jews (Hebrew Christians) can contribute to the Church's new and lasting consciousness of its Jewish roots. They can also make a special contribution to the encounter between Jews and Christians.

(b) The Holocaust and its Consequences

1. The Holocaust and the history of anti-Judaism as a whole present a far-reaching challenge to Christian doctrine and practice. Already when interpreting the Holy Scripture, anti-Jewish motifs and patterns of interpretation have to be identified and overcome in teaching and

preaching. Although, from a historical point of view, Christianity and Judaism have developed in mutual conflict, anti-Judaism does not belong to the doctrine of the Church. Nor can it be part of Christian teaching and practice.

2. Christian triumphalism, which has long been weighing heavily on the relationship between Christians and Jews, is incompatible with a serious encounter and an honest witness. Therefore, rethinking is necessary, within the Churches, with regard to theology and behaviour. Triumphalism is a feeling of superiority that compares the ideals of one's own religious tradition with the historical reality of others. Christian triumphalism – an expression of a *theologia gloriae* that disregards the cross of Christ – distorts assertions about Jesus by making them into assertions about the reality of the Church. In this context, Judaism in the time of Jesus is shown as a dark background against which the Church, then and now, can shine all the brighter. This attitude has often been used for justifying oppression and persecution.

3. We as a Church must learn to repent, in order to find a new relationship with Jews.

4. Jews and Christians are in search of salvation and redemption, and find different answers. According to the New Testament, salvation is revealed in Jesus Christ, who is preached as the way of salvation for Jews and Gentiles. All the more, we Christians need to meet our Jewish partners with humility, love and respect. We must listen to their expression of faith concerning reconciliation and redemption, and we must take it seriously. The last judgment on man will be passed by God and will remain His mystery.

The Evangelical Lutheran Church in America

To the Jewish Community

Statement adopted by the ELCA Church Council on April 18, 1994

In the long history of Christianity there exists no more tragic development than the treatment accorded the Jewish people on the part of Christian believers. Very few Christian communities of faith were able to escape the contagion of anti-Judaism and its modern successor, anti-Semitism. Lutherans belonging to the Lutheran World Federation and the Evangelical Lutheran Church in America feel a special burden in this regard because of certain elements in the legacy of the reformer Martin Luther and the catastrophes, including the Holocaust of the twentieth century, suffered by Jews in places where the Lutheran churches were strongly represented.

The Lutheran communion of faith is linked by name and heritage to the memory of Martin Luther, teacher and reformer. Honoring his name in our own, we recall his bold stand for truth, his earthy and sublime words of wisdom, and above all his witness to God's saving Word. Luther proclaimed a gospel for people as we really are, bidding us to trust a grace sufficient to reach our deepest shames and address the most tragic truths.

In the spirit of truth-telling, we who bear his name and heritage must with pain acknowledge also Luther's anti-Judaic diatribes and the violent recommendations of his later writings against the Jews. As did many of Luther's own contemporaries in the sixteenth century, we reject his violent invective, and yet more do we express our deep and abiding sorrow over its tragic effects on subsequent generations. In concert with the Lutheran World Federation, we particularly deplore the appropriation of Luther's words by modern anti-Semites for the teaching of hatred toward Judaism or toward the Jewish people in our day.

Grieving the complicity of our own tradition within this history of hatred, moreover, we express our urgent desire to live out our faith in Jesus Christ with love and respect for the Jewish people. We recognize in anti-Semitism a contradiction and an affront to the Gospel, a violation of our hope and calling, and we pledge this Church to oppose the deadly working of such bigotry, both within our own circles and in the society around us. Finally, we pray for the continued blessing of the Blessed One upon the increasing cooperation and understanding between Lutheran Christians and the Jewish community.

The Evangelical Lutheran Church in Canada, at its Fifth Biannual Convention, July 12–16, 1995, adopted an almost identical statement – addressed, like its American predecessor, to the Jewish community.

The Evangelical Lutheran Church in America

On Lutheran-Jewish Relations

Introduction to Guidelines adopted by the ELCA Church Council on November 16, 1998

As Lutherans, we seek to renew and enhance our relationship with the Jewish people, a relationship long distorted by misunderstanding and prejudice. In its 1994 Declaration to the Jewish Community, the Evangelical Lutheran Church in America publicly repudiated the anti-Jewish views of Martin Luther, expressed repentance for Christian complicity in hatred and violence against the Jews through the centuries, and committed itself to building a relationship with the Jewish people based on love and respect. For Lutherans to read, understand and acknowledge this Declaration can be a first step in renewing our relationship with the Jewish community. Reconciliation always begins with an understanding of the offense and a willingness to repent and amend one's ways. Only then can further steps be taken to forge a new relationship.

We as Christians share deep and common roots with Jews, not least books of Scripture revered by both communities. There is much to be gained in exploring those common roots, as well as the reasons for the "parting of the ways" during the first generations of the followers of Jesus. New Testament texts reflect at many points the hostility between the two communities, but also point to ways in which a new spirit of mutual respect and understanding can be achieved.

We as Christians also need to learn of the rich and varied history of Judaism since New Testament times, and of the Jewish people as a diverse, living community of faith today. Such an encounter with living and faithful Judaism can be profoundly enriching for Christian self-understanding. It is to nurture this blessing that we offer these guidelines for honest and faithful conversation and cooperation between Lutherans and Jews.

The World Council of Churches
On Authentic Christian Witness

Extract from conference paper on Christian-Jewish relations
adopted by the Jerusalem Conference of the
World Council of Churches Consultation on the
Church and the Jewish People, June 20–23, 1977

1. Proselytism, as distinct from Mission or Witness, is rejected in the strongest terms by the wcc: "Proselytism embraces whatever violates the right of the human person, Christian or non-Christian, to be free from external coercion in religious matters, or whatever, in the proclamation of the Gospel, does not conform to the ways God draws free men to Himself in response to His calls to serve in spirit and in truth" (*Ecumenical Review* 1/1971, p. 11).

We now realize more than ever before that the world in which we live is a world of religious pluralism. This demands from us that we treat those who differ from us with respect and that we strongly support the religious liberty of all.

2. This rejection of proselytism and our advocacy of respect for the integrity and identity of all peoples and faith-communities is the more urgent where Jews are concerned. For our relationship to the Jews is of a unique and very close character. Moreover, the history of "Christian" anti-Semitism and forced baptisms of Jews in the past makes it understandable that Jews are rightly sensitive towards all religious pressures from outside and all attempts as proselytizing.

3. We reject proselytism both in its gross and in its more refined forms. This implies that all triumphalism and every kind of manipulation are to be abrogated. We are called upon to minimize the

power dimension in our encounter with the Jews and to speak at every level from equal to equal. We have to be conscious of the pain and the perception of the others, and we have to respect their right to define themselves.

4. We are called upon to witness to God's love for and claim upon the whole of humankind. Our witness to Christ as Lord and Savior, however, is challenged in a special way where Jews are concerned. It has become discredited as a result of past behavior on the part of Christians. We therefore are seeking authentic and proper forms of Christian witness in our relations with the Jews. Some of us believe that we have to bear witness also to the Jews; some among us are convinced, however, that Jews are faithful and obedient to God even though they do not accept Jesus Christ as Lord and Savior. Many maintain that, as a separate and specific people, the Jews are an instrument of God with a specific God-given task and, as such, a sign of God's faithfulness to all humankind on the way towards ultimate redemption.

The World Council of Churches

On Jewish-Christian Dialogue

Excerpts from a study entitled "Ecumenical Considerations
on Jewish-Christian Dialogue," commended to the churches
by the Executive Committee of the World Council of
Churches at Geneva on July 16, 1982

1. Preface

1.1 One of the functions of dialogue is to allow participants to describe and witness to their faith in their own terms. This is of primary importance since self-serving descriptions of other peoples' faith are one of the roots of prejudice, stereotyping and condescension. Listening carefully to the neighbours' self-understanding enables Christians better to obey the commandment not to bear false witness against their neighbours, whether those neighbours be of long-established religious, cultural or ideological traditions or members of new religious groups. It should be recognized by partners in dialogue that any religion or ideology claiming universality, apart from having an understanding of itself, will also have its own interpretations of other religions and ideologies as part of its own self-understanding. Dialogue gives an opportunity for a mutual questioning of the understanding partners have about themselves and others. It is out of a reciprocal willingness to listen and learn that significant dialogue grows. (WCC Guidelines on Dialogue, III.4)

...

1.4 In the case of Jewish-Christian dialogue, a specific historical and theological asymmetry is obvious. While an understanding of

Judaism in New Testament times becomes an integral and indispensable part of any Christian theology, for Jews, a "theological" understanding of Christianity is of a less than essential or integral significance. Yet, neither community of faith has developed without awareness of the other.

1.5 The relations between Jews and Christians have unique characteristics because of the ways in which Christianity historically emerged out of Judaism. Christian understandings of that process constitute a necessary part of the dialogue and give urgency to the enterprise. As Christianity came to define its own identity over against Judaism, the Church developed its own understandings, definitions and terms for what it had inherited from Jewish traditions, and for what it read in the Scriptures common to Jews and Christians. In the process of defining its own identity, the Church defined Judaism and assigned to the Jews definite roles in its understanding of God's acts of salvation. It should not be surprising that Jews resent those Christian theologies in which they as a people are assigned to play a negative role. Tragically, such patterns of thought in Christianity have often led to overt acts of condescension, persecutions and worse.

1.6 Bible-reading and worshipping Christians often believe that they "know Judaism" since they have the Old Testament, the records of Jesus' debates with Jewish teachers and the early Christian reflections on the Judaism of their times. Furthermore, no other religious tradition has been so thoroughly "defined" by preachers and teachers in the Church as has Judaism. This attitude is often enforced by lack of knowledge about the history of Jewish life and thought through the 1,900 years since the parting of the ways of Judaism and Christianity.

1.7 For these reasons there is special urgency for Christians to listen, through study and dialogue, to ways in which Jews understand their history and their traditions, their faith and their obedience "in their own terms." Furthermore, a mutual listening to how each is perceived by the other may be a step towards understanding the hurts, overcoming the fears and correcting the misunderstandings that have thrived on isolation.

1.8 Both Judaism and Christianity comprise a wide spectrum of opinions, options, theologies and styles of life and service. Since generalizations often produce stereotyping, Jewish-Christian dialogue becomes the more significant by aiming at as full as possible a representation of views within the two communities of faith.

2. Towards a Christian Understanding of Jews and Judaism

2.1 Through dialogue with Jews, many Christians have come to appreciate the richness and vitality of Jewish faith and life in the covenant and have been enriched in their own understandings of God and the divine will for all creatures.

2.2 In dialogue with Jews, Christians have learned that the actual history of Jewish faith and experiences does not match the images of Judaism that have dominated a long history of Christian teaching and writing, images that have been spread by Western culture and literature into other parts of the world.

2.3 A classical Christian tradition sees the Church replacing Israel as God's people, and the destruction of the Second Temple of Jerusalem as a warrant for this claim. The covenant of God with the people of Israel was only a preparation for the coming of Christ, after which it was abrogated.

2.4 Such a theological perspective has had fateful consequences. As the Church replaced the Jews as God's people, the Judaism that survived was seen as a fossilized religion of legalism – a view now perpetuated by scholarship which claims no theological interests. Judaism of the first centuries before and after the birth of Jesus was therefore called "Late Judaism." The Pharisees were considered to represent the acme of legalism, Jews and Jewish groups were portrayed as negative models, and the truth and beauty of Christianity were thought to be enhanced by setting up Judaism as false and ugly.

2.5 Through a renewed study of Judaism and in dialogue with Jews, Christians have become aware that Judaism in the time of Christ was in an early stage of its long life. Under the leadership of the Pharisees, the Jewish people began a spiritual revival of remarkable power, which gave them the vitality capable of surviving the catastrophe of the loss of the temple. It gave birth to Rabbinic Judaism, which produced the Mishnah and Talmud and built the structures for a strong and creative life through the centuries.

2.6 As a Jew, Jesus was born into this tradition. In that setting he was nurtured by the Hebrew Scriptures, which he accepted as authoritative and to which he gave a new interpretation in his life and teaching. In this context Jesus announced that the Kingdom of God was at hand, and in his resurrection his followers found the confirmation of his being both Lord and Messiah.

2.7 Christians should remember that some of the controversies reported in the New Testament between Jesus and the "Scribes and Pharisees" find parallels within Pharisaism itself and its heir, Rabbinic Judaism. These controversies took place in a Jewish context, but when the words of Jesus came to be used by Christians who did not identify with the Jewish people as Jesus did, such sayings often became weapons in anti-Jewish polemics, and thereby their original intention was tragically distorted. An internal Christian debate is now taking place on the question of how to understand passages in the New Testament that seem to contain anti-Jewish references.

2.8 Judaism, with its rich history of spiritual life, produced the Talmud as the normative guide for Jewish life, in thankful response to the grace of God's covenant with the people of Israel. Over the centuries, important commentaries, profound philosophical works and poetry of spiritual depth have been added. For Judaism the Talmud is central and authoritative. Judaism is more than the religion of the Scriptures of Israel. What Christians call the Old Testament has received in the Talmud and later writings interpretations that for Jewish tradition share in the authority of Moses.

2.9 For Christians the Bible with the two Testaments is also followed by traditions of interpretation from the Church Fathers to the present time. Both Jews and Christians live in the continuity of their Scripture and Tradition.

2.10 Christians as well as Jews look to the Hebrew Bible as the story recording Israel's sacred memory of God's election and covenant with this people. For Jews it is their own story, in historical continuity with the present. Christians, mostly of gentile background since early in the life of the Church, believe themselves to be heirs to this same story by grace in Jesus Christ. The relationship between the two communities, both worshipping the God of Abraham, Isaac and Jacob, is a given historical fact, but how it is to be understood theologically is a matter of internal discussion among Christians, a discussion that can be enriched by dialogue with Jews....

3. Hatred and Persecution of Jews – A Continuing Concern

3.1 Christians cannot enter into dialogue with Jews without the awareness that hatred and persecution of Jews have a long, persistent history, especially in countries where Jews constitute a minority among Christians. The tragic history of the persecution of Jews includes massacres in Europe and the Middle East by the Crusaders, the Inquisition, pogroms and the Holocaust. The World Council of Churches Assembly at its first meeting in Amsterdam, 1948, declared: "We call upon the churches we represent to denounce antisemitism, no matter what its origin, as absolutely irreconcilable with the profession and practice of the Christian faith. Antisemitism is a sin against God and man." This appeal has been reiterated many times. Those who live where there is a record of acts of hatred against Jews can serve the whole Church by unmasking the ever-present danger they have come to recognize.

3.2 Teachings of contempt for Jews and Judaism in certain Christian traditions proved a spawning ground for the evil of the Nazi Holocaust. The Church must learn so to preach and teach the Gospel as to make sure that it cannot be used towards contempt for Judaism and against the Jewish people. A further response to the Holocaust by Christians, and one which is shared by their Jewish partners, is a resolve that it will never happen again to the Jews or to any other people.

3.3 Discrimination against and persecution of Jews have deep-rooted socio-economic and political aspects. Religious differences are magnified to justify ethnic hatred in support of vested interests. Similar phenomena are also evident in many interracial conflicts. Christians should oppose all such religious prejudices, whereby people are made scapegoats for the failures and problems of societies and political regimes.

3.4 Christians in parts of the world with a history of little or no persecution of Jews do not wish to be conditioned by the specific experiences of justified guilt among other Christians. Rather, they explore in their own ways the significance of Jewish-Christian relations from the earliest times to the present, for their life and witness....

The Council of Churches in The Netherlands

On Persistent Antisemitism

Introduction to the Council's Declaration on the subject intended for Dutch Christians and Churches, issued at Amersfoort in 1981

Antisemitism is an age-old phenomenon that time and again raises its head in many different forms: It seems to be ineradicable. Whoever had imagined that after the horrors of the Second World War it would have disappeared forever from our society has been sorely deceived.

Since the War, expressions of Jew-hatred have been heard many times. True, in most cases it was not a mass phenomenon, but even so it is of alarming persistence. Small fanatical groups may be responsible for desecrations of cemeteries, for abusive words on the street or over the telephone, and for painting anti-Jewish slogans and swastikas on synagogues and Jewish shops. But the incidental eruptions of Jew-hatred occasion great alarm and uncertainty among Jews. By such events, many are violently reminded of the Jewish persecutions before and during the Second World War; anxiously they ask themselves: Is it all starting again?

We should not forget that in the 1920s antisemitism began in Germany with small splinter groups, which originally nobody took seriously. Yet, as time went by, antisemitism – and other expressions of discrimination – ultimately found a fertile soil within wide strata of the population, due to disastrous economic regression. It is understandable, therefore, that Jewish fellow-citizens – and not only they – draw parallels between then and now. Today we also live in a time of economic regression and growing unemployment. Feelings of fear and hatred against "the other" are being fed, moreover, by the growing number of aliens in our country.

The Church cannot leave in doubt that she watches attentively and opposes any form of discrimination against minorities. That she calls special attention to the ever-recurrent flaring-up of antisemitism is due to the fact that a special tie exists between the Jewish people and the Church. Therefore she can and should speak about antisemitism in a special way.

The Presbyterian Church (USA)

A Theological Understanding of the
Relationship Between Christians and Jews

Text adopted by the 199th General Assembly of the
Presbyterian Church (USA) in June 1987

Background

This theological study is not unprecedented. Since World War II, state-ments and study documents dealing with Jewish-Christian relations have been issued by a number of churches and Christian bodies. Among these are the Vatican's Nostra Aetate (1965), the Report of the Faith and Order Commission of the World Council of Churches (1968), the statement of the Synod of the Reformed Church of Hol-land (1970), the statement of the French Bishops' Committee for Relations with the Jews (1973), the report of the Lutheran World Fed-eration (1975), the statement of the Synod of the Rhineland Church in West Germany (1980), the report of the Christian/Jewish Con-sultation Group of the Church of Scotland (1985) and the study of the World Alliance of Reformed Churches (1986).

The present study has been six years in preparation. It is the product of a project begun in 1981 within the former Presbyterian Church, US, then redeveloped and greatly expanded in scope and participation in 1983 upon the reunion which brought into being the Presbyterian Church (USA). The study has been developed under the direction of the church's Council on Theology and Culture, through a process which involved many people reflecting diverse interests and backgrounds, both in the United States and in the Middle East.

In the course of addressing this subject, our church has come to see many things in a new light. The study has helped us to feel the pain of our Jewish neighbors who remember that the Holocaust was carried out in the heart of "Christian Europe" by persons many of whom were baptized Christians. We have come to understand in a new way how our witness to the gospel can be perceived by Jews as an attempt to erode and ultimately to destroy their own communities. Similarly, we have been made sensitive to the difficult role of our Arab Christian brothers and sisters in the Middle East. We have listened to the anguish of the Palestinians, and we have heard their cry.

The paper which we here present to the church does not attempt to address every problem nor to say more than we believe that we are able truly to say. It consists of seven theological affirmations, with a brief explication of each. Together they seek to lay the foundation for a new and better relationship under God between Christians and Jews. They are –

1. a reaffirmation that the God who addresses both Christians and Jews is the same – the living and true God;
2. a new understanding by the church that its own identity is intimately related to the continuing identity of the Jewish people;
3. a willingness to ponder with Jews the mystery of God's election of both Jews and Christians to be a light to the nations;
4. an acknowledgment by Christians that Jews are in covenant relationship with God and the consideration of the implications of this reality for evangelism and witness;
5. a determination by Christians to put an end to "the teaching of contempt" for the Jews;
6. a willingness to investigate the continuing significance of the promise of "land" and its associated obligations and to explore the implications for Christian theology;
7. a readiness to act on the hope which we share with the Jews in God's promise of the peaceable kingdom.

These seven theological affirmations with their explications are offered to the church not to end debate but to inform it and thus to serve as a basis for an ever deepening understanding of the mystery of God's saving work in the world....

AFFIRMATIONS AND EXPLICATIONS

Affirmation

1. We affirm that the living God whom Christians worship is the same God who is worshiped and served by Jews. We bear witness that the God revealed in Jesus, a Jew, to be the Triune Lord of all, is the same one disclosed in the life and worship of Israel.

Explication

Christianity began in the context of Jewish faith and life. Jesus was a Jew, as were his earliest followers. Paul, the apostle of the Gentiles, referred to himself as a "Hebrew of the Hebrews." The life and liturgy of the Jews provided the language and thought forms through which the revelation in Jesus was first received and expressed. Jewish liturgical forms were decisive for the worship of the early church and are influential still, especially in churches of the Reformed tradition.

Yet the relationship of Christians to Jews is more than one of common history and ideas. The relationship is significant for our faith because Christians confess that the God of Abraham and Sarah and their descendants is the very One whom the apostles addressed as "the God and Father of our Lord Jesus Christ." The one God elected and entered into covenant with Israel to reveal the divine will and point to a future salvation in which all people will live in peace and righteousness. This expectation of the reign of God in a Messianic Age was described by the Hebrew prophets in different ways. The Scriptures speak of the expectation of a deliverer king anointed by God, of the appearing of a righteous teacher, of a suffering servant, or of a people enabled through God's grace to establish the Messianic Age. Early Christian preaching proclaimed that Jesus had become Messiah and Lord, God's anointed who has inaugurated the kingdom of peace and righteousness through his life, death and resurrection.

While some Jews accepted this message, the majority did not, choosing to adhere to the biblical revelation as interpreted by their teachers and continuing to await the fulfillment of the messianic promises given through the prophets, priests and kings of Israel.

Thus the bond between the community of Jews and those who came to be called Christians was broken, and both have continued as vital but separate communities through the centuries. Nonetheless, there are ties which remain between Christians and Jews: the faith of both in the one God whose loving and just will is for the redemption of all humankind, and the Jewishness of Jesus whom we confess to be the Christ of God.

In confessing Jesus as the Word of God incarnate, Christians are not rejecting the concrete existence of Jesus who lived by the faith of Israel. Rather, we are affirming the unique way in which Jesus, a Jew, is the being and power of God for the redemption of the world. In him, God is disclosed to be the Triune One who creates and reconciles all things. This is the way in which Christians affirm the reality of the one God who is sovereign over all.

Affirmation

2. We affirm that the church, elected in Jesus Christ, has been engrafted into the people of God established by the covenant with Abraham, Isaac and Jacob. Therefore, Christians have not replaced Jews.

Explication

The church, especially in the Reformed tradition, understands itself to be in covenant with God through its election in Jesus Christ. Because the church affirms this covenant as fundamental to its existence, it has generally not sought nor felt any need to offer any positive interpretation of God's relationship with the Jews, lineal descendants of Abraham, Isaac and Jacob, and Sarah, Rebekah, Rachel and Leah, with whom God covenanted long ago. The emphasis has fallen on the new covenant established in Christ and the creation of the church.

Sometime during the second century of the Common Era, a view called "supersessionism," based on the reading of some biblical texts and nurtured in controversy, began to take shape. By the beginning of the third century, this teaching that the Christian church had superseded the Jews as God's chosen people became the orthodox understanding of God's relationship to the church. Such a view influenced the church's understanding of God's relationship with the Jews and allowed the church to regard Jews in an inferior light.

Supersessionism maintains that because the Jews refused to receive Jesus as Messiah, they were cursed by God, are no longer in covenant with God, and that the church alone is the "true Israel" or the "spiritual Israel." When Jews continue to assert, as they do, that they are the covenant people of God, they are looked upon by many Christians as impertinent intruders, claiming a right which is no longer theirs. The long and dolorous history of Christian imperialism, in which the church often justified anti-Jewish acts and attitudes in the name of Jesus, finds its theological base in this teaching.

We believe and testify that this theory of supersessionism or replacement is harmful and in need of reconsideration as the church seeks to proclaim God's saving activity with humankind. The scriptural and theological bases for this view are clear enough; but we are prompted to look again at our tradition by events in our own time and by an increasing number of theologians and biblical scholars who are calling for such a reappraisal. The pride and prejudice which have been justified by reference to this doctrine of replacement themselves seem reason enough for taking a hard look at this position.

For us, the teaching that the church has been engrafted by God's grace into the people of God finds as much support in Scripture as the view of supersessionism and is much more consistent with our Reformed understanding of the work of God in Jesus Christ. The emphasis is on the continuity and trustworthiness of God's commitments and God's grace. The issue for the early church concerned the inclusion of the Gentiles in God's saving work, not the exclusion of the Jews. Paul insists that God is God of both Jews and Gentiles and justifies God's redemption of both on the basis of faith (Romans 3:29–30). God's covenants are not broken. "God has not rejected his people whom he foreknew" (Romans 11:2). The church has not "replaced" the Jewish people. Quite the contrary! The church, being made up primarily of those who were once aliens and strangers to the covenants of promise, has been engrafted into the people of God by the covenant with Abraham (Romans 11:17–18).

The continued existence of the Jewish people and of the church as communities elected by God is, as the apostle Paul expressed it, a "mystery" (Romans 11:25). We do not claim to fathom this mystery, but we cannot ignore it. At the same time we can never forget that we stand in a covenant established by Jesus Christ (Hebrews 8), and that faithfulness to that covenant requires us to call all women and men to faith in Jesus Christ. We ponder the work of God, including the wonder of Christ's atoning work for us.

Affirmation

3. We affirm that both the church and the Jewish people are elected by God for witness to the world, and that the relationship of the church to contemporary Jews is based on that gracious and irrevocable election of both.

Explication

God chose a particular people, Israel, as a sign and foretaste of God's grace toward all people. It is for the sake of God's redemption of the world that Israel was elected. The promises of God, made to Abraham and Sarah and to their offspring after them, were given so that blessing might come upon "all families of the earth" (Genesis 12:1–3). God continues that purpose through Christians and Jews. The church, like the Jews, is called to be a light to the nations (Acts 13:47). God's purpose embraces the whole creation.

In the electing of peoples, God takes the initiative. Election does not manifest human achievement but divine grace. Neither Jews nor Christians can claim to deserve this favor. Election is the way in which God creates freedom through the Holy Spirit for a people to be for God and for others. God, who is ever faithful to the word which has been spoken, does not take back the divine election. Whenever either the Jews or the church have rejected God's ways, God has judged but not rejected them. This is a sign of God's redeeming faithfulness toward the world.

Both Christians and Jews are elected to service for the life of the world. Despite profound theological differences separating Christians and Jews, we believe that God has bound us together in a unique relationship for the sake of God's love for the world. We testify to this election, but we cannot explain it. It is part of the purpose of God for the whole creation. Thus there is much common ground where Christians and Jews can and should act together.

Affirmation

4. We affirm that the reign of God is attested both by the continuing existence of the Jewish people and by the church's proclamation of the gospel of Jesus Christ. Hence, when speaking with Jews about matters of faith, we must always acknowledge that Jews are already in a covenantal relationship with God.

Explication

God, who acts in human history by the Word and Spirit, is not left without visible witnesses on the earth. God's sovereign and saving reign in the world is signified both by the continuing existence of and faithfulness within the Jewish people who, by all human reckoning, might be expected to have long since passed from the stage of history, and by the life and witness of the church.

As the cross of Jesus has always been a stumbling block to Jews, so also the continued existence and faithfulness of the Jews is often a stumbling block to Christians. Our persuasion of the truth of God in Jesus Christ has sometimes led Christians to conclude that Judaism should no longer exist, now that Christ has come, and that all Jews ought properly to become baptized members of the church. Over the centuries, many afflictions have been visited on the Jews by Christians holding this belief – not least in our own time. We believe that the time has come for Christians to stop and take a new look at the Jewish people and at the relationship which God wills between Christian and Jew.

Such reappraisal cannot avoid the issue of evangelism. For Jews, this is a very sensitive issue. Proselytism by Christians seeking to persuade, even convert, Jews often implies a negative judgment on Jewish faith. Jewish reluctance to accept Christian claims is all the more understandable when it is realized that conversion is often seen by them as a threat to Jewish survival. Many Jews who unite with the church sever their bonds with their people. On the other hand, Christians are commissioned to witness to the whole world about the good news of Christ's atoning work for both Jew and Gentile. Difficulty arises when we acknowledge that the same Scripture which proclaims that atonement and which Christians claim as God's word clearly states that Jews are already in a covenant relationship with God who makes and keeps covenants.

For Christians, there is no easy answer to this matter. Faithful interpretation of the biblical record indicates that there are elements of God's covenant with Abraham that are unilateral and unconditional. However, there are also elements of the covenant which appear to predicate benefits upon faithfulness (see Gen. 17:1 ff.). Christians, historically, have proclaimed that true obedience is impossible for a sinful humanity and thus have been impelled to witness to the atoning work of Jesus of Nazareth, the promised Messiah, as the way to a right relationship with God. However, to the present day, many Jews have been unwilling to accept the Christian claim and have continued in their covenant tradition. In light of Scripture, which testifies to God's repeated offer of forgiveness to Israel, we do not presume to judge in God's place. Our commission is to witness to the saving work of Jesus Christ; to preach good news among all the "nations" (ethne).

Dialogue is the appropriate form of faithful conversation between Christians and Jews. Dialogue is not a cover for proselytism. Rather, as trust is established, not only questions and concerns can be shared but faith and commitments as well. Christians have no reason to be reluctant in sharing the good news of their faith with anyone.

However, a militancy that seeks to impose one's own point of view on another is not only inappropriate but also counterproductive. In dialogue, partners are able to define their faith in their own terms, avoiding caricatures of one another, and are thus better able to obey the commandment, "Thou shalt not bear false witness against thy neighbor." Dialogue, especially in light of our shared history, should be entered into with a spirit of humility and a commitment to reconciliation. Such dialogue can be a witness that seeks also to heal that which has been broken. It is out of a mutual willingness to listen and to learn that faith deepens and a new and better relationship between Christians and Jews is enabled to grow.

Affirmation

5. We acknowledge in repentance the church's long and deep complicity in the proliferation of anti-Jewish attitudes and actions through its "teaching of contempt" for the Jews. Such teaching we now repudiate, together with the acts and attitudes which it generates.

Explication

Anti-Jewish sentiment and action by Christians began in New Testament times. The struggle between Christians and Jews in the first century of the Christian movement was often bitter and marked by mutual violence. The depth of hostility left its mark on early Christian and Jewish literature, including portions of the New Testament.

In subsequent centuries, after the occasions for the original hostility had long since passed, the church misused portions of the New Testament as proof texts to justify a heightened animosity toward Jews. For many centuries, it was the church's teaching to label Jews as "Christ-killers" and a "deicide race." This is known as the "teaching of contempt." Persecution of Jews was at times officially sanctioned and at other times indirectly encouraged or at least tolerated. Holy Week became a time of terror for the Jews.

To this day, the church's worship, preaching and teaching often lend themselves, at times unwittingly, to a perpetuation of the "teaching of contempt." For example, the public reading of Scripture without explicating potentially misleading passages concerning "the Jews," preaching which uses Judaism as a negative example in order to commend Christianity, public prayer which assumes that only the prayers of Christians are pleasing to God, teaching in the church school which reiterates stereotypes and non-historical ideas about the Pharisees and Jewish leadership – all of these contribute, however subtly, to a continuation of the church's "teaching of contempt."

It is painful to realize how the teaching of the church has led individuals and groups to behavior that has tragic consequences. It is agonizing to discover that the church's "teaching of contempt" was a major ingredient that made possible the monstrous policy of annihilation of Jews by Nazi Germany. It is disturbing to have to admit that the churches of the West did little to challenge the policies of their governments, even in the face of the growing certainty that the Holocaust was taking place. Though many Christians in Europe acted heroically to shelter Jews, the record reveals that most churches as well as governments the world over largely ignored the pleas for sanctuary for Jews.

As the very embodiment of anti-Jewish attitudes and actions, the Holocaust is a sober reminder that such horrors are actually possible in this world and that they begin with apparently small acts of disdain or expedience. Hence, we pledge to be alert for all such acts of denigration from now on, so that they may be resisted. We also pledge resistance to any such actions perpetrated by anyone, anywhere.

The church's attitudes must be reviewed and changed as necessary, so that they never again fuel the fires of hatred. We must be willing to admit our church's complicity in wrongdoing in the past, even as we try to establish a new basis of trust and communication with Jews. We pledge, God helping us, never again to participate in, to contribute to, or (insofar as we are able) to allow the persecution or denigration of Jews or the belittling of Judaism.

Affirmation
6. We affirm the continuity of God's promise of land along with the obligations of that promise to the people Israel.

Explication

As the Church of Scotland's (1985) report says:

> We are aware that in dealing with this matter we are entering a
> minefield of complexities across which is strung a barbed-wire
> entanglement of issues, theological, political and humanitarian.

However, a faithful explication of biblical material relating to the
covenant with Abraham cannot avoid the reality of the promise of
land. The question with which we must wrestle is how this promise is to be understood in the light of the existence of the modem
political State of Israel which has taken its place among the nations
of the world.

The Genesis record indicates that "the land of your sojourn-
ings" was promised to Abraham and his and Sarah's descendants.
This promise, however, included the demand that "you shall keep
my covenant..." (Genesis 17:7–9). The implication is that the blessings of the promise were dependent upon fulfillment of covenant
relationships. Disobedience could bring the loss of land, even while
God's promise was not revoked. God's promises are always kept, but
in God's own way and time.

The establishment of the State of Israel in our day has been seen
by many devout Jews as the fulfillment of God's divine promise. Other
Jews are equally sure that it is not, and regard the State of Israel as
an unauthorized attempt to flee divinely imposed exile. Still other
Jews interpret the State of Israel in purely secular terms. Christian
opinion is equally diverse. As Reformed Christians, however, we
believe that no government at any time can ever be the full expression of God's will. All, including the State of Israel, stand account-
able to God. The State of Israel is a geopolitical entity and is not to
be validated theologically.

God's promise of land bears with it obligation. Land is to be
used as the focus of mission, the place where a people can live and
be a light to the nations. Further, because land is God's to be given,
it can never be fully possessed. The living out of God's covenant in
the land brings with it not only opportunity but also temptation. The

history of the people of Israel reveals the continual tension between sovereignty and stewardship, blessing and curse.

The Hebrew prophets made clear to the people of their own day – as well, indeed, as any day – that those in possession of "land" have a responsibility and obligation to the disadvantaged, the oppressed and the "strangers in their gates." God's justice, unlike ours, is consistently in favor of the powerless (Ps. 103:6). Therefore we, whether Christian or Jew, who affirm the divine promise of land, however land is to be understood, dare not fail to uphold the divine right of the dispossessed. We have indeed been agents of the dispossession of others. In particular, we confess our complicity in the loss of land by Palestinians, and we join with those of our Jewish sisters and brothers who stand in solidarity with Palestinians as they cry for justice as the dispossessed.

We disavow any teaching which says that peace can be secured without justice through the exercise of violence and retribution. God's justice upholds those who cry out against the strong. God's peace comes to those who do justice and mercy on the earth. Hence we look with dismay at the violence and injustice occurring in the Middle East.

For three thousand years the covenant promise of land has been an essential element of the self-understanding of the Jewish people. Through centuries of dispersion and exile, Jews have continued to understand themselves as a people in relation to the God they have known through the promise of land. However, to understand that promise solely in terms of a specific geographical entity on the eastern shore of the Mediterranean is, in our view, inadequate.

"Land" is understood as more than place or property; "land" is a biblical metaphor for sustainable life, prosperity, peace and security. We affirm the rights to these essentials for the Jewish people. At the same time, as bearers of the good news of the gospel of Jesus Christ, we affirm those same rights in the name of justice to all peoples. We are aware that those rights are not realized by all persons in our day. Thus we affirm our solidarity with all people to whom those rights of "land" are currently denied.

We disavow those views held by some dispensationalists and some Christian Zionists that see the formation of the State of Israel as a signal of the end time, which will bring the Last Judgment, a conflagration which only Christians will survive. These views ignore the word of Jesus against seeking to set the time or place of the consummation of world history.

We therefore call on all people of faith to engage in the work of reconciliation and peacemaking. We pray for and encourage those who would break the cycles of vengeance and violence, whether it be the violence of states or of resistance movements, of terror or of retaliation. We stand with those who work toward nonviolent solutions, including those who choose nonviolent resistance. We also urge nation states and other political institutions to seek negotiated settlements of conflicting claims.

The seeking of justice is a sign of our faith in the reign of God.

Affirmation

7. We affirm that Jews and Christians are partners in waiting. Christians see in Christ the redemption not yet fully visible in the world, and Jews await the messianic redemption. Christians and Jews together await the final manifestation of God's promise of the peaceable kingdom.

Explication

Christian hope is continuous with Israel's hope and is unintelligible apart from it. New Testament teaching concerning the Kingdom of God was shaped by the messianic and apocalyptic vision of Judaism. That prophetic vision was proclaimed by John the Baptist, and the preaching of Jesus contained the same vision. Both Jews and Christians affirm that God reigns over all human destiny and has not abandoned the world to chaos and that, despite many appearances to the contrary, God is acting within history to establish righteousness and peace.

Jews still await the kingdom which the prophets foretold. Some look for a Messianic Age in which God's heavenly reign will be ushered in upon the earth. Christians proclaim the good news that in Christ "the Kingdom of God is at hand," yet, we too wait in hope for the consummation of the redemption of all things in God. Though the waiting of Jews and Christians is significantly different on account of our differing perception of Jesus, nonetheless, we both wait with eager longing for the fulfillment of God's gracious reign upon the earth – the kingdom of righteousness and peace foretold by the prophets. We are in this sense partners in waiting.

Both Christians and Jews are called to wait and to hope in God. While we wait, Jews and Christians are called to the service of God in the world. However that service may differ, the vocation of each shares at least these elements: a striving to realize the word of the prophets, an attempt to remain sensitive to the dimension of the holy, an effort to encourage the life of the mind, and a ceaseless activity in the cause of justice and peace. These are far more than the ordinary requirements of our common humanity; they are elements of our common election by the God of Abraham, Isaac and Jacob, and Sarah, Rebekah, Rachel and Leah. Precisely because our election is not to privilege but to service, Christians and Jews are obligated to act together in these things. By so acting, we faithfully live out our partnership in waiting. By so doing, we believe that God is glorified.

Fundamental Agreement Between the Holy See and the State of Israel

Signed in Jerusalem December 30, 1993

PREAMBLE

The Holy See and the State of Israel,

Mindful of the singular character and universal significance of the Holy Land;

Aware of the unique nature of the relationship between the Catholic Church and the Jewish people, and of the historic process of reconciliation and growth in mutual understanding and friendship between Catholics and Jews;

Having decided on July 29, 1992, to establish a Bilateral Permanent Working Commission in order to study and define together issues of common interest, and in view of normalizing their relations;

Recognizing that the work of the aforementioned commission has produced sufficient material for a first and fundamental agreement;

Realizing that such agreement will provide a sound and lasting basis for the continued development of their present and future relations and for the furtherance of the commission's task,

Agree upon the following articles:

ARTICLE 1

1. The State of Israel, recalling its Declaration of Independence, affirms its continuing commitment to uphold and observe the human right to freedom of religion and conscience, as set forth in the Universal

Declaration of Human Rights and in other international instruments to which it is a party.

2. The Holy See, recalling the Declaration on Religious Freedom of the Second Vatican Council, Dignitatis Humanae, affirms the Catholic Church's commitment to uphold the human right to freedom of religion and conscience, as set forth in the Universal Declaration of Human Rights and in other international instruments to which it is a party. The Holy See wishes to affirm as well the Catholic Church's respect for other religions and their followers as solemnly stated by the Second Vatican Council in its Declaration on the Relation of the Church to Non-Christian Religions, Nostra Aetate.

ARTICLE 2

1. The Holy See and the State of Israel are committed to appropriate cooperation in combating all forms of anti-Semitism and all kinds of racism and of religious intolerance, and in promoting mutual understanding among nations, tolerance among communities and respect for human life and dignity.

2. The Holy See takes this occasion to reiterate its condemnation of hatred, persecution and all other manifestations of anti-Semitism directed against the Jewish people and individual Jews anywhere, at any time and by anyone. In particular, the Holy See deplores attacks on Jews and desecration of Jewish synagogues and cemeteries, acts which offend the memory of the victims of the Holocaust, especially when they occur in the same places which witnessed it.

ARTICLE 3

1. The Holy See and the State of Israel recognize that both are free in the exercise of their respective rights and powers, and commit themselves to respect this principle in their mutual relations and in their cooperation for the good of the people.

2. The State of Israel recognizes the right of the Catholic Church to carry out its religious, moral, educational and charitable functions,

and to have its own institutions, and to train, appoint and deploy its own personnel in the said institutions or for the said functions to these ends. The Church recognizes the right of the state to carry out its functions, such as promoting and protecting the welfare and the safety of the people. Both the State and the Church recognize the need for dialogue and cooperation in such matters as by their nature call for it.

3. Concerning the Catholic legal personality at canon law, the Holy See and the State of Israel will negotiate on giving it full effect in Israeli law, following a report from a joint subcommission of experts.

ARTICLE 4

1. The State of Israel affirms its continuing commitment to maintain and respect the status quo in the Christian holy places to which it applies and the respective rights of the Christian communities thereunder. The Holy See affirms the Catholic Church's continuing commitment to respect the aforementioned status quo and the said rights.

2. The above shall apply notwithstanding an interpretation to the contrary of any article in this fundamental agreement.

3. The State of Israel agrees with the Holy See on the obligation of continuing respect for and protection of the character proper to Catholic sacred places, such as churches, monasteries, convents, cemeteries and their like.

4. The State of Israel agrees with the Holy See on the continuing guarantee of the freedom of Catholic worship.

ARTICLE 5

1. The Holy See and the State of Israel recognize that both have an interest in favoring Christian pilgrimages to the Holy Land. Whenever the need for coordination arises, the proper agencies of the church and of the state will consult and cooperate as required.

2. The State of Israel and the Holy See express the hope that such pilgrimages will provide an occasion for better understanding between the pilgrims and the people and religions of Israel.

ARTICLE 6
The Holy See and the State of Israel jointly reaffirm the right of the Catholic Church to establish, maintain and direct schools and institutes of study at all levels, this right being exercised in harmony with the rights of the state in the field of education.

ARTICLE 7
The Holy See and the State of Israel recognize a common interest in promoting and encouraging cultural exchanges between Catholic institutions worldwide and educational, cultural and research institutions in Israel, and in facilitating access to manuscripts, historical documents and similar source materials, in conformity with applicable laws and regulations.

ARTICLE 8
The State of Israel recognizes that the right of the Catholic Church to freedom of expression in the carrying out of its functions is exercised also through the church's own communications media, this right being exercised in harmony with the rights of the state in the field of communications media.

ARTICLE 9
The Holy See and the State of Israel jointly reaffirm the right of the Catholic Church to carry out its charitable functions through its health care and social welfare institutions, this right being exercised in harmony with the rights of the state in this field.

ARTICLE 10
1. The Holy See and the State of Israel jointly reaffirm the right of the Catholic Church to property.

2. Without prejudice to rights relied upon by the parties:

    a. The Holy See and the State of Israel will negotiate in good faith a comprehensive agreement, containing solutions acceptable to both parties, on unclear, unsettled and disputed issues concerning property, economic and fiscal matters relating to the Catholic Church generally or to specific Catholic Communities or institutions.

    b. For the purpose of the said negotiations, the Bilateral Permanent Working Commission will appoint one or more bilateral subcommissions of experts to study the issues and make proposals.

    c. The parties intend to commence the aforementioned negotiations within three months of entry into force of the present Agreement, and aim to reach agreement within two years from the beginning of the negotiations.

    d. During the period of these negotiations, actions incompatible with these commitments shall be avoided.

ARTICLE 11

1. The Holy See and the State of Israel declare their respective commitment to the promotion of the peaceful resolution of conflicts among states and nations, excluding violence and terror from international life.

2. The Holy See, while maintaining in every case the right to exercise its moral and spiritual teaching office, deems it opportune to recall that, owing to its own character, it is solemnly committed to remaining a stranger to all merely temporal conflicts, which principle applies specifically to disputed territories and unsettled borders.

ARTICLE 12

The Holy See and the State of Israel will continue to negotiate in good faith in pursuance of the agenda agreed upon in Jerusalem on July 15, 1992, and confirmed at the Vatican on July 29, 1992; likewise on issues arising from articles of this present Agreement, as well as on other issues bilaterally agreed upon as objects of negotiation.

ARTICLE 13

1. In this Agreement, the parties use these terms in the following sense:
   a. The Catholic Church and the Church – including, inter alia, its Communities and institutions.
   b. Communities of the Catholic Church – meaning the Catholic religious entities considered by the Holy See as Churches *sui iuris* and by the State of Israel as recognized religious communities.
   c. The State of Israel and the State – including, inter alia, its authorities established by law.

2. Notwithstanding the validity of this Agreement as between the parties, and without detracting from the generality of any applicable rule of law with reference to treaties, the parties agree that this Agreement does not prejudice rights and obligations arising from existing treaties between either party and a state or states, which are known and in fact available to both parties at the time of the signing of this Agreement.

ARTICLE 14

1. Upon the signing of the present Fundamental Agreement, and in preparation for the establishment of full diplomatic relations, the Holy See and the State of Israel exchange Special Representatives, whose rank and privileges are specified in an Additional Protocol.

2. Following the entry into force and immediately upon the beginning of the implementation of the present Fundamental Agreement, the Holy See and the State of Israel will establish full diplomatic relations, at the level of Apostolic Nunciature on the part of the Holy See, and Embassy on the part of the State of Israel.

ARTICLE 15

This Agreement shall enter into force on the date of the latter notification of ratification by a party.

Done in two original copies, in the English and Hebrew languages, both texts being equally authentic. In case of divergency, the English text shall prevail.

Signed in Jerusalem, this 30th day of the month of December, in the year 1993, which corresponds to the 16th day of the month of Tevet, in the year 5754.

[Signed by:]

For the State of Israel
Mr. Yossi Beilin
Deputy Foreign Minister

For the Holy See
Msgr. Claudio Maria Celli
Assistant Secretary of State

The Alliance of Baptists
On Jewish-Christian Relations

Statement adopted at Vienna, Virginia, on March 4, 1995

Background

Thirty years ago the Vatican document, Nostra Aetate, was adopted by the Second Vatican Council. This statement heralded a significant change in Jewish-Christian relations, first among Roman Catholics and soon thereafter among Protestant Christian bodies. As Baptists, we too have been influenced by this invitation to dialogue begun by Vatican II. Certain Baptists – persons like A. Jase Jones, Joe R. Estes, George Sheridan, Glenn Ingleheart and others – modeled out, for a brief moment in time, a different way to relate to the Jewish people and the Jewish faith. Regrettably, in recent years this effort at Jewish-Baptist dialogue has been reduced to a theology of conversion.

Fifty years ago the world stood in shocked disbelief at the evidence of humankind's inhumanity to its own, as the reality of places like Auschwitz-Birkenau, Treblinka, Sobibor, Belzec, Dachau, Buchenwald, Bergen-Belsen and Ravensbruck were forever etched into conscience and history. The madness, the hatred, the dehumanizing attitudes which led to the events known collectively as the Holocaust did not occur overnight or within the span of a few years, but were the culmination of centuries of Christian teaching and Church-sanctioned action directed against the Jews simply because they were Jews.

As Baptist Christians, we are the inheritors of – and, in our turn, have been the transmitters of – a theology which lays the blame for the death of Jesus at the feet of the Jews; a theology which has taken the anti-Jewish polemic of the Christian Scriptures out of its first century context and has made it normative for Christian-Jewish relations; a theology which has usurped for the Church the biblical promises and prerogatives given by God to the Jews; a theology which ignores nineteen centuries of Jewish development by viewing contemporary Jews as modern versions of their first century co-religionists; a theology which views the Jewish people and Jewish nationhood merely as pieces in an eschatological chess game; a theology which has valued conversion over dialogue, invective over understanding, and prejudice over knowledge; a theology which does not acknowledge the vibrancy, vitality and efficacy of the Jewish faith.

It is in recognition of a past and present among Baptists that is complicit in perpetuating negative stereotypes and myths concerning Jews, that we, the Alliance of Baptists meeting in convocation on March 4, 1995, at Vienna Baptist Church, Vienna, Virginia –

Confess our sin of complicity.

Confess our sin of silence.

Confess our sin of interpreting our sacred writings in such a way that we have created enemies of the Jewish people.

Confess our sin of indifference and inaction to the horrors of the Holocaust.

Confess our sins against the Jewish people.

Offer this confession with humility and with hope of reconciliation between Christians and Jews.

We call upon all Baptists to join us in –

1. Affirming the teaching of the Christian Scriptures that God has not rejected the community of Israel, God's covenant people (Romans 11:1–2), since "the gifts and calling of God are irrevocable" (Romans 11:29);

2. Renouncing interpretations of Scripture which foster religious stereotyping and prejudice against the Jewish people and their faith;

3. Seeking genuine dialogue with the broader Jewish community, a

dialogue built on mutual respect and the integrity of each other's faith;

4. Lifting our voices quickly and boldly against all expressions of antisemitism;

5. Educating ourselves and others on the history of Jewish-Christian relations from the first century to the present, so as to understand our present by learning from our past.

Joseph Cardinal Bernardin

Antisemitism: The Historical Legacy and the Continuing Challenge for Christians

Excerpts from an address delivered at the
Hebrew University of Jerusalem on March 23, 1995

In recent years the Catholic Church has undertaken important efforts to acknowledge guilt for the legacy of antisemitism and to repudiate as sinful any remaining vestiges of that legacy in its contemporary teaching and practice....antisemitism has deep roots in Christian history, which go back to the earliest days of the Church.... Inclusion of this history, as painful as it is for us to hear today, is a necessary requirement for authentic reconciliation between Christians and Jews in our time.

At the dawn of the twentieth century, the theology of perpetual divine judgment upon Jewish people... continued to exercise a decisive role in shaping Catholicism's initial reactions, for example, to the proposal for restoring a Jewish national homeland in Palestine. It also was of central importance in shaping popular Christian attitudes towards the Nazis and their stated goal of eliminating all Jews from Europe and beyond through deliberate extermination.... there is little doubt that this persistent tradition provided an indispensable seedbed for the Nazis' ability to succeed as far as they did in their master plan. They would not have secured the popular support they enjoyed, were it not for the continuing influence of traditional Christian antisemitism on the masses of baptized believers in Europe.

In the three decades or so since the beginning of the Second Vatican Council, the negative theology of the Jewish people has lost its theological foundations.... With its positive affirmation of continued covenantal inclusion on the part of the Jewish People after the coming of Christ Jesus, following St. Paul in Romans 9–11, the Council permanently removed all basis for the long-held "perpetual wandering" theology and the social deprivation and suffering that flowed from it. The Second Vatican Council's removal of the classical "displacement / perpetual wandering" theology from contemporary Catholic catechesis has been enhanced in subsequent documents from the Holy See and Pope John Paul II:

> ...the text of the new Catechism of the Catholic Church... reaffirms the two major points on which the Council built its new theological approach to the Jewish People. In Paragraph #597 the Catechism rejects any idea that all Jews then or now can be charged with the responsibility for Jesus' death....And #849 speaks of the distinctiveness of Jewish faith as an authentic response to God's original revelation and underlines the permanence of the divine promise made to the people Israel....

The Holy See's action in formally recognizing Israel through the [Holy See-Israel] Accords represents a final seal on the process begun at the Second Vatican Council to rid Catholicism of all vestiges of "displacement theology" and the implied notion of perpetual Jewish homelessness. The Accords represent the Catholic Church's full and final acknowledgment of Jews as a people, not merely as individuals....

For many baptized Christians, traditional Christian beliefs about Jews and Judaism constituted the primary motivation for their support, active or tacit, of the Nazi movement.... In the Church today, we must not minimize the extent of Christian collaboration with Hitler and his associates. It remains a profound moral challenge that we must continue to confront for our own integrity as a religious community....

Confronting the legacy of antisemitism will not prove easy, but confront it we must. Allow me to discuss several ways in which this can be done:

1. The history of antisemitism and of anti-Judaic theology must be restored to our teaching materials....

2. We also need an integral understanding of the Holocaust.... We need to re-emphasize the protest statements and oppositional actions of Christian leaders and grassroots groups and individuals....To be sure, there were not enough. But these Christians preserved a measure of moral integrity in the Church during these years of Nazi darkness. Nevertheless, the witness of these courageous Christian leaders, groups and individuals should never be used to argue against the need for a full scrutiny of Church activities by reputable scholars. We must be prepared to deal honestly and candidly with the genuine failures of some in the Christian Churches during that critical period....

3. Education about the Holocaust should become a prominent feature in Catholic education at every level....

4. Nostra Aetate and subsequent documents from the Holy See, as well as Pope John Paul ii, have not merely removed the classical prejudices against Jews and Judaism from Catholic teaching. They have laid out the basis for a positive theology of reconciliation and bonding. This, too, must become part of our current effort in education.... In this connection, I wish to add that it is my hope that, at the same time as we seek to develop a positive Christian understanding, Jewish educators will also be able to rethink the Jewish community's understanding of its relationship with the Church.

5. Liturgy and preaching are additional areas that require continued attention by the Church.... The great challenge of these liturgical seasons [Lent/Holy Week and Easter] is that they become times of reconciliation between Jews and Christians rather than conflict and division as they were in past centuries....

6. But education and preaching will not prove completely effective unless we also have women and men of vision and reconciliation who embody the new spirit of Jewish-Christian bonding....

7. Above all, in light of the history of antisemitism and the Holocaust, the Church needs to engage in public repentance....

Here in Jerusalem, where the vision of peace may seem very far off at times, there is need to find ways to cooperate for the development of a genuine peace among Christians, Jews and Muslims, Arabs and Israelis, that includes living faith communities with full opportunity for economic justice. Jerusalem, my brothers and sisters, cannot become a mere monument to peace. It must be a true city of living communities of peace, a true Neve Shalom. That is my prayer. That is my hope. That is my dream!

The Catholic Bishops of Germany

On the 50th Anniversary of the Liberation of the Death Camp at Auschwitz

Statement issued in Würzburg on January 23, 1995

(Excerpts in English translation)

On January 27, 1945, the concentration camps of Auschwitz I and Auschwitz-Birkenau were liberated. Countless human beings were murdered there in horrible fashion: Poles, Russians, Shintos and Gypsies, as well as members of other nations. The overwhelming majority of the prisoners and victims at this camp were Jews. That is why Auschwitz is the symbol of the destruction of European Jewry, designated as the Holocaust – or, using the Hebrew term, the Shoah.

The crime against the Jews was planned and set in motion by the Nazi authorities in Germany. The "unprecedented crime" of the Shoah (Pope John Paul II, June 13, 1991) still raises many questions, which we must not try to evade. The memory of the fiftieth anniversary of the liberation of Auschwitz represents, for German Catholics, an opportunity to re-examine their relationship with the Jews....

The fact weighs heavily upon us, today, that there were but few individual initiatives on behalf of persecuted Jews, and that even the pogroms of November 1938 did not elicit any public and explicit protest, when hundreds of synagogues were burned down and destroyed, cemeteries were violated, thousands of Jewish businesses were demolished, countless homes of Jewish families were damaged and plundered, and people were mocked, abused and even murdered. A retrospective look at the events of November 1938, and on the 12-year Nazi regime of terror, brings home to us the heavy burden of history. It reminds us "that the Church, which we hold to be sacred and which we honor as mystery, is also a Church that has sinned and is in need of repentance" (Statement of the German-speaking Bishops on the occasion of the 50th anniversary of the pogroms of November 1938).

The denial and guilt of that time are linked with the Churches as well. We are reminded of this by the testimony of the Joint Synod of the Bishoprics of the Federal Republic of Germany:

> Ours is the country whose most recent political history has been darkened by the attempt to systematically wipe out the Jewish people. And, during this Nazi era, notwithstanding the exemplary conduct of individual persons and groups, we were, on the whole, an ecclesiastical community that, to too great an extent, continued its daily life while turning its back on the fate of this persecuted Jewish people; whose eyes were fixed too much on the threat to its own institutions; and which remained silent in the face of the crimes being perpetrated against the Jews and against Judaism... In practice, the integrity of our will to renewal hinges also on our confession of this guilt and on our readiness to learn the painful lessons of this history of the guilt of our country and our Church.
>
> (*Our Hope* – Resolution adopted November 22, 1975)

We beg the Jewish people that it lend an ear to this statement of repentance and our will to renewal.

Auschwitz confronts us Christians with the question concerning our relationship with the Jews, and whether this relationship corresponds to the spirit of Jesus Christ. Antisemitism is "a sin against God and humankind," as Pope John Paul II has repeatedly stated. In the Church, there is no place for, and there must be no acquiescence in, hostility towards Jews. Christians must not harbor feelings of aversion or repugnance, and certainly not hatred, against Jews and Judaism. Wherever such an attitude makes its appearance, we are duty-bound publicly and explicitly to resist it.

The Church respects the autonomy of Judaism. At the same time, it must learn anew that it is descended from Israel and remains linked to its patrimony concerning faith, ethos and liturgy. Wherever possible, Christian and Jewish communities should cultivate mutual contacts. We must do everything in our power to enable Jews and Christians in our country to live together as good neighbors. In this way they will make their own distinctive contribution to a Europe whose past was darkened by the Shoah but which, in the future, is to become a continent of solidarity.

The Catholic Bishops of France

A Declaration of Repentance

Read on the 57th anniversary of the passage of antisemitic laws by the collaborationist Vichy government during the Nazi occupation of France, September 30, 1997

(Excerpts in English translation)

The time has come for the Church to submit her own history, especially that of this period, to critical examination, to recognize without hesitation the sins committed by members of the Church, and to beg forgiveness of God and humankind.

In France, the violent persecution did not begin immediately. But very soon, in the months that followed the 1940 defeat, antisemitism was sown at the state level, depriving French Jews of their rights and foreign Jews of their freedom; all of our national institutions were drawn into the applications of these legal measures. By February 1941, some 40,000 Jews were in French internment camps. At this point, in a country which had been beaten, lay prostrate and was partially occupied, the hierarchy saw the protection of its own faithful as its first priority, ensuring as much as possible its own institutions. The absolute priority which was given to these objectives, in themselves legitimate, had the unhappy effect of casting a shadow over the biblical demand of respect for every human being created in the image of God.

This retreat into a narrow vision of the Church's mission was compounded by a lack of appreciation on the part of the hierarchy of the immense global tragedy which was being played out and which was a threat to Christianity's future. Yet many members of the

Church and many non-Catholics yearned for the Church to speak out at a time of such spiritual confusion and to recall the message of Jesus Christ.

For the most part, those in authority in the Church, caught up in a loyalism and docility which went far beyond the obedience traditionally accorded to civil authorities, remained stuck in conformity, prudence and abstention. This was dictated in part by their fear of reprisals against the Church's activities and youth movements. They failed to realize that the Church, called at that moment to play the role of defender within a social body that was falling apart, did in fact have considerable power and influence, and that, in the face of the silence of other institutions, the words of the Church could have aroused reverberations that might have stemmed the tidal wave of irretrievable events.

It must be borne in mind: During the occupation no one knew the full extent of the Hitlerian genocide. While it is true that mention could be made of a great number of gestures of solidarity, we have to ask ourselves whether acts of charity and help are enough to fulfill the demands of justice and respect for the rights of human persons.

So it is that, given the antisemitic legislation enacted by the French government – beginning with the October 1940 law on Jews and that of June 1941, which deprived a whole section of the French people of their rights as citizens, which hounded them out and treated them as inferior beings within the nation – and given the decision to put into internment camps foreign Jews who had thought they could rely on the right of asylum and hospitality in France, we are obliged to admit that the bishops of France made no public statements, thereby acquiescing by their silence in the flagrant violation of human rights and leaving the way open to a death-bearing chain of events.

We can pass no judgment on the consciences of the people of that era. Nor are we ourselves guilty of the things that were done then. We can, however, and we must be fully aware of the cost of such behavior and actions. It is our Church, and we are obliged to acknowledge objectively today that ecclesiastical interests, understood in an overly restrictive sense, took priority over the demands of conscience – and we must ask ourselves why...

Before the war, Jacques Maritain, both in articles and in lectures, tried to open Christians up to a different perspective on the Jewish people. He also forcefully warned against the perversity of the anti-semitism that was developing. Just before the war broke out, Cardinal Saliege advised Catholics of the 20th century to seek light in the teaching of Pius xi rather than in that of the 13th-century edicts of Innocent iii. During the war, theologians and exegetes in Paris and in Lyons spoke out prophetically about the Jewish roots of Christianity, underlining how the shoot of Jesse flowered in Israel, that the two Testaments were indissolubly linked, that the Virgin, Christ and the Apostles were all Jews and that Christianity is linked to Judaism like a branch to the trunk that has borne it. Why was so little attention paid to such words?

...

In the process which led to the Shoah, we are obliged to admit the role, indirect if not direct, played by commonly held anti-Jewish prejudices, which Christians were guilty of maintaining. In fact, in spite of (and to some extent because of) the Jewish roots of Christianity, and because of the Jewish people's fidelity throughout its history to the one God, the "original separation" dating back to the first century became a divorce, then an animosity and ultimately a centuries-long hostility between Christians and Jews....

In the judgment of historians, it is a well-proved fact that for centuries, up until Vatican Council ii, an anti-Jewish tradition stamped its mark in differing ways on Christian doctrine and teaching, in theology, apologetics, preaching and in the liturgy. It was on such ground that the venomous plant of hatred for the Jews was able to flourish. Hence, the heavy inheritance we still bear in our century, with all its consequences which are so difficult to wipe out. Hence our still open wounds.

To the extent that the pastors and those in authority in the Church let such a teaching of disdain develop for so long, along with an underlying basic religious culture among Christian communities which shaped and deformed people's attitudes, they bear a grave responsibility. Even if they condemned antisemitic theologies as being pagan in origin, they did not enlighten people's minds as they ought, because they failed to call into question these centuries-old ideas and attitudes. This had a soporific effect on people's consciences, reducing their capacity to resist when the full violence of Nazi antisemitism rose up, the diabolical and ultimate expression of hatred of the Jews, based on categories of race and blood, and which was explicitly directed to the physical annihilation of the Jewish people – "total and premeditated destruction," in the words of Pope John Paul ii.

Subsequently, when the persecution became worse and the genocidal policy of the Third Reich was unleashed within France itself, shared by the Vichy government, which put its own force at the disposition of the occupier, some brave bishops raised their voices in a clarion call, in the name of human rights, against the rounding up of the Jewish population. These public statements, though few in number, were heard by many Christians. Neither should the many actions undertaken by ecclesiastical authorities to save men, women and children in danger of death be forgotten; nor the outpouring of Christian charity by the ordinary faithful, shown in generosity of every kind, often at great risk, in saving thousands and thousands of Jews....

Nevertheless, while it may be true that some Christians – priests, religious and lay people – were not lacking in acts of courage in defense of fellow human beings, we must recognize that indifference won the day over indignation in the face of the persecution of the Jews and that, in particular, silence was the rule in face of the multifarious laws enacted by the Vichy government, whereas speaking out in favor of the victims was the exception. As François Mauriac wrote, "A crime of such proportions falls, in no small part, on the shoulders of those witnesses who failed to cry out, and this whatever the reason for their silence."

The end result is that the attempt to exterminate the Jewish people, instead of being perceived as a central question, in human and spiritual terms, remained a secondary consideration. In the face of so great and utter a tragedy, too many of the Church's pastors committed an offense, by their silence, against the Church itself and its mission.

Today we confess that such silence was a sin. In so doing, we recognize that the Church of France failed in her mission as teacher of consciences, and that therefore she carries, along with the Christian community as a whole, the responsibility for failing to lend their aid, from the very first moments, when protest and rescue were still possible, as well as necessary – even if, subsequently, a great many acts of courage were performed.

This is a fact that we acknowledge today. This failure of the Church of France and of her responsibility toward the Jewish people are part of our history. We confess this sin. We beg God's pardon, and we call upon the Jewish people to hear our words of repentance.

This act of remembering calls us to an ever keener vigilance on behalf of humankind today and in the future.

The United Methodist Church, USA

Building New Bridges in Hope

Statement adopted by the UMC's General Conference in April 1996

"God, whom Christians have come to know in Jesus Christ, has created all human beings in the divine image, and...God desires that all people live in love and righteousness...While we are committed to the promotion of mutual respect and understanding among people of all living faiths, we as Christians recognize a special relationship between Christians and Jews because of our shared roots in biblical revelation."
(From Statement adopted at Sigtuna, Sweden, by the Consultation on the Church and the Jewish People, sponsored by the World Council of Churches, 1988)

A Quest For New Understanding

What is the relationship that God intends between Christianity and Judaism, between Christians and Jews? In The United Methodist Church, a search for understanding and appropriate response to this important theological and relational question has been under way for some time. A significant step in the development of United Methodist understanding of and intention for Christian-Jewish relations was taken in 1972 when the General Conference adopted a position statement under the title, Bridge in Hope. This denominational statement urged church members and congregations to undertake "serious new conversations" with Jews in order to promote "growth in mutual understanding." As it has been studied and used, Bridge in

Hope has served as a strong foundation for United Methodist-Jewish dialogue in many settings.

Since 1972 other Christian denominations, as well as ecumenical bodies in which The United Methodist Church participates, such as the World Council of Churches, have also made statements on Christian-Jewish relations. Those voices have contributed to our further knowledge, reflection and understanding. At the same time, we have learned much from the many relationships and dialogues that have flourished between Jews and Christians locally, nationally and internationally.

Especially crucial for Christians in our quest for understanding has been the struggle to recognize the horror of the Holocaust as the catastrophic culmination of a long history of anti-Jewish attitudes and actions in which Christians, and sometimes the Church itself, have been deeply implicated. Dialogues with Jewish partners have been central for Christians in our process of learning of the scope of the Holocaust atrocities, acknowledgment of complicity and responsibility, repentance and commitment to work against anti-Semitism in all its forms in the future.

We are aware, however, that the Christian-Jewish bridge of understanding has only begun to be constructed. The United Methodist Church is committed to continuing clarification and expansion of our knowledge of Judaism and to strengthening our relationships with Jewish people. We seek mutual exploration of the common ground underlying Christianity and Judaism as well as that which makes each faith unique. This statement is an expression of the principles of that commitment.

As with all theological questions, United Methodists approach the issues of interfaith relationships, including Christian-Jewish dialogue, by seeking understanding of God's will in scripture in the context of tradition, reason and experience. In that spirit and with that intention, we affirm the following principles for continued study, discussion and action within The United Methodist Church, with other Christians, and especially with Jews.

Guiding Principles for Christian-Jewish Relations

In order to increase our understanding of and with peoples of other living faith traditions, of ourselves as followers of Jesus Christ and of God and God's truth, The United Methodist Church encourages dialogue and experiences with those of other faiths. For important and unique reasons, including a treasury of shared scripture and an ancient heritage that belong to us in common but which also contain our dividedness, we look particularly for such opportunities with Jews. United Methodist participation in Christian-Jewish dialogue and relationships is based on the following understandings:

1. There is one living God in whom both Jews and Christians believe.
While the Jewish and Christian traditions understand and express their faith in the same God in significantly different ways, we believe with Paul that God, who was in Christ reconciling the world to God's own self (11 Corinthians 5:18–19), is none other than the God of Israel, maker of heaven and earth. Above all else, Christians and Jews are bonded in our joyful and faithful response to the one God, living our faith as each understands God's call.

2. Jesus was a devout Jew, as were many of his first followers.
We know that understanding our Christian faith begins by recognizing and appreciating this seminal fact. Neither the ministry of Jesus and his apostles, nor the worship and thought of the early Church, can be understood apart from the Jewish tradition, culture and worship of the first century. Further, we believe that God's revelation in Jesus Christ is unintelligible apart from the story of what God did in the life of the people of Israel.

Because Christianity is firmly rooted in biblical Judaism, we understand that knowledge of these roots is essential to our faith. As expressed in a statement from the Consultation on the Church and the Jewish People of the World Council of Churches: "We give thanks to God for the spiritual treasure we share with the Jewish people: faith in the living God of Abraham, Isaac and Jacob; knowledge of the name of God and of the commandments; the prophetic proclamation of judgment and grace; the Hebrew scriptures; and the hope of the coming kingdom. In all these we find common roots in biblical revelation and see spiritual ties that bind us to the Jewish people."

3. Judaism and Christianity are living and dynamic religious movements that have continued to evolve since the time of Jesus, often in interaction with each other and with God's continual self-disclosure in the world.

Christians often have little understanding of the history of Judaism as it has developed since the lifetime of Jesus. As a World Council of Churches publication points out: "Bible-reading and worshiping Christians often believe that they 'know Judaism' since they have the Old Testament, the records of Jesus' debates with Jewish teachers and the early Christian reflections on the Judaism of their times...This attitude is often reinforced by lack of knowledge about the history of Jewish life and thought through the 1900 years since the parting of the ways of Judaism and Christianity."

As Christians, it is important for us to recognize that Judaism went on to develop vital new traditions of its own after the time of Jesus, including the Rabbinic Judaism that is still vibrant today in shaping Jewish religious life. This evolving tradition has given the Jewish people profound spiritual resources for creative life through the centuries. We increase our understanding when we learn about the rich variety of contemporary Jewish faith practice, theological interpretation and worship, and discover directly through dialogue how Jews understand their own history, tradition and faithful living.

4. Christians and Jews are bound to God though biblical covenants that are eternally valid.

As Christians, we stand firm in our belief that Jesus was sent by God as the Christ to redeem all people, and that in Christ the biblical covenant has been made radically new. While Church tradition has taught that Judaism has been superseded by Christianity as the "new Israel," we do not believe that earlier covenantal relationships have been invalidated or that God has abandoned Jewish partners in covenant.

We believe that just as God is steadfastly faithful to the biblical covenant in Jesus Christ, likewise God is steadfastly faithful to the biblical covenant with the Jewish people. The covenant God established with the Jewish people through Abraham, Moses and others continues because it is an eternal covenant. Paul proclaims that the gift and call of God to the Jews is irrevocable (Romans 11:29). Thus we believe that the Jewish people continue in covenantal relationship with God.

Both Jews and Christians are bound to God in covenant, with no covenantal relationship invalidated by any other. Though Christians and Jews have different understandings of the covenant of faith, we are mysteriously bound to one another through our covenantal relationships with the one God and creator of us all.

5. As Christians, we are clearly called to witness to the gospel of Jesus Christ in every age and place. At the same time, we believe that God has continued, and continues today, to work through Judaism and the Jewish people.

Essential to the Christian faith is the call to proclaim the good news of Jesus Christ to all people. Through the announcement of the gospel in word and work comes the opportunity for others to glimpse the glory of God which we have found through Jesus Christ. Yet we also understand that the issues of the evangelization of persons of other faiths, and of Jews in particular, are often sensitive and difficult. These issues call for continuing serious and respectful reflection and dialogue among Christians and with Jews.

While we as Christians respond faithfully to the call to proclaim the gospel in all places, we can never presume to know the full extent of God's work in the world, and we recognize the reality of God's activity outside the Christian Church. It is central to our faith that salvation is not accomplished by human beings but by God. We know that judgment as to the ultimate salvation of persons from any faith community, including Christianity and Judaism, belongs to God alone.

It is our belief that Jews and Christians are co-workers and companion pilgrims who have made the God of Israel known throughout the world. Through common service and action, we jointly proclaim the God we know. Together, through study and prayer, we can learn how the God we believe to be the same God speaks and calls us continually into closer relationship with each other as well as with God.

6. As Christians, we are called into dialogue with our Jewish neighbors. Christians and Jews hold a great deal of scripture, history and culture in common. And yet, we also share two thousand painful years of anti-Semitism and the persecution of Jews by Christians. These two apparently discordant facts move Christians to seek common experiences with Jews, and especially to invite them into dialogue to explore the meaning of our kinship and our differences. Our intention is to learn about the faith of one another and to build bridges of understanding.

While, for Christians, dialogue will always include testimony to God's saving acts in Jesus Christ, it will include in equal measure listening to and respecting the understanding of Jews as they strive to live in obedience and faithfulness to God as they understand the conditions of their faith.

Productive interfaith dialogue requires focused, sustained conversation based on willingness to recognize and probe genuine differences while also seeking that which is held in common. We are called to openness, so that we may learn how God is speaking through our dialogue partners. As stated in the World Council of Churches Guidelines on Dialogue, "One of the functions of dialogue is to allow participants to describe and witness to their faith on their own terms... Participants seek to hear each other in order to better understand each other's faith, hopes, insights and concerns." Fruitful and respectful dialogue is centered in a mutual spirit of humility, trust, openness to new understanding and commitment to reconciliation and the healing of the painful wounds of our history.

7. As followers of Jesus Christ, we deeply repent of the complicity of the Church, and the participation of many Christians, in the long history of persecution of the Jewish people. The Christian Church has a profound obligation to correct historical and theological teachings that have led to false and pejorative perceptions of Judaism and contributed to persecution and hatred of Jews. It is our responsibility as Christians to oppose anti-Semitism whenever and wherever it occurs.

We recognize with profound sorrow that, repeatedly and often in the last two thousand years, the worship, preaching and teaching of the Christian Church have allowed and sometimes even incited and directed persecution against Jews.

The Church today carries grave responsibility to counter the evil done by Christians to Jews in the Crusades, the Inquisition, the pogroms of Eastern Europe and elsewhere, carried out in the name of Jesus Christ. In the twentieth century there is the particular shame in the failure of most of the Church to challenge the policies of governments that were responsible for the unspeakable atrocities of the Holocaust.

Historically and today, both the selective use and the misuse of scripture have fostered negative attitudes toward and actions against Jews. Use of New Testament passages that blame "the Jews" for the crucifixion of Jesus have throughout history been the basis of many acts of discrimination against Jews, frequently involving physical violence. There is no doubt that traditional and often officially sanctioned and promulgated Christian teachings, including the uncritical use of anti-Jewish New Testament writings, have caused untold misery and form the basis of modern anti-Semitism.

Misinterpretations and misunderstanding of historical and contemporary Judaism continue, including the mistaken belief that Judaism is a religion solely of law and judgment while Christianity is a religion of love and grace. The characterizations of God in the Hebrew Bible (called the Old Testament by Christians) are rich and diverse; strong images of a caring, compassionate and loving deity are dominant for Jews as well as for Christians. Further, there are parallels between New Testament Christian understandings of the "spirit of the law" and contemporaneous theological developments in first-century Jewish theology.

The Church has an obligation to correct erroneous and harmful past teachings and to ensure that the use of scripture, as well as the preparation, selection and use of liturgical and educational resources, does not perpetuate misleading interpretations and misunderstanding of Judaism.

It is also essential for Christians to oppose forcefully anti-Jewish acts and rhetoric that persist in the present time in many places. We must be zealous in challenging overt and subtle anti-Semitic stereotypes and bigoted attitudes that ultimately made the Holocaust possible, and that stubbornly and insidiously continue today. These lingering patterns are a call to Christians for ever-new educational efforts and continued vigilance, so that we, remembering and honoring the cries of the tortured and dead, can claim with Jews around the world to be faithful to the post-Holocaust cry of "Never Again!"

8. As Christians, we share a call with Jews to work for justice, compassion and peace in the world, in anticipation of the fulfillment of God's reign.

Together, Jews and Christians honor the commandment to love God with all our heart, soul and might. It is our task to join in common opposition to those forces – nation, race, power, money – that clamor for ultimate allegiance. Together, we honor the commandment to love neighbor as self. It is our task to work in common for those things that are part of God's work of reconciliation. Together, we affirm the sacredness of all persons and the obligation of stewardship for all God has created.

Jews still await the messianic reign of God foretold by the prophets. Christians proclaim the good news that in Jesus Christ "the kingdom of God is at hand"; yet we, as Christians, also wait in hope for the consummation of God's redemptive work. Together, Jews and Christians long for and anticipate the fulfillment of God's reign. Together, we are "partners in waiting." In our waiting, we are called to witness and to work for God's reign together.

9. As United Methodist Christians, we are deeply affected by the anguish and suffering that continue for many people who live in the Middle East region which includes modern Israel. We commit ourselves, through prayer and advocacy, to bring about justice and peace for those of every faith.

Within The United Methodist Church, we struggle with our understanding of the complexity and the painfulness of the controversies in which Christians, Jews and Muslims are involved in the Middle East. The issues include disputed political questions of sovereignty and control, and concerns over human rights and justice. We recognize the theological significance of the holy land as central to the worship, historical traditions, hope and identity of the Jewish people. We are mindful of this land's historic and contemporary importance for Christians and Muslims. We are committed to the security, safety and well-being of Jews and Palestinians in the Middle East, to respect for the legitimacy of the State of Israel, to justice and sovereignty for the Palestinian people and to peace for all who live in the region.

As we join with others of many religious communities in wrestling with these issues and searching for solutions, we seek to work together with other Christians, Jews and Muslims to honor the religious significance of this land and to bring about healthy, sustainable life, justice and peace for all.

New Bridges to Christian-Jewish Understanding

The above statements of principle and affirmation offer a foundation for theological reflection within The United Methodist Church and with other Christians on our understanding of our relationships with the Jewish people. They are meant to be the basis of study, discussion and action as we strive for greater discernment within the Church.

Further, we hope that these statements of guiding principle will be important as bases of cooperative efforts, and especially for dialogue between United Methodists (sometimes in the company of other Christians) and Jewish communities, as we mutually explore the meaning of our kinship and our differences.

Using the foregoing foundation and principles, The United

Methodist Church encourages dialogue with Jews at all levels of the Church, including, and especially, local congregations. It is also hoped that there will be many other concrete expressions of Jewish-Christian relationships, such as participating in special occasions of interfaith observance, joint acts of common service and programs of social transformation. These offer great opportunity to Christians and Jews to build relationships and, together, work for justice and peace (shalom) in their communities and in the world, serving humanity as God intends.

We dare to believe that such conversations and acts will build new bridges in hope between Christians and Jews, and that they will be among the signs and first fruits of our sibling relationship under our parent God. Together, we await and strive for the fulfillment of God's reign.

Dabru Emet
"Speak the Truth" Zech. 8:16
A Jewish Statement on
Christians and Christianity

Published in *The New York Times* and *The Baltimore Sun*
on September 11, 2000

In recent years, there has been a dramatic and unprecedented shift
in Jewish and Christian relations. Throughout the nearly two millennia of Jewish exile, Christians have tended to characterize Judaism as a failed religion or, at best, a religion that prepared the way
for, and is completed in, Christianity. In the decades since the Holocaust, however, Christianity has changed dramatically. An increasing
number of official Church bodies, both Roman Catholic and Protestant, have made public statements of their remorse about Christian
mistreatment of Jews and Judaism. These statements have declared,
furthermore, that Christian teaching and preaching can and must be
reformed so that they acknowledge God's enduring covenant with
the Jewish people and celebrate the contribution of Judaism to world
civilization and to Christian faith itself.

We believe these changes merit a thoughtful Jewish response.
Speaking only for ourselves – an interdenominational group of Jewish scholars – we believe it is time for Jews to learn about the efforts
of Christians to honor Judaism. We believe it is time for Jews to
reflect on what Judaism may now say about Christianity. As a first
step, we offer eight brief statements about how Jews and Christians
may relate to one another.

1. Jews and Christians worship the same God. Before the rise of
Christianity, Jews were the only worshipers of the God of Israel. But

Christians also worship the God of Abraham, Isaac and Jacob, creator of heaven and earth. While Christian worship is not a viable religious choice for Jews, as Jewish theologians we rejoice that, through Christianity, hundreds of millions of people have entered into relationship with the God of Israel.

2. Jews and Christians seek authority from the same book – the Bible (what Jews call "Tanakh" and Christians call the "Old Testament"). Turning to it for religious orientation, spiritual enrichment and communal education, we each take away similar lessons: God created and sustains the universe; God established a covenant with the people Israel; God's revealed word guides Israel to a life of righteousness; and God will ultimately redeem Israel and the whole world. Yet, Jews and Christians interpret the Bible differently on many points. Such differences must always be respected.

3. Christians can respect the claim of the Jewish people upon the land of Israel. The most important event for Jews since the Holocaust has been the re-establishment of a Jewish state in the Promised Land. As members of a biblically based religion, Christians appreciate that Israel was promised – and given – to Jews as the physical center of the covenant between them and God. Many Christians support the State of Israel for reasons far more profound than mere politics. As Jews, we applaud this support. We also recognize that Jewish tradition mandates justice for all non-Jews who reside in a Jewish state.

4. Jews and Christians accept the moral principles of Torah. Central to the moral principles of Torah is the inalienable sanctity and dignity of every human being. All of us were created in the image of God. This shared moral emphasis can be the basis of an improved relationship between our two communities. It can also be the basis of a powerful witness to all humanity for improving the lives of our fellow human beings and for standing against the immoralities and idolatries that harm and degrade us. Such witness is especially needed after the unprecedented horrors of the past century.

5. Nazism was not a Christian phenomenon. Without the long history of Christian anti-Judaism and Christian violence against Jews, Nazi ideology could not have taken hold nor could it have been carried out. Too many Christians participated in, or were sympathetic to, Nazi atrocities against Jews. Other Christians did not protest sufficiently against these atrocities. But Nazism itself was not an inevitable outcome of Christianity. If the Nazi extermination of the Jews had been fully successful, it would have turned its murderous rage more directly to Christians. We recognize with gratitude those Christians who risked or sacrificed their lives to save Jews during the Nazi regime. With that in mind, we encourage the continuation of recent efforts in Christian theology to repudiate unequivocally contempt of Judaism and the Jewish people. We applaud those Christians who reject this teaching of contempt, and we do not blame them for the sins committed by their ancestors.

6. The humanly irreconcilable difference between Jews and Christians will not be settled until God redeems the entire world as promised in Scripture. Christians know and serve God through Jesus Christ and the Christian tradition. Jews know and serve God through Torah and the Jewish tradition. That difference will not be settled by one community insisting that it has interpreted Scripture more accurately than the other; nor by exercising political power over the other. Jews can respect Christians' faithfulness to their revelation, just as we expect Christians to respect our faithfulness to our revelation. Neither Jew nor Christian should be pressed into affirming the teaching of the other community.

7. A new relationship between Jews and Christians will not weaken Jewish practice. An improved relationship will not accelerate the cultural and religious assimilation that Jews rightly fear. It will not change traditional Jewish forms of worship, nor increase intermarriage between Jews and non-Jews, nor persuade more Jews to convert to Christianity, nor create a false blending of Judaism and Christianity. We respect Christianity as a faith that originated within Judaism and that still has significant contacts with it. We do not see it as an extension of Judaism. Only if we cherish our own traditions can we pursue this relationship with integrity.

8. Jews and Christians must work together for justice and peace. Jews and Christians, each in their own way, recognize the unredeemed state of the world as reflected in the persistence of persecution, poverty and human degradation and misery. Although justice and peace are finally God's, our joint efforts, together with those of other faith communities, will help bring the kingdom of God for which we hope and long. Separately and together, we must work to bring justice and peace to our world. In this enterprise, we are guided by the vision of the prophets of Israel:

> *It shall come to pass in the end of days*
> *that the mountain of the Lord's house shall be established*
> *at the top of the mountains and be exalted above the hills,*
> *and the nations shall flow unto it...*
> *and many peoples shall go and say,*
> *"Come ye and let us go up to the mountain of the Lord,*
> *to the house of the God of Jacob, and*
> *He will teach us of His ways and we will walk in his paths."*
>
> (Isaiah 2:2–3)

(The statement bears the signatures of 173 leading rabbis and scholars in the USA, Canada, the UK and Israel. By March 2002, fifty more names had been appended.)

Bibliography

The Holy Scriptures: Hebrew Masoretic Text

TANAKH: A New Translation of the Holy Scriptures According to the Traditional Hebrew Text, Jewish Publication Society, Philadelphia / New York / Jerusalem, 1985

The Holy Bible: New International Version, Containing the Old Testament and the New Testament, American Bible Society, Zondervan Bible Publishers, Inc., International Bible Society, 1984

Beck, Norman A.: *Mature Christianity in the 21st Century – The Recognition and Repudiation of the Anti-Jewish Polemic in the New Testament*, American Interfaith Institute / World Alliance, Crossroad, New York, 1994

Boys, Mary C.: *Jewish-Christian Dialogue – One Woman's Experience*, Paulist Press, New York / Mahwah, 1997

Carroll, James: *Constantine's Sword: The Church and the Jews*, Houghton Mifflin, Boston, 2001

Charlesworth, James H. (Ed.): *Jews and Christians – Exploring the Past, Present and Future*, Crossroad, New York, 1990

Charlesworth, James H. (Ed.): *Overcoming Fear Between Jews and Christians*, American Interfaith Institute, Crossroad, New York, 1992

Croner, Helga: *Stepping Stones to Further Jewish-Christian Relations – An Unabridged Collection of Christian Documents*, Stimulus Books, London / New York, 1977

Croner, Helga: *More Stepping Stones to Jewish-Christian Relations – An Unabridged Collection of Christian Documents 1975–1983*, Stimulus Books / Paulist Press, New York / Mahwah, 1985

Dacy, Marianne (Ed.): *Pathways to Understanding – A Handbook on*

Christian-Jewish Relations, Victorian Council of Churches, Melbourne, 1994

Duvernoy, Claude: *Controversy of Zion – A Biblical View of the History and Meaning of Zion,* Forewords by Dr. David Flusser and Dr. David Allen Lewis, New Leaf Press, 1987

Eckstein, Yechiel Z. (with Lloyd John Ogilvie): *How Firm a Foundation: A Gift of Jewish Wisdom for Christians and Jews,* Paraclete Press, 1997

Eckstein, Yechiel Z.: *What You Should Know About Jews and Judaism,* World Books Publisher, Waco, Texas, 1984

Eiklor, Frank: *A Time for Trumpets, Not Piccolos! – Action Against Anti-Semitism: A Call to Christian Conscience,* Foreword by Rabbi Harold S. Kushner, Promise Publishing Co., Orange, CA, 1988

Eiklor, Frank: *God, Ghettos, Genocide, Glory,* Printing Connection, Inc., Riverside, CA, 1995

Erst, Anna Marie: *Discovering Our Jewish Roots – A Simple Guide to Judaism,* Paulist Press, New York / Mahwah, 1996

Feldman, Louis H.: *Jew and Gentile in the Ancient World,* Princeton University Press, 1996

Fisher, Eugene J. (Ed.): *Visions of the Other – Jewish and Christian Theologians Assess the Dialogue,* Stimulus Books / Paulist Press, New York / Mahwah, 1994

Flusser, David, with Notley, R. Steven: *Jesus,* Magnes Press, Hebrew University, Jerusalem, 1997

Givati, Zvi: *Haver Zvi of Israel* (General Zvi Givati is the liaison for Israel at the International Christian Embassy Jerusalem), Joseph S. and Elizabeth W. Rigell, 1995

Hagee, John: *Final Dawn Over Jerusalem,* Thomas Nelson Publishers, Nashville, 1998

Hess, Tom: *Let My People Go! – The Struggle of the Jewish People to Return to Israel,* Progressive Vision, Washington, DC, 1988

Interreligious Coordinating Council in Israel (ICCI) & Israel Jewish Council on Interreligious Relations (IJCIR): *Christian Documents on Jewish-Christian Relations in the Contemporary Era,* Initiation and Coordination: Dr. Ron Kronish, ICCI, 1996

Kenny, Anthony J.: *Catholics, Jews and the State of Israel,* Stimulus Books / Paulist Press, New York / Mahwah, 1993

Klein Halevi, Yossi: *At the Entrance to the Garden of Eden: A Jew's Search for God with Christians and Muslims in the Holy Land,* William Morrow, New York, 2001

Klenicki, Leon & Wigoder, Geoffrey: *A Dictionary of the Jewish-Christian Dialogue,* Stimulus Books / Paulist Press, New York / Ramsey, 1984

Larsson, Göran: *Fact or Fraud? The Protocols of the Elders of Zion,* AMI-Jewish Center for Biblical Study and Research, Jerusalem / San Diego / Basel / Tuberg / Nijkerk / Tokyo / Gisborne, 1994

Larsson, Göran: *Bound for Freedom – The Book of Exodus in Jewish and Christian Traditions,* Hendrickson Publishers, 1999

Lewis, David Allen: *Can Israel Survive in a Hostile World?* Foreword by Stanley M. Horton, New Leaf Press, 1994

Lewis, David Allen: *New 95 Theses – Christian and Jewish Relations,* Menorah Press, Springfield, MO, 1995

Lowe, Malcolm (Ed.): *People, Land and State of Israel – Jewish and Christian Perspectives,* Ecumenical Theological Research Fraternity in Israel, Issue 22/23 of *Immanuel* series, 1989

Lowe, Malcolm (Ed.): *Orthodox Christians and Jews on Continuity and Renewal – The Third Academic Meeting Between Orthodoxy and Judaism (including a history and bibliography of dialogue between Orthodox Christians and Jews),* Ecumenical Theological Research Fraternity in Israel, Issue 26/27 of *Immanuel* series, 1994

McQuaid, Elwood: *The Zion Connection – Evangelical Christians and the Jewish Community,* Harvest House Publishers, Eugene, OR, 1996

Merkley, Paul Charles: *Christian Attitudes Towards the State of Israel,* McGill-Queen's University Press, Montreal, 2001

Pontifical Biblical Commission: *The Jewish People and Their Sacred Scriptures in the Christian Bible,* Preface by Joseph Cardinal Ratzinger, Rome, 2001

Pragai, Michael J.: *Faith and Fulfilment – Christians and the Return to the Promised Land,* Vallentine, Mitchell, London 1985

Rottenberg, Isaac: *The Turbulent Triangle – Christians/Jews/Israel,* Red Mountain Associates, Hawley, PA, 1989

Schlink, Basilea: *Israel, My Chosen People – A German Confession Before God and the Jews,* Chosen Books, Fleming H. Revell Co., Old Tappan, NJ, 1987

Simon, Merrill: *Jerry Falwell and the Jews,* Foreword by Emanuel Rackman, Jonathan David Publishers, Inc., Middle Village, NY, 1984

Stitskin, Leon D. (Ed.): *Studies in Judaica,* Ktav Publishing House, Inc. / Yeshiva University Press, New York, 1964–1974

Tal, Eliyahu: *You Don't Have to be Jewish to be a Zionist: A Review of 400 Years of Christian Zionism,* International Forum for a United Jerusalem, 2000. (Order directly from Publisher, at POB 6771, Tel Aviv 61067, Israel.)

Vatican Library: *Fifteen Years of Catholic-Jewish Dialogue 1970–1985,* Libreria Editrice Vaticana / Libreria Editrice Lateranense, 1988

Wagner, Clarence H., Jr.: *Lessons from the Land of the Bible – Revealing More of God's Word,* Bridges for Peace, Jerusalem, 1998

Wilson, Marvin R.: *Our Father Abraham – Jewish Roots of the Christian Faith,* William B. Eerdmans Publishing Co., Grand Rapids, MI / Center for Judaic-Christian Studies, Dayton, OH, 1992

Index

About the Author

Of Moshe Aumann's 35 years of active service in Israel's Foreign Ministry, the last four were devoted largely to the intensive study and practice of Jewish-Christian and Israel-Christian relations. This included a 3-year tour of duty at Israel's Embassy in Washington as Consul General and Minister-Counselor for Relations with the Churches. Since his retirement in 1991, Aumann has continued to maintain close contact with Christian leaders and communities in Israel and abroad. He serves as Editor of *Christians and Israel*, a quarterly publication of the Association of Christians and Jews in Israel, and he is a sought-after speaker and lecturer for local organizations and visiting groups as well as overseas institutions.

A graduate of CCNY with a Social Science degree in English and Journalism, Aumann came to Israel in 1950 and settled in Jerusalem. For five years he wrote and edited *Chronicles: News of the Past*, an authentic journalistic treatment of the Bible and post-biblical Jewish history. After one year as Managing Editor of the weekly *Here and Now*, Aumann joined the Foreign Ministry, where his diplomatic career included three periods of service in the USA and eight years as the Ministry's Chief Writer and Editor.

His publications include *Land Ownership in Palestine, 1880–1948, Jerusalem, The Palestinian Labyrinth, Facts About Israel* (1985 edition) and numerous articles, booklets and translations on a variety of subjects.